U0018821

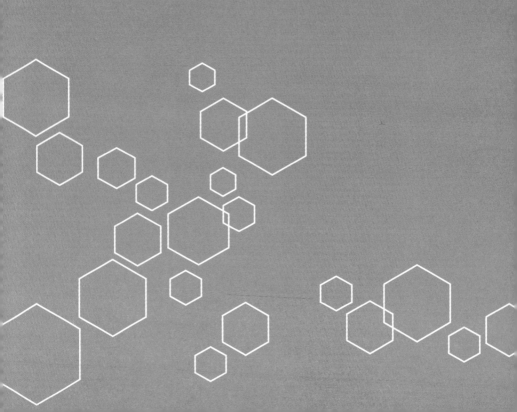

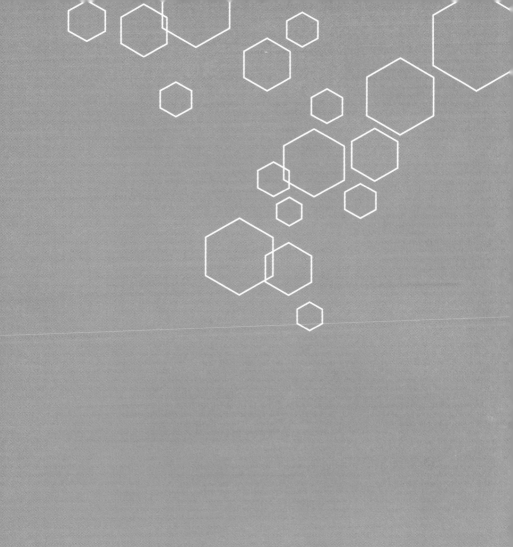

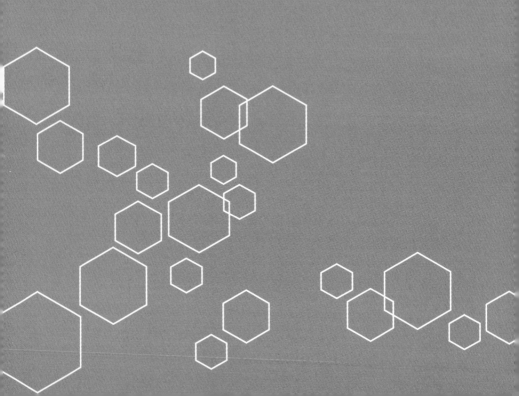

The Quotable Asshole

More Than 1200 Bitter Barbs,
Cutting Comments, and Caustic Comebacks for Aspiring Assholes Alike

這些話,
為什麼
這麼有哏?!

—— 名人毒舌語錄1200句

Eric Grzymkowski

艾瑞克·格茲莫考斯基 著

王定春 譯

獻給

我的父母，儘管取了這種書名，

他們還是會很驕傲地把這本書展示在茶几上。

引言

當我們所愛的人碎念著生活裡的雞毛蒜皮，我們還是會口頭支持他們滔滔不絕的廢話；當咖啡師搞砸我們點的咖啡，我們會說服自己：那才是自己真正想要的咖啡；老闆要求週末加班，我們會禮貌性地微笑，感謝他給我們機會遠離家人。這個世界到處都是亂開車的人、課稅永遠課不到有錢人、嬰兒一直哭卻沒有人管，以及無視這些混亂、仍持續表演的街頭藝人，但是絕大多數的我們忍住了原本想脫口而出的話。不過，某些白目竟然一臉無懼，勇於告訴全世界他們到底在想什麼。

翻開歷史，這些該死的傢伙們可真不少，他們把所有的禮節與禮儀一腳踢開，把家人、朋友、工作到政治上的一切，全給狠狠酸了一番。溫斯頓‧邱吉爾、約瑟夫‧史達林與梅‧蕙絲等大人物說出這些話，你可能還可以接受；但在這本書裡，你還會發現原本是好人的，也會因為一時失去理性而飆出肺腑之言。畢竟，好人也是人，如果你發現自己正對著車陣中插你隊的白癡大吼的話，又怎能期望華特‧迪士尼、聖雄甘地及黛安娜王妃在各方面都是完美的呢？不論你是想加入這些無禮傢伙們的行列一起開罵，還是只想帶點敬畏聽他們大放厥詞而發笑就夠了，你都可以在這本書裡找到你想要的。

政治諷刺作家 P・J・歐羅克說：「要閱讀一些會讓你看起來很棒的書，如果你讀到一半死掉的話。」放心，名人毒舌語錄不會是那本書。不過，在這本書裡，可以盡情擁抱你內心深處的黑暗，而且你會愛上這裡頭每一句過度自信、過度誇大、言過其實的狂妄言論。好好享受吧！

CONTENTS

第一篇

和混蛋打交道

我喜歡長途散步，尤其去散步的是我覺得很討厭的人。
—— 佛瑞德‧亞倫，美國喜劇演員

I like long walks, especially when they are taken by people that annoy me.
—Fred Allen, American comedian

第一章
家人

　　大部分的人都很愛他們的家人。畢竟，他們與你有血緣關係，在你人生困頓時會無條件愛你。但與你血脈相連，並不表示他們所做的每一件事情都會讓你開心。人生當中某些時刻，可能會發生這樣的事：你的手足或是某個行為不端的叔叔在一個重要場合遲到、宿醉，還穿著前一晚的衣服；你的小孩對你大吼：「我恨你！」；或是你的另一半領光了你戶頭裡的錢……或忘了把碗盤放進洗碗機裡。不過，好消息是，你並不孤單。你以為你是全世界第一個必須拆掉撞球桌，就為了替岳母騰出點空間的倒楣鬼時，事實上，早在你之前就已經有十億人在應付這些家庭裡狗屁倒灶的事情。不少人會翻白眼，或用一頓來得快、去得也快的大爆炸來回應這些狀況，不過有些傢伙卻能說出至理名言，將這一切帶往另一個完全不同的層次：

基因庫的問題，就是池邊沒有救生員。

　　——大衛·傑羅德，美國科幻小說作家

The problem with the gene pool is that there's no lifeguard.

—David Gerrold, American science fiction author

如果你不相信世界上有鬼，那表示你從沒參加過家庭聚會。

　　——艾希莉·布理恩特，美國漫畫家

If you don't believe in ghosts, you've never been to a family reunion.

—Ashleigh Brilliant, American cartoonist

我應該要認識你們，但認識的人還不到一半；我應該要喜歡你們，但我喜歡的人不到一半，喜愛的程度也不及一半。

　　——比爾博·巴金斯，出自小說《魔戒現身》

I don't know half of you half as well as I should like, and I like less than half of you half as well as you deserve.

—Bilbo Baggins, *The Fellowship of the Ring*

我根本不需要去查我們的家族樹，因為我很清楚我是枝幹裡面的樹液❶。　　——佛瑞德·亞倫，美國喜劇演員

I don't have to look up my family tree, because I know that I'm the sap.

—Fred Allen, American comedian

---

❶ sap，樹液，也是笨蛋的意思。

親情就像牆上剝落的壁紙，凌亂、黏著、惱人而且都是重複的圖案。——弗里德里希·尼采，德國哲學家

Family love is messy, clinging, and of an annoying and repetitive pattern, like bad wallpaper.

—Friedrich Nietzsche

幸福就是擁有一個關係親密、充滿愛與溫情的大家庭，不過這個家是在另一個城市。——喬治·伯恩斯，美國喜劇演員與演員

Happiness is having a large, loving, caring, close-knit family in another city.

—George Burns, American comedian and actor

你不會因為有了小孩就更有父母的樣子，就像擁有一架鋼琴不會讓你變成鋼琴家。——麥可·萊文，美國作家

Having children makes you no more a parent than having a piano makes you a pianist.

—Michael Levine, American author

家庭是個麻煩的累贅，尤其當一個人未婚的時候。
——保羅王子，出自奧斯卡·王爾德的著作《薇拉，那些虛無主義者》

A family is a terrible encumbrance, especially when one is not married.

—Prince Paul, Oscar Wilde's *Vera, or The Nihilists*

聖誕老人的想法是對的，一年只拜訪人們一次。

——維克多‧伯治，丹麥喜劇演員

Santa Claus has the right idea—visit people only once a year.

—Victor Borge, Danish comedian

我們一起度過了這麼些難關，而且大部分都是你的錯。

——艾希莉‧布理恩特，美國漫畫家

We've been through so much together, and most of it was your fault.

—Ashleigh Brilliant, American cartoonist

跟某些人相處一個小時，比跟其他人相處一個星期還痛苦得多。

——威廉‧迪安‧豪威爾斯，美國作家

Some people stay longer in an hour than others can in a week.

—William Dean Howells, American author

　　雖然沒有一套絕對的標準可以用來為父親打分數，你還是可以從他們的行為來判斷很多事。例如，會帶小孩出去玩傳接球遊戲或出門吃冰淇淋的，可能就是個不錯的老爸；但讓小孩帶著五塊美金跟一張寫著「請給我一包駱駝牌香菸，一包M&Ms巧克力給小孩」的紙條去街角雜貨店的，可能就不是個好老爸。不論你的老爸是落在光譜的哪一端，每個老爸都有他們各自的缺點，而那些缺點讓我們成為了今天的我們，不論是男人還是女人。但有些人對這個議題，可就沒這麼客氣了……

當代住在郊區的家庭，父親的地位已經夠渺小了，尤其如果他還打高爾夫球的話。——伯特蘭‧羅素，英國哲學家

The place of the father in the modern suburban family is a very small one, particularly if he plays golf.
—Bertrand Russell, British philosopher

成功父親的鐵則是：當你有了小孩，頭兩年看都別看他一眼。
——厄尼斯特‧海明威，美國作家

To be a successful father, there's one absolute rule: when you have a kid, don't look at it for the first two years.
—Ernest Hemingway

老爸一直認為笑聲是最好的解藥，我想這就是為什麼我們之中有幾個是死於肺結核。——傑克‧韓第，美國喜劇演員

Dad always thought laughter was the best medicine, which I guess is why several of us died of tuberculosis.
—Jack Handey, American comedian

我從不知道該買什麼生日禮物給老爸，所以我拿了一百元美金給他，說：「給自己買點會讓日子好過一點的東西吧。」結果他買了禮物給我媽。——麗塔‧羅德納，美國女演員與喜劇演員。

I never know what to get my father for his birthday. I gave him a $100 and said, "Buy yourself something that will make your life easier." So

he went out and bought a present for my mother.
—Rita Rudner, American actress and comedian

我記得被綁架那次，歹徒把我的一截手指頭寄給我爸。結果，他說他需要更多證據。

—— 羅德尼‧丹傑菲爾德，美國喜劇演員。

I remember the time I was kidnapped and they sent a piece of my finger to my father. He said he wanted more proof.
—Rodney Dangerfield, American comedian

父親影響我至深。他是個瘋子。 —— 史派克‧密里根，愛爾蘭喜劇演員
My father had a profound influence on me. He was a lunatic.
—Spike Milligan, Irish comedian

　　很多媽媽會常常親她們的小寶貝，讀讀床邊故事。但是，對某些混蛋來說，老媽更像電影《親愛的媽咪》❷裡頭那個可怕的母親一樣。如果你想用這些話來形容你媽，請便。不過，要是你決定這樣做，請千萬當心點。比方，好幾個星期沒打電話給你媽這種小事，你很清楚她會有什麼反應。接下來會發生什麼事……我們只能用想像的。

---

❷《親愛的媽咪》為女星瓊‧克勞馥的傳記電影，作者克莉絲汀娜‧克勞馥是她的養女，影片描述酗酒成性的瓊‧克勞馥虐待兒女以及對小孩漠不關心等行徑。

食物、愛、事業、母親，是四大罪惡集團。

——凱西・葛絲薇特，美國漫畫家

Food, love, career, and mothers, the four major guilt groups.

—Cathy Guisewite, American cartoonist

我們問這位有著三個無法無天死小孩的媽媽，如果可以重來，還會想要小孩嗎？她說，她想，但不是同一群孩子。

——大衛・芬克斯坦，喬治亞理工學院教授

The mother of three notoriously unruly youngsters was asked whether or not she'd have children if she had it to do over again. Yes, she replied. But not the same ones.

—David Finkelstein, professor at the Georgia Institute of Technology

燙衣服是我第二喜歡做的家事，僅次於在上鋪把自己的頭撞到昏過去。——爾瑪・龐貝克，美國幽默作家

My second favorite household chore is ironing, my first being hitting my head on the top bunk bed until I faint.

—Erma Bombeck, American humorist

搖籃曲是母親試圖將自己從怪物變回聖人所用的咒語。

——詹姆斯・芬頓，英國詩人

The lullaby is the spell whereby the mother attempts to transform herself back from an ogre to a saint.

—James Fenton, English poet

該死，妳這卑鄙的女人！從妳討厭死的子宮逃出來那天起，妳就一直礙著我。 ── 史杜伊‧格里芬，美國電視影集《蓋酷家庭》

Damn you, vile woman! You've impeded my work since the day I escaped from your wretched womb.

—Stewie Griffin, *Family Guy*

我媽很厲害，她有超殺的眼神，即使門是關上的，她光靠瞄一眼就能阻止你做任何事；她也可以一言不發就把你的扁桃腺拉出來。 ── 琥碧‧戈柏，美國演員、作家、歌手

My mother's great. She has the major looks. She could stop you from doing anything, through a closed door even, with a single look. Without saying a word, she has that power to rip out your tonsils.

—Whoopi Goldberg

明明量杯只量過水，老媽卻用清潔劑刷洗，她一定有毛病。 ── 爾瑪‧龐貝克，美國幽默作家

There's something wrong with a mother who washes out a measuring cup with soap and water after she's only measured water in it.

—Erma Bombeck, American humorist

時至今日，生小孩已經不需要做任何測驗或填表格。不論是有計畫地生育，還是拜廉價避孕用品所賜，每年都有成千上萬的人變成父母。放心吧，某個後代子孫一定會抱怨自己為何被帶到這世上。

父母是世上最不該有小孩的人。
　　——塞繆爾·巴特勒，英國維多利亞時代小說家
Parents are the last people on earth who ought to have children.
—Samuel Butler, Victorian novelist

如果你不曾被自己的小孩痛恨過，那表示你根本沒當過父母。
　　——貝蒂·戴維斯，美國電影、電視、戲劇女演員
If you've never been hated by your child, you've never been a parent.
—Bette Davis

每個人都知道該怎麼養育小孩，除了那些有小孩的人以外。
　　——P·J·歐羅克，美國政治諷刺作家
Everybody knows how to raise children, except the people who have them.
—P. J. O'Rourke, American political satirist

四十五年來，我的父母只吵過一次架，那次吵架持續四十三年了。——凱西‧萊德曼，美國喜劇演員

My parents only had one argument in forty-five years. It lasted forty-three years.

—Cathy Ladman, American comedian

大人只是過氣的孩子，管他們去死。
——蘇斯博士，美國著名童書作家、漫畫家

Adults are just obsolete children and the hell with them.

—Dr. Seuss

父母常用一種與他們無關的態度談論年輕一代。
——海姆‧吉諾特，以色列心理學家

Parents often talk about the younger generation as if they didn't have anything to do with it.

—Haim Ginott, Israeli child psychologist

因為體型尺寸的關係，父母很難被好好管教。
——P‧J‧歐羅克，美國政治諷刺作家

Because of their size, parents may be difficult to discipline properly.

—P. J. O'Rourke, American political satirist

沒有東西可以視而不見，孩子不會開心，這就是父母存在的意義。──奧頓‧納許，美國詩人

Children aren't happy without something to ignore, and that's what parents were created for.

—Ogden Nash

　　沒有任何經驗比得上懷抱一名初生嬰兒更美妙，因為這個活生生、有呼吸心跳的東西是由生命與愛所創造的奇蹟。這種美好通常可以持續約十五秒，直到這個奇蹟把奶吐在你的袖子上或者換尿布之前為止。通常，孩子交還到他們父母手上時，你可能還會加上一抹微笑或一句「沒關係」。但有時候，隨著微笑而來的則是乾洗費用帳單以及類似以下的意見：

一定要用母音來當小孩名字的結尾，這樣在你大吼的時候，名字才會傳得夠遠。──比爾‧寇司比，美國諧星

Always end the name of your child with a vowel, so that when you yell, the name will carry.

—Bill Cosby

擁有一個小孩，讓你成為父母；擁有兩個小孩，你就變成裁判。──大衛‧佛斯特，英國記者

Having one child makes you a parent; having two, you are a referee.

—David Frost, British journalist

養小孩一半是喜悅，一半是打游擊戰。　——愛德華‧阿斯納，美國演員

Raising kids is part joy and part guerrilla warfare.

—Ed Asner, American actor

我的小孩總覺得浴室是個等待我把所有生活用品從車上搬下來的地方。　——爾瑪‧龐貝克，美國幽默作家

My kids always perceived the bathroom as a place where you wait it out until all the groceries are unloaded from the car.

—Erma Bombeck, American humorist

我娶你媽是因為我想要小孩，你可以想像當你出生後我有多失望。——格魯喬‧馬克斯，美國電影與喜劇演員

I married your mother because I wanted children; imagine my disappointment when you came along.

—Groucho Marx

兩歲孩子就像是一台攪拌機，不過缺了蓋子。

——傑里‧賽恩菲爾德，美國喜劇演員、劇作家

A two-year-old is kind of like having a blender, but you don't have a top for it.

—Jerry Seinfeld

當我看到陪我洗澡的玩具是烤麵包機和收音機時，我明白原來我是個不被期待的孩子。—— 瓊·瑞佛斯，美國演員、電視節目主持人

I knew I was an unwanted baby when I saw that my bath toys were a toaster and a radio.

—Joan Rivers

結婚前，我有六套養育小孩的理論；現在我有六個小孩，卻沒有任何理論。—— 約翰·威爾默特，英國詩人

Before I got married, I had six theories about bringing up children; now I have six children and no theories.

—John Wilmot, English poet

想知道小孩把溜冰鞋丟在哪兒，試著在黑暗中繞著房子走一圈看看。—— 李奧波德·費克納，美國作家

If you wonder where your child left his roller skates, try walking around the house in the dark.

—Leopold Fechtner, American author

醜嬰兒令人討厭，可愛的嬰兒卻令人害怕。—— 英國維多利亞女王

An ugly baby is a very nasty object—and the prettiest is frightful.

—Queen Victoria

很多孩子不時威脅要離家出走，這卻是讓某些父母能夠撐下去的唯一理由。——菲莉絲‧狄樂，美國喜劇演員與女演員

Most children threaten at times to run away from home. This is the only thing that keeps some parents going.
—Phyllis Diller, American comedian and actress

人類是地球上唯一會讓小孩回家的生物。——比爾‧寇司比，美國諧星

Human beings are the only creatures on earth that allow their children to come back home.
—Bill Cosby

千萬別對你的小孩舉起手來，那會讓你的身體核心部位毫無防備。——羅伯特‧奧本，美國喜劇演員與魔術師

Never raise your hand to your children—it leaves your midsection unprotected.
—Robert Orben, American magician and comedian

避孕藥應該要用在任何想像得到的❸場合。
——史派克‧米利根，愛爾蘭喜劇演員

Contraceptives should be used on every conceivable occasion.
—Spike Milligan, Irish comedian

---

❸ conceivable, 可想像的，來自 conceive, 動詞，受孕的意思。

我從沒遇過能讓我喜歡的小孩。——W‧C‧菲爾茲，美國喜劇演員

I never met a kid I liked.

—W. C. Fields

　　再也沒有任何親屬關係比姻親還煩人，而且就是這麼令人吐血。自己的親戚要求你幫個忙已經夠討厭了，但比不上婆婆想跟你們一起去結婚週年旅行，或是岳父堅持可以把你的車修得比專業技師還好更讓你怒氣沖天。當你無法拒絕岳父的時候，你可以把修車師傅電話號碼加到常用聯絡人，保證你絕對有很多事情要跟他說，至少你就這麼想吧。

和岳父之間的關係是很難拿捏的。你得證明你夠格，同時對他又要帶著敬意，這有點像是在走鋼索。順道一提，我真的會走鋼索，因為我上過雜耍學校。——菲爾‧鄧菲，美國電視影集《摩登家庭》

A relationship with your fatherin-law is tough. You need to prove you can stand up to him, while being respectful. It's like walking a tightrope, which by the way I can do, because I went to trapeze school.

—Phil Dunphy, *Modern Family*

幽默總是奠基在一點點事實之上，你有聽過關於岳父的笑話嗎？——狄克‧克拉克，美國節目主持人

Humor is always based on a modicum of truth. Have you ever heard a

joke about a father-in-law?
—Dick Clark

我跟我的婆婆說我家就是妳家，然後她就說：「滾出我的房子。」
—— 瓊‧瑞佛斯，美國演員、電視節目主持人

I told my mother-in-law that my house was her house, and she said,
"Get the hell off my property."
—Joan Rivers

為了躲避姻親干涉，美國夫妻已經淪落到要花錢請婚姻諮商專家
來干涉他們的婚姻。—— 弗洛倫斯‧金，美國小說家

American couples have gone to such lengths to avoid the interference
of in-laws that they have to pay marriage counselors to interfere
between them.
—Florence King, American novelist

檀香山擁有一切：給小孩玩的沙灘，給老婆曬的太陽，以及給岳
母的鯊魚。—— 肯‧杜德，英國喜劇演員

Honolulu—it's got everything. Sand for the children, sun for the wife,
sharks for the wife's mother.
—Ken Dodd, British comedian

我看到六個男人在對丈母娘又踢又打。鄰居問我：「你不去幫忙嗎？」我說：「不用，六個人應該夠了。」
—— 萊斯‧道森，英國喜劇演員。

I saw six men kicking and punching the motherin-law. My neighbor said, "Are you going to help?" I said, "No, six should be enough."
—Les Dawson, British comedian

很多時候，我早該要轟掉自己的腦袋，但一想到這會讓我岳母開心，我就放棄了；就算我能夠變成鬼去嚇她，我也不想停留在這些無聊的家庭瑣事上。 —— 拜倫勳爵，英國詩人

I should, many a good day, have blown my brains out, but for the recollection that it would have given pleasure to my mother-inlaw; and, even then, if I could have been certain to haunt her—but I won't dwell upon these trifling family matters.
—Lord Byron

所有我研究過的人，不論是住在城市還是峭壁，至少有一半的人都希望在他們與婆婆（或岳母）之間隔著一座叢林。
—— 瑪格麗特‧米德，美國人類學家

Of all the peoples whom I have studied, from city dwellers to cliff dwellers, I always find that at least 50 percent would prefer to have at least one jungle between themselves and their mothers-in-law.
—Margaret Mead

亞當是全世界最幸運的男人，因為他沒有岳母。
—— 馬克·吐溫，美國作家

Adam was the luckiest man; he had no mother-in-law.
—Mark Twain

我婆婆不在挪亞方舟上的唯一理由就是，他們找不到另一個跟她長得一模一樣的動物。—— 菲莉絲·狄樂，美國喜劇演員與女演員

The only reason my mother-inlaw wasn't on Noah's Ark was because they couldn't find another animal that looked like her.
—Phyllis Diller, American comedian and actress

　　提到祖父母時，你可能會聯想到打毛衣與熱茶，或是門廊上的鞦韆與老人家說很久很久以前的故事給你聽；但也有可能你想起來的是喋喋不休、不會使用網路、而且還嚴重耳背聽不見你說話的老男人與老女人。不過他們聽不見，不代表你可以在他們背後說壞話⋯⋯就像下面這些不肖子孫一樣。

一個透露自己年齡的女人，不是太年輕、還沒有什麼東西好失去，就是老到無法得到任何東西。—— 中國諺語

The woman who tells her age is either too young to have anything to lose or too old to have anything to gain.
—Chinese proverb

如果我知道會活這麼久，我以前會更小心照顧自己。

——尤比·布雷克，美國爵士音樂家

If I'd known I was going to live this long, I'd have taken better care of myself.

—Eubie Blake, American jazz musician

老人是很危險的，因為對他們來說，世界會變得怎樣根本無關緊要。——蕭伯納，愛爾蘭劇作家與作家

Old men are dangerous: It doesn't matter to them what is going to happen to the world.

—George Bernard Shaw, Irish playwright and author

我想像我祖父一樣在睡夢中死去，而不是像他開車載的乘客那樣，在驚聲尖叫中死亡。——威爾·史萊納，美國喜劇演員

I want to die in my sleep like my grandfather ... Not screaming and yelling like the passengers in his car.

—Will Shriner, American comedian

為什麼爺爺奶奶與孫子可以處得好？因為他們有共同的敵人，媽媽。——克勞黛·考爾白，法國女演員

Why do grandparents and grandchildren get along so well? They have the same enemy—the mother.

—Claudette Colbert, French actress

譴責年輕人對老人的養生是必要的，因為這有助於血液循環。
——羅根‧P‧史密斯，美國作家與評論家

The denunciation of the young is a necessary part of the hygiene of older people, and greatly assists the circulation of the blood.
—Logan P. Smith, American writer and critic

　　有時候，過一段沒有親密愛人陪伴的日子，會比與他們共享時光更美好。這聽起來不太合理，但獨處的確有許多好處。很不幸，你們這些人都有老婆、老公、寵物、女友、稅金與小孩⋯⋯他們不會等你中場休息。所以當你想放鬆的夜晚被一串愚蠢的嘮叨打斷時，你有兩個選擇：暫停比賽，拾起你的耐心處理眼前的狀況，或是追隨以下這些王八蛋的腳步，大聲說出這些至理名言：

我不知道，也不在乎，那根本沒差！
——阿爾伯特‧愛因斯坦，物理哲學家

I don't know, I don't care, and it doesn't make any difference!
—Albert Einstein

有時候，我需要一樣只有你能給的東西：你不在場。
——艾希莉‧布理恩特，美國漫畫家

Sometimes I need what only you can provide: your absence.
—Ashleigh Brilliant, American cartoonist

我不是想獨自一人，我只是不想被打擾。

—— 奧黛麗‧赫本，知名電影演員

I don't want to be alone; I want to be left alone.

—Audrey Hepburn

男人對女人跟內褲的要求是一樣的：一點支持，跟一點自由。

—— 傑里‧賽恩菲爾德，美國喜劇演員

Men want the same thing from their underwear that they want from women: a little bit of support, and a little bit of freedom.

—Jerry Seinfeld

當男人需要、而她不在身邊，這是女人最重的罪，僅次於當男人不需要她時，她還在身邊。 —— 教皇保祿六世

Failing to be there when a man wants her is a woman's greatest sin, except to be there when he doesn't want her.

—Pope Paul VI

沒有妳，我覺得好痛苦，這程度跟妳在我身邊是一樣的。

—— 史蒂芬‧畢夏普，美國歌手與作曲家

I feel so miserable without you; it's almost like having you here.

—Stephen Bishop, American singer and songwriter

不被打擾的權利確實是所有自由的起點。——威廉·奧維爾·道格拉斯，美國最高法院大法官

The right to be let alone is indeed the beginning of all freedom. —William Orville Douglas, Associate Justice of the United States Supreme Court

第二章
朋友

　　朋友，幾乎會是你希望能夠擁有的家人。他們傾聽你的問題，讓你趴在他們肩上哭泣，並在你有麻煩的時候支持你。雖然你的朋友可以讓你倚靠，不代表他們不會考驗你的耐心。當然，你的好兄弟幫你搬進你的第一間公寓，但別忘了那次他在感恩節晚餐喝醉，並告訴你的小孩，他們是你收養來的。你認為不論如何，多數人都會對那些與他們禍福與共的人很好，畢竟，他們知道你所有的祕密，包括你收藏《星艦迷航記》紀念版以及對歌手辛蒂・羅波的過度癡迷，他們可以用這些資訊摧毀你。不管你信不信，還是有些王八蛋才不管那麼多，偏偏要用這些意見來回敬他們的朋友：

我不相信他，我們是朋友。—— 貝托爾特・布萊希特，德國詩人與劇作家
I don't trust him. We're friends.
—Bertolt Brecht, German poet and playwright

我的朋友？世上沒有朋友這種東西。—— 可可・香奈兒

My friends? There are no friends.

─Coco Chanel

三十多歲時，我們想要交朋友；到了四十多歲才會知道，朋友跟愛情一樣，都無法拯救我們。──F・史考特・費茲傑羅，美國作家

It is in the thirties that we want friends. In the forties we know they won't save us any more than love did.

─F. Scott Fitzgerald

對麻煩事一笑置之的人肯定會失去許多朋友，因為他們喪失了對他的特權，這萬不可原諒。──H・L・曼肯，美國記者

When a man laughs at his troubles,he loses a great many friends. They never forgive the loss of their prerogative.

─H. L. Mencken, American journalist

友誼是如此甜美、穩固、忠誠又至死不渝的神聖情感，只要他們不跟你借錢。── 馬克・吐溫，美國作家

The holy passion of friendship is of so sweet and steady and loyal and enduring a nature that it will last through a whole lifetime, if not asked to lend money.

─Mark Twain

根據合理的數據指出，每四個美國人當中，就有一個正遭受某種精神疾病的折磨。想想你最好的三個好友。如果他們都很好，剩下那個就是你了。——李查‧巴哈，美國作家

The statistics on sanity are that one out of every four Americans is suffering from some form of mental illness. Think of your three best friends. If they're okay, then it's you.

—Richard Bach, American author

男人把友情當足球踢來踢去，似乎永遠踢不壞；女人對待友情像捧玻璃杯一樣小心翼翼，但總是碎了一地。

——安‧莫洛‧林白，美國飛行員、作家、探險家查爾斯‧林白之妻

Men kick friendship around like a football, but it doesn't seem to crack. Women treat it like glass and it goes to pieces.

—Anne Morrow Lindbergh, American aviator and wife of Charles Lindbergh

我曾觀察我老婆跟她朋友講電話。老天！她們會彼此分享生活中所有私密的小細節。而男人呢？一旦我們跟另一個男人成為朋友，可能永遠也不會跟他說上一句話，除非有什麼值得交換的資訊，像是：「嘿，吉姆，你的襯衫著火了。」

——傑夫‧福克斯渥西，美國喜劇演員

I notice my wife when she's on the phone with her friends. Man, they will share every intimate detail of their lives with each other. See, men, once we become friends with another man, we may never say another

word to him, unless there's valuable information that needs to be exchanged. Things like, "Hey, Jim, your shirt's on fire."
—Jeff Foxworthy, American comedian

　　殘忍的誠實只能在兩個密友間分享。當你老婆或女友問你，她看起來胖不胖的時候，她最不需要的就是誠實的答案。但如果你無法信任你的朋友，讓他們告訴你實話，那你又可以相信誰？他們通常心口如一，反之亦然。不過，你可能還是會想避開以下那些舌尖口快的犀利言語：

信任朋友，才能夠對他坦白你的錯；若要讓他知道他錯，則需要更多的信任。——班傑明·富蘭克林，美國政治家
Tis a great confidence in a friend to tell him your faults; greater to tell him his.
—Benjamin Franklin

你在你的詩裡說我是蠢蛋，就在我快要同意的那一剎那，我發現凡是跟愚蠢有關的，你才真是專家，朋友。
——法蘭茲·格里帕策，奧地利作家
You even called me stupid in your verse, and I'm almost agreeing, for where stupidity is involved, you are quite an expert, friend.
—Franz Grillparzer, Austrian writer

他沒得潰瘍，他讓人得潰瘍。——漢尼‧楊曼，英國喜劇演員

He doesn't get ulcers—he gives them.

—Henny Youngman, British comedian

摧毀美好的一天需要兩個人。第一個人在你背後說了一些很糟的壞話，第二個人是你好朋友，他可以保證你立刻聽到那些壞話。——來源不詳

It takes two people to ruin a perfectly good day. First a person who says something downright nasty about you, and second, a dear friend who makes sure you hear about it immediately.

—Unknown

每個人都有愚蠢的權利，有些人卻濫用這個特權。——史達林，蘇聯前領導人

Everyone has a right to be stupid. Some people abuse the privilege.

—Joseph Stalin

文字有很強的力量，如果你不把太多字拴在一起的話。——亨利‧威勒‧蕭，美國幽默作家

There's a great power in words, if you don't hitch too many of them together.

—Henry Wheeler Shaw, American humorist

有時候我貼心到連我自己都受不了。

── 茱莉・安德魯斯，英國女演員，電影《真善美》女主角

Sometimes I'm so sweet even I can't stand it.

—Julie Andrews

和茱莉・安德魯斯共事就像是被情人敲到頭一樣。

── 克里斯多福・柏麥，加拿大演員，電影《真善美》男主角

Working with Julie Andrews is like getting hit over the head with a valentine.

—Christopher Plummer, Canadian actor

我不需要一個在我改變時跟著改變、點頭時跟著點頭的朋友，我的影子可以更勝任這工作。── 普魯塔克，羅馬時代的希臘作家

I don't need a friend who changes when I change and who nods when I nod; my shadow does that much better.

—Plutarch

也許你不明白發生了什麼事，但往你的牙齒踢上一腳可能是世上最適合你的一件事。── 華特・迪士尼，美國著名電影製片人

You may not realize it when it happens, but a kick in the teeth may be the best thing in the world for you.

—Walt Disney

緊挨著你親密盟友的是，滿是寄生蟲的糞坑，這就是俗稱「亦敵亦友」的狀態。這些人是朋友，也是敵人，是你樂於痛恨的對象。你可能永遠也不會知道他們為什麼對你存心不良，不過，你很確定他們每個月的第二個星期天都會聚在一起，密謀要把你搞垮。有些混蛋大膽地決定要來些犀利的言語讓這些人一刀斃命。如果你決定要做同樣的事，為了達到最好的效果，不妨借用以下任何一句話。

你怎麼不在自己身上鑽個洞，好讓那些愚蠢流出來？
——格魯喬·馬克斯，美國喜劇演員
Why don't you bore a hole in yourself and let the sap run out?
—Groucho Marx

他就是那種死了以後可以變得更好的人。
——H·H·孟若，英國作家，使用「薩基」為筆名寫作
He is one of those people who would be enormously improved by death.
—H. H. Munro, British author who wrote under the pen name "Saki"

你爸那時候真該拔出來的。❹ ——約翰·韋恩，美國電影演員
Your father should have pulled out.
—John Wayne

---

❹ 此指該把陰莖拔出來，意指「你根本不該被生下來。」

睿智的人說話是因為有話要說，蠢蛋說話則是因為得說些話。

── 柏拉圖，古希臘哲學家

Wise men talk because they have something to say; fools talk because they have to say something.

—Plato

如何區分不幸和災難？如果格萊斯頓掉進泰晤士河，那是不幸。但如果有人再把他拖上岸，那就會是場災難。 ── 班傑明・迪斯雷利，前英國首相，文內指的是他的繼任者威廉・尤爾特・格萊斯頓

The difference between a misfortune and a calamity? If Gladstone fell into the Thames, it would be a misfortune. But if someone dragged him out again, it would be a calamity.

—Benjamin Disraeli, former British prime minister referring to his successor, William Ewart Gladstone

「做你自己。」大概是你能給人最糟的意見了。

── 湯瑪斯・L・麥森，美國作家

"Be yourself" is about the worst advice you can give some people.

—Thomas L. Masson, American author

我可以罵他是虐待狂、變態戀屍癖，但那只是對牛彈琴。
——伍迪・艾倫，美國電影導演
I'd call him a sadistic, hippophilic necrophiliac, but that would be beating a dead horse.
—Woody Allen

如果我發現她浮在我的游泳池裡，我會處罰我的狗。
——小野洋子，日裔美籍音樂家，約翰・藍儂之妻
If I found her floating in my pool, I'd punish my dog.
—Yoko Ono

　　不論友情再怎麼穩固，對嫉妒這個綠色小怪獸都是無法免疫的。儘管打從包著尿布起你就認識了你的好朋友，但很有可能在你的哥兒們又一次升官、而你的老闆卻連你的名字都記不住時，你還是會覺得噁心。不過問題究竟是出於嫉妒？還是你真的被打壓？下面這些王八蛋們一定覺得是後者。

很多人都會樂見他們最好的朋友失勢、出糗。
——切斯特菲爾德領主，17世紀英國貴族
Most people enjoy the inferiority of their best friends.
—Lord Chesterfield, seventeenth century British nobleman

不可能沒有朋友沒有那麼一點討人厭的地方。

——愛德嘉‧華生‧浩威，美國小說家

Probably no man ever had a friend that he did not dislike a little.

—Edgar Watson Howe, American novelist

如果你無法回應一個男人的論點，也沒什麼好損失的，你還是可以用下流的名字來叫他。——阿爾伯特‧哈伯德，美國作家

If you cannot answer a man's argument, all is not lost; you can still call him vile names.

—Elbert Hubbard, American writer

女人生活中最刺激的事，就是發現比自己胖的女人。

——海倫‧羅蘭德，美國記者

The chief excitement in a woman's life is spotting women who are fatter than she is.

—Helen Rowland, American journalist

嘲笑我們的朋友，就報復了他們帶給我們的失望。

——梅森‧庫利，英國教授與作家

Laughing at our friends, we avenge the disappointment they have caused.

—Mason Cooley, English professor and writer

要忍受敵人造就的困難非常容易，朋友的成功才是難以承受的事。——奧斯卡·王爾德，愛爾蘭作家

It is very easy to endure the difficulties of one's enemies. It is the successes of one's friends that are hard to bear.

—Oscar Wilde

你失敗，會讓朋友感到優越。你成功，會讓他們覺得憤恨。——梅森·庫利，英國教授與作家

Fail, and your friends feel superior. Succeed, and they feel resentful.

—Mason Cooley, English professor and writer

不是人人都能宣稱自己交友滿天下，但多數人還是會有一些朋友，哪怕是想像出來的也行。這麼多人選擇踏入友誼圈時，按常理而言，一定是有些好處的，即使那好處非常渺小。究竟這些傢伙喜歡朋友的哪些地方？而他們又是如何表達對朋友的欣賞？讀下去就知道了。

一個好朋友可以立刻告訴你，你究竟是怎麼搞的。不過，以後他可能就沒那麼像好朋友了。——亞瑟·布里斯班，美國報紙編輯

A good friend can tell you what is the matter with you in a minute. He may not seem such a good friend after telling.

—Arthur Brisbane, American newspaper editor

友誼的特權就是言不及義，而且這些屁話會被尊重。
──查爾斯·蘭姆，英國作家

'Tis the privilege of friendship to talk nonsense, and have her nonsense respected.
─Charles Lamb, British author

真正的朋友就是假裝沒看見你失敗，並忍受你成功。
──道格·拉森，美國專欄作家

A true friend is one who overlooks your failures and tolerates your success.
─Doug Larson, American columnist

遇到比我們還蠢的人是多麼愉快的事！我們會因此立刻愛上他們。──傑羅姆·K·傑羅姆，英國作家

It is so pleasant to come across people more stupid than ourselves. We love them at once for being so.
─Jerome K. Jerome, English author

老朋友的好處之一，就是你受得了跟他們一起幹蠢事。
──拉爾夫·沃爾多·愛默生，美國文學家

It is one of the blessings of old friends that you can afford to be stupid with them.
─Ralph Waldo Emerson

他是我認識唯一有橡膠口袋的人，這樣可以偷些湯。

——威爾森‧米茲納，美國劇作家

He's the only man I ever knew who had rubber pockets so he could steal soup.

—Wilson Mizner, American playwright

　　雖然多數人珍愛並重視友誼，但還是有一些個性古怪、憤世嫉俗的人認為，普通朋友大概就像兩人三腳競賽中那種雖跛腳但堪用的狀態。這些怪咖還不怕讓他們的「朋友」知道自己真正的想法。

他媽真該把他丟掉，留下送子鳥就好。

——梅‧蕙絲，美國演員

His mother should have thrown him away and kept the stork.

—Mae West

如果我有一把槍、兩顆子彈，然後跟希特勒、賓拉登、托比在同一個房間裡，我會射托比兩次。

——麥可‧史考特，美國電視劇《辦公室瘋雲》

And if I had a gun, with two bullets, and I was in a room with Hitler, Bin Laden, and Toby, I would shoot Toby twice.

—Michael Scott, *The Office*

我認清一個事實，就是如果所有人都知道別人怎麼說他們，這世上沒有任何四個人能成為朋友。——布萊茲·帕斯卡，法國數學家

I lay it down as a fact that if all men knew what others say of them, there would not be four friends in the world.

—Blaise Pascal, French mathematician

就像大自然一樣。你能擁有多少動物，取決於生態系統的支撐量，而你能擁有的朋友數量，則取決於你能容忍多少牢騷。

——R·K·米爾荷蘭，美國漫畫家，最有名作品為網路漫畫《來點正面的》

It's a lot like nature. You only have as many animals as the ecosystem can support, and you only have as many friends as you can tolerate the bitching of.

—Randy K. Milholland, American cartoonist most famous for the webcomic, *Something Positive*

朋友就是跟我借書，然後把濕玻璃杯放在我書上的人。

——埃德溫·阿靈頓·羅賓森，美國詩人

Friends: people who borrow my books and set wet glasses on them.

—Edwin Arlington Robinson, American poet

保持小型交友圈的好處是，每四件謀殺案中有三件是由被害人所認識的傢伙幹的。——喬治·卡林，美國喜劇演員

One good reason to only maintain a small circle of friends is that three out of four murders are committed by people who know the victim.

—George Carlin, American comedian

你想跟我共患難，但我只想當一個討厭鬼。

——喬·E·路易斯，美國喜劇演員與歌手

Show me a friend in need and I'll show you a pest.

—Joe E. Lewis, American comedian and singer

把友誼的屍體給埋了，它不值得防腐保存。

——威廉·赫茲利特，英國作家

Bury the carcass of friendship: It is not worth embalming.

—William Hazlitt, British writer

有些友誼是如此堅定，可以在迂迴的人生故事中一路追溯至包尿布時期，或是互相取笑彼此的睏氣。但是，哎，世事難料，即使是這樣的密友，也會有分開的一天。對某些混蛋來說，好友的死亡不是用來哀悼，而是讓他們終於可以肆無忌憚地說出內心對那個老混蛋極度不爽的觀感。當然，仍願他安息。

我沒殺過人，但我閱讀了很多訃聞，而且非常開心。

──克萊倫斯‧蘇厄德‧丹諾，美國律師，為教授演化論的高中生物老師約翰‧T‧斯科普斯辯護，也是後來著名的「斯科普斯猴子審判」。

I have never killed a man, but I have read many obituaries with great pleasure.

—Clarence Seward Darrow, American lawyer famous for his defense of John T. Scopes in the "Scopes Monkey Trial"

說「我道歉」和「我很抱歉」，兩者的意思是一模一樣的，除非你是在喪禮上。❺ ──狄米崔‧馬丁，美國喜劇演員

Saying I apologize is the very same thing as saying I'm sorry. They're the same. Unless you're at a funeral.

—Demetri Martin, American comedian

「別說死者壞話」真是去你的狗屎！人不會因為死掉就變得更好；你只是講得好像他們變好了一樣。但這不是真的！王八蛋還是王八蛋，只是變成死王八蛋。

──伊恩‧弗雷澤‧萊米‧基爾麥思特，英國重金屬樂家

Fuck this "Don't speak ill of the dead" shit! People don't become better when they are dead; you just talk about them as if they are. But it's not true! People are still a**holes; they are just dead a**holes!

—Ian Fraser "Lemmy"Kilmister, British heavy metal musician

---

❺「I'm sorry.」有多種意思，前文指的是我很抱歉，喪禮時則是表達遺憾之意。

我無法原諒我的朋友死去，因為我一點也不覺得他們搞出這種消失行徑是有趣的事。——羅根‧P‧史密斯，美國作家與評論家

I cannot forgive my friends for dying; I do not find these vanishing acts of theirs at all amusing.

—Logan P. Smith, American writer and critic

他在地表上一無是處，他應該要在地底下，當高麗菜的肥料。
——馬克‧吐溫，美國作家

He is useless on top of the ground; he aught to be under it, inspiring the cabbages.

—Mark Twain

他本身是具非常好看的屍體，而且還那麼剛好地成為自己的棺材。——奧利佛‧戈得史密斯，愛爾蘭作家

He makes a very handsome corpse and becomes his coffin prodigiously.

—Oliver Goldsmith, Irish writer

老年，就是在電話簿裡刪掉很多名字。
——羅納德‧布萊斯，英國作家與編輯

Old age is—a lot of crossed off names in an address book.

—Ronald Blythe, British writer and editor

他是個偉大的愛國者、人道主義者與忠實的朋友。前提是，他真的死了。 ──伏爾泰，法國哲學家

He was a great patriot, a humanitarian, a loyal friend—provided, of course, that he really is dead.
—Voltaire, French philosopher

我沒有參加葬禮，不過我好好寫了封信，來表達我同意舉行。
── 馬克·吐溫，美國作家

I didn't attend the funeral, but I sent a nice letter saying I approved of it.
—Mark Twain

第三章
室友

任何一個曾經與別人同住在一起的人，都能了解室友有多難搞。想想這個情況：你搬去跟你的朋友同住，本來以為住在一起會很有趣。他們一開始看起來人很好，很貼心也很正常，但之後卻變了，那個你認識了一輩子、乾淨有禮、沉默寡言的人，變成一個把髒碗盤丟在水槽、拒絕清理浴室，並在三更半夜用小韋恩❻的饒舌歌當鈴聲把你吵醒的人。聽起來不錯吧？

當蜜月期過去，很多人會決定面對現實，一臉尷尬地說：「我要搬出去了。」不過有些氣壞了的傢伙可不會善罷干休。雖然室友總是有辦法拿到他們的牙刷，也知道他們在哪兒睡覺，不過他們從不做無謂的抵抗，相反地，他們使出一些你想也想不到的糟糕行為，來反制壞室友……

---

❻ Lil Wayne 為美國饒舌歌手。

我不需要付錢給治療師讓他們給我那些垃圾，因為我有個室友可以免費提供。 ——卡莉絲塔‧弗洛克哈特，美國女演員

I don't need to pay a therapist to give me crap. I have a roommate that does it for free.

—Calista Flockhart, American actress

跟別人當室友真的很難，尤其如果你的行李箱比他們的好太多。 ——霍爾頓‧考菲爾德，《麥田捕手》男主角

It's really hard to be roommates with people if your suitcases are much better than theirs.

—Holden Caulfield, *The Catcher in the Rye*

我對你的那些憂傷情緒真是一丁點兒都不在意。 ——茱蒂絲‧沙因德林，美國電視劇《茱蒂法官》

I couldn't give a rat's tutu about your emotional distress.

—Judith Sheindlin, *Judge Judy*

跟我住一起不是件容易的事，因為我算是個邋遢的人。所以如果要我考慮室友的話，可能得是我的姊妹之類的。 ——凱蒂‧荷姆斯，美國女演員

I'm not the easiest person to live with. I'm kind of a slob. So for me to consider a roommate, it would have to be one of my sisters or something.

—Katie Holmes

我曾經有個室友，不過我媽搬去佛羅里達了。
──瑞克‧莫拉尼斯，加拿大演員、喜劇演員

I used to have a roommate, but my mom moved to Florida.
──Rick Moranis

你真他媽的煩死了，真的，閉上你他媽的嘴，因為這屋裡沒有人
喜歡你。──史努奇對麥可說的話，美國真人實鏡秀節目《玩咖日記》

You're fucking annoying, seriously, just shut the fuck up because no one
likes you in the house.
──Snooki to Mike "The Situation" Sorrentino, *Jersey Shore*

我寧願花一小時跟壞蛋共處，也不想花兩分鐘跟無聊的人在一
起。──史黛芬妮‧巴倫，《珍與史卡葛瑞夫莊園的不愉快》

I would rather spend an hour among the notorious than two minutes
with the dull.
──Stephanie Barron, *Jane and the Unpleasantness at Scargrave Manor*

　　老實說，如果可以選擇，一般人都會盡量避免有室友。因
為，比起更新家事輪值表跟搞清楚童山濯濯的室友究竟是如何把
浴室水槽塞住，大家通常都有更重要的事要做。既然室友不能
免，唯一可以讓我們和平共存的就是相互了解一些基本禮儀。
　　這些禮儀規範可以複雜到連整理抹布也有準則表，也可以簡
單到像是別讓室友的貓在你房間尿尿。不論你是事先訂好基本規

則，還是等到事情發生再說，對於成功的同居生活來說，都是不可或缺的。當然，有些規則以及必須經由交談確認的內容會有點繁瑣……

文明的最高表現就是你可以討厭我，而我也可以討厭你，但我們發展出一套禮儀讓我們可以相處。如果光憑衝動行事，那我們很可能會大戰。── 史丹利‧克勞區，美國流行文化評論家

The high point of civilization is that you can hate me and I can hate you, but we develop an etiquette that allows us to deal with each other because if we acted solely upon our impulse, we'd probably go to war.
—Stanley Crouch, American pop culture critic

我不在乎你喜歡我或討厭我……我只要求你尊重我是個人。
── 傑基‧羅賓森，美國職棒大聯盟第一位非裔美國球員

I'm not concerned with your liking or disliking me ... All I ask is that you respect me as a human being.
—Jackie Robinson

我可能有些缺點，但「我是錯的」這件事並不是缺點之一。
── 吉米‧荷法，美國工會組織領袖

I may have faults, but being wrong ain't one of them.
—Jimmy Hoffa

問題不在於我是否無禮地對待你，而是你可曾聽過我對別人更好。——亨利·希金斯教授，《窈窕淑女》

The question is not whether I treat you rudely, but whether you've ever heard me treat anyone else better.

—Professor Henry Higgins, *My Fair Lady*

禮儀就是比必要的禮貌還要更有禮一點。

——威爾·卡比，美國文學評論家

Etiquette means behaving yourself a little better than is absolutely essential.

—Will Cuppy, American literary critic

唯一能超越你的無禮的，只有你的無禮。——戴爾·卡內基，美國作家

Your lack of manners is only exceeded by your lack of manners.

—Dale Carnegie, American author

你對地點、人與時間一點尊重也沒有嗎？

——威廉·莎士比亞，英國戲劇家

Is there no respect of place, persons, nor time in you?

—William Shakespeare

在動物界裡，群體中最暴力、最具攻擊性的成員通常也是最

沒安全感的一個，這在室友身上也適用。當然，當你把碗盤留在水槽裡的時候，你的室友可能會踤腳或是用爪子刨地板，一副就要展開攻擊的樣子，但其實他是在唬人。無論你是要讓他坐下好好討論這個問題，還是你要堅持自己是主導這段關係的人，看看以下這些讓爛室友知道自己本分的言論。

她就是個廚房女僕而且油膩膩的，我不知道除了拿她身上的油來做油燈並用那盞燈逃離她之外，她還有什麼用。

——威廉・莎士比亞，英國戲劇家。

She is the kitchen wench and all grease, and I know not what use to put her to than to make a lamp from her and run from her by her own light.

—William Shakespeare

我會用簡單的字來解釋，保證你一定懂，你這個疣豬臉小丑。

——男主角衛斯理，出自電影《公主新娘》

I'll explain and I'll use small words so that you'll be sure to understand, you warthog-faced buffoon.

—Wesley, *The Princess Bride*

他以為自己舉止合宜，這其實是錯覺。

——華特・柯爾，美國作家與戲劇評論家

He had delusions of adequacy.

—Walter Kerr, American writer and theater critic

有時候大家會覺得我說的笑話帶著優越感⋯⋯那就是你以高人一
等的態度對人講話時的模樣。——吉米・卡爾，英國喜劇演員

People sometimes say my jokes are condescending. ... That's when you
talk down to people.

—Jimmy Carr, British comedian

噢，是嗎？剛剛混蛋專賣店打電話來，說你賣光、缺貨了呢！
——喬治・康斯坦札，美國電視劇《歡樂單身派對》

Oh, yeah? Well the Jerk Store called, and they're running out of you!
—George Costanza, *Seinfeld*

我從來不會忘了恭喜別人表現幽默，即使他們不是有意的。
——克里斯多福・希欽斯，英國作家

I never miss an opportunity to congratulate someone on being
humorous, even if unintentionally.

—Christopher Hitchens, British author

　　有一個或好幾個室友已經夠慘了，不需要再多加幾個人進來
攪和。不過，有些室友偶爾會帶幾個討厭的客人回來，緩衝一
下。最終，這些客人會因為用光了乾淨的毛巾，於是再跑去別人
家揩油。雖然班・富蘭克林說過：「客人，就像魚一樣，三天後
就開始發臭。」如果這些訪客拜訪的人不是你，難堪的局面可能

會來得更快。幸好，下面的這些混蛋已經為你該如何掌控事態開了先例。

每位客人都痛恨其他客人，而主人則痛恨他們所有人。
—— 阿爾巴尼亞諺語。
Every guest hates the others, and the host hates them all.
—Albanian proverb

客人是貪得無厭的時間吞噬者，而且適合那些不出門拜訪就什麼也不做的人。—— 威廉・古柏，英國詩人
Visitors are insatiable devourers of time, and fit only for those who, if they did not visit, would do nothing.
—William Cowper, English poet

我一直覺得與客人道別時，有兩個必須盡的責任：首先確認他沒忘記任何屬於他的東西；另一個是確認他沒有拿走我的東西。
—— 阿爾弗雷德・諾斯・懷海德，英國數學家與哲學家
I always feel that I have two duties to perform with a parting guest: one, to see that he doesn't forget anything that is his; the other, to see that he doesn't take anything that is mine.
—Alfred North Whitehead, British mathematician and philosopher

你們要互相熱情款待，不發怨言。—— 聖經，彼得前書 4：9

Offer hospitality to one another without grumbling.

—Bible, 1 Peter 4:9

跟別人住在一起，你不能我行我素，他們也不能想怎樣就怎樣。
—— 馬騰·馬騰斯，比利時足球員

Staying with people consists in your not having your own way, and their not having theirs.

—Maarten Martans, Belgian footballer

沒有任何人可以在朋友家裡受到三天歡迎後卻還沒變成討厭的
人。—— 提圖斯·馬丘斯·普勞圖斯，古羅馬劇作家

No guest is so welcome in a friend's house that he will not become a nuisance after three days.

—Titus Maccius Plautus, Roman playwright

　　室友有個舉世皆然的事實，那就是他們痛恨任何形式的工作勝於其他事物。如果他們拿出逃避家事十分之一的時間來做家事，房子就會變得一塵不染，你也不用只為了讓他們拖廚房地板而得每週與他們進行一場決死賽。因此當你回到家，發現室友躺在一堆披薩盒和空啤酒罐之間，專心按著電玩遙控器，你卻只能翻白眼、咬牙切齒的時候，想想在同樣的情況下，那些快被逼瘋的傢伙會脫口而出哪些話。

你是個看了就刺眼的寄生蟲。

——格雷戈里·拉托夫，俄羅斯導演、演員與製作人

You're a parasite for sore eyes.

—Gregory Ratoff, Russian director, actor, and producer

拖延讓你有些事可以期待。 ——瓊·柯納，美國記者與作家

Procrastination gives you something to look forward to.

—Joan Konner, American journalist and author

懶惰不過是一個在你覺得累之前就先休息的習慣。

——朱爾·勒納爾，法國作家

Laziness is nothing more than the habit of resting before you get tired.

—Jules Renard, French author

像顆拔出來的牙一樣沒用。 ——瑪麗·羅伯茲·萊因哈特，美國作家

Useless as a pulled tooth.

—Mary Roberts Rinehart, American author

雖然家事不會讓你丟了小命，不過為什麼要冒險呢？

——菲莉絲·狄樂，美國喜劇演員與女演員

Housework can't kill you, but why take a chance?

—Phyllis Diller, American comedian and actress

有懶室友，就有笨室友。不然，怎麼會在你出差的時候，你都把垃圾處理、包好了，他們還不會拿出去丟？有千百個理由你可以討厭一起住的人，但是很有可能這並不全是他們的錯，不過，王八蛋們可不接受這個說法，他們閉不了嘴。

對沒受過教育的人而言，成績拿A就只是三條槓。

——A·A·米恩，英國作家，以《小熊維尼》聞名

To the uneducated, an A is just three sticks.

—A. A. Milne

沒必要給聰明人建議，笨蛋才需要。　——比爾·寇司比，美國諧星

A word to the wise ain't necessary—it's the stupid ones that need the advice.

—Bill Cosby

你的出生是個你必須花一輩子矯正的錯誤。

——恰克·帕拉尼克，美國小說家

Your birth is a mistake you'll spend your whole life trying to correct.

—Chuck Palahniuk, American novelist

你比一群爬過花生醬的烏龜還要遲鈍。　——呆伯特，出自《呆伯特》

You're slower than a herd of turtles stampeding through peanut butter.
—Dilbert, *Dilbert*

就算你在交配季充滿飢渴線索的原野上，身上塗滿麝香並跳著求偶舞讓自己充滿線索，你也還是得不到任何線索。
—— 愛德華・弗萊厄帝，美國作家

You couldn't get a clue during the clue mating season in a field full of horny clues if you smeared your body with clue musk and did the clue mating dance.
—Edward Flaherty, American author

我是低期望值的集大成者。 —— 喬治・W・布希，前美國總統，為與同樣擔任過美國總統的父親區別，另稱「小布希」

I'm the master of low expectations.
—George W. Bush

按理說，他是個瘋子，不過他也有只是愚蠢的清醒時刻。
—— 海因里希・海涅，德國詩人

Ordinarily he is insane. But he has lucid moments when he is only stupid.
—Heinrich Heine, German poet

雖然他沒比牛笨，卻也沒比牛聰明。

——詹姆斯‧瑟伯，美國漫畫家與作家

While he was not dumber than an ox, he was not any smarter either.

—James Thurber, American cartoonist and writer

他那自願的持續性無知，要為所有無知所造成的罪行負責。

——塞繆爾‧詹森，英國作家

He that voluntarily continues in ignorance is guilty of all crimes which ignorance produces.

—Samuel Johnson, British author

他們每次開口都讓人類知識的總和又減少了一些。

——湯瑪斯‧布拉克特‧里德，前美國眾議院議長

They never open their mouths without subtracting from the sum of human knowledge.

—Thomas Brackett Reed, former Speaker of the House

一個人是聰明的；而一群人，你很清楚，就會變成是愚蠢、危險，一點什麼就會恐慌失措的動物。 ——湯米‧李‧瓊斯，美國演員

A person is smart. People are dumb, dangerous, panicky animals and you know it.

—Tommy Lee Jones

在理想的世界裡，雖然你很不幸得跟他們共處一室，卻可以合得來，或至少可以容忍彼此的存在。相反的，在你那不甚完美的世界裡，可能充斥著以退為進的攻擊性紙條，以及人類最糟糕的發明之一：家庭會議。這個糟糕的主意讓大家聚在一起並分享所有你們彼此無法忍受的小怪癖，真的很糟糕。但對於根本不把這件事當回事的王八蛋來說，原本有禮的談話最後流於幼稚的謾罵，而他們還可以吐出超厲害的話羞辱人時，家庭會議絕對很有娛樂性。

你介意我往後坐一點嗎？因為你的嘴巴真的很臭。
—— 唐納・川普，美國第45任總統；商業大亨
Do you mind if I sit back a little? Because your breath is very bad.
—Donald Trump

你可以認為我是錯的，但那不是停止思考的理由。
—— 格瑞利・豪斯醫生，出自美國電視劇《怪醫豪斯》
You can think I'm wrong, but that's no reason to stop thinking.
—Dr. Gregory House, *House*

我絕不會犯下這種錯誤，去跟意見不值得尊重的人吵架。
—— 愛德華・吉本，英國歷史學家
I never make the mistake of arguing with people for whose opinions I

have no respect.

—Edward Gibbon, British historian

別看了，在這房裡有個多餘的人，我想那個人就是你。

——格魯喬·馬克斯，美國電影與喜劇演員

Don't look now, but there's one too many in this room and I think it's you.

—Groucho Marx

我不會藉由暗示你真的相信你剛剛所說的話來侮辱你的智慧。

——小威廉·F·巴克利，美國保守派作家與政論雜誌《國家評論》創辦人

I won't insult your intelligence by suggesting that you really believe what you just said.

—William F. Buckley Jr., American conservative author and founder of *The National Review*

如果你正在說話的對象看起來不像在聽你說，請保持耐心。可能只是他耳朵裡有一小團毛。 ——小熊維尼，出自《噗噗熊的逍遙遊》

If the person you are talking to doesn't appear to be listening, be patient. It may simply be that he has a small piece of fluff in his ear.

—Winnie the Pooh, *Pooh's Little Instruction Book*

女士，妳還有什麼想法沒表達嗎？—— 喬治·S·考夫曼，美國劇作家
Madam, have you no unexpressed thoughts?
—George S. Kaufman, American playwright

　　和尚擁有一種忽視周遭環境並進入禪定的神奇能力。經由多年的冥想與認真訓練，他們達到精神的統一性，超脫人生無數的煩惱。當然，一般而言，和尚不需要跟裸體主義者及演奏風笛的室友住在一起。然而，即使是長期飽受折磨的室友，都可以從和尚那學習對那些教人難以忍受的惱人習慣視而不見……或者也可以追隨下列這些混蛋的腳步，低聲抱怨。

當他們發現宇宙中心時，很多人會因為發現他們不是宇宙中心而大失所望。—— 伯納德·貝利，漫畫藝術家
When they discover the center of the universe, a lot of people will be disappointed to discover they are not it.
—Bernard Baily, comic book artist

我很想認真看待你，但這樣做是侮辱你的智慧。
—— 蕭伯納，愛爾蘭劇作家與作家。
I would like to take you seriously, but to do so would be an affront to your intelligence.
—George Bernard Shaw, Irish playwright and author

只有傻子才會與臭鼬、騾子或廚師爭辯。

—— 哈利・奧利佛，美國電影藝術總監

Only a fool argues with a skunk, a mule, or the cook.

—Harry Oliver, American director

沒說出來的話永遠不會造成傷害。 —— 科蘇特，匈牙利律師與政治家

The unspoken word never does harm.

—Kossuth, Hungarian lawyer and politician

絕學無憂。 —— 老子，中國哲學家

Stop thinking, and end your problems.

—Lao Tzu, ancient Chinese philosopher

你知道嗎？也許驢子不該講話是有道理的。

—— 史瑞克，出自《史瑞克》

You know what? Maybe there's a good reason donkeys shouldn't talk.

—Shrek, *Shrek*

唯一比自以為什麼都懂的人還傻的，就是跟他爭辯的人。

—— 斯坦尼斯拉夫・耶日・萊斯，波蘭詩人

The only fool bigger than the person who knows it all is the person who argues with him.

—Stanislaw Jerszy Lec, Polish poet

當室友之間的關係緊張了起來，甚至連想好好做人的意圖都失敗時，受挫的室友就會退回老方法：迴避。雖然房東要求你按時付租金，但那不代表你得跟同住的人攪和在一起。不過這也不是意味著你得跟室友公開宣戰，你們只需要避開彼此就好了，這簡單得多，也比較和平。然而，某些白目鬼就是無法閉上他們的嘴巴，而且還經常打破沉默提醒室友他們正在做什麼。

親密無間是很好，但僅限於連體嬰。
—— 維多利亞・比林斯，美國作家
Constant togetherness is fine—but only for Siamese twins.
—Victoria Billings, American author

我的幸福來源之一就是不要老想知道別人的事。
—— 多莉・麥迪遜，美國前總統詹姆斯・麥迪遜之妻
It is one of my sources of happiness never to desire a knowledge of other people's business.
—Dolley Madison

有人認為，會話是個失落的藝術；我真希望它曾經是。
—— 愛德華・R・默羅，美國廣播與電視記者
People say conversation is a lost art; how often I have wished it were.
—Edward R. Murrow, American radio and television journalist

隱士沒有同儕壓力。 ——史蒂芬‧萊特，美國喜劇演員

Hermits have no peer pressure.

—Steven Wright, American comedian

石頭經常會彈回投擲者的頭上。 ——伊麗莎白一世

The stone often recoils on the head of the thrower.

—Elizabeth I

別動！我想忘記你的樣子。 ——漢尼‧楊曼，英國喜劇演員

Don't move! I want to forget you just the way you are.

—Henny Youngman, British comedian

　　跟室友之間的對峙就像史詩般的世仇，到最後沒有人會記得當初是為了什麼事而開始爭吵。是他忘了把衛生紙撿起來？還是他老穿你的襪子卻不自己花錢買？一開始，答案似乎很重要，但也到了差不多可以讓過去的事就過去了的時候。以下的論調，可以證明一筆勾銷這種事，對混蛋來說，實在是太陌生了。

別走開！我正想試著道歉呢，你這個蠢蛋！

——卡爾文，出自漫畫《卡爾文與霍布斯》

Don't walk away! I'm trying to apologize, you dumb noodleloaf!

—Calvin, *Calvin and Hobbes*

雖然錯誤總是可以被原諒，但很少情有可原，而且永遠讓人無法接受。 ──羅伯特‧弗里普，樂團《深紅之王》的吉他手

A mistake is always forgivable, rarely excusable, and always unacceptable.
─Robert Fripp, guitarist for King Crimson

基於我靈活運用英語的能力，我什麼也不說。
──羅伯特‧本奇利，美國幽默作家與作家

Drawing on my fine command of the British language, I said nothing.
─Robert Benchley, American humorist and writer

你真是個悲哀、奇怪的小男人，我真同情你。再會了。
──巴斯光年，出自《玩具總動員》

You are a sad, strange little man, and you have my pity. Farewell.
─Buzz Lightyear, *Toy Story*

跟不用冗長艱深字彙而用簡短的語句像是「午餐吃啥？」的人講話有趣多了。 ──小熊維尼，出自《小熊維尼和老灰驢的家》

It is more fun to talk with someone who doesn't use long, difficult words but rather short, easy words like "What about lunch?"
─Winnie the Pooh, *House at Pooh Corner*

第四章
其他讓你幹譙的白癡

即使你已經是個幸運兒，不僅有愛你的家人、忠實的朋友以及超棒的室友，但你還是無法倖免於等著毀掉你一天的討厭傢伙。想像一下殭屍大舉入侵宛如世界末日的情境，然後把那些嗜食大腦的殭屍換成並排停車的人、亂插隊的傢伙、滑手機成癮者以及那些張著嘴大聲咀嚼的人。

你以為把自己搞得像胎兒一樣蜷縮在房裡，可以是一種對付混蛋的方式，但這絕對不理想。畢竟，你會肚子餓嘛。所以當你終於要冒險踏入這個世界時，用以下這些混蛋的言論來武裝自己吧。這樣一來，就算你只是在你安全上鎖的車裡一遍又一遍地重複咕噥著這些話，你還是會覺得你痛罵了這些混蛋一頓。

評論家就像是後宮的太監；他們知道要怎麼做，也每天看著別人做，但他們自己就是無法做。——布倫丹・貝漢，愛爾蘭作家
Critics are like eunuchs in a harem; they know how it's done, they've seen it done every day, but they're unable to do it themselves.
—Brendan Behan, Irish author

她的問題是欠缺對話的能力，而不是發表高論的能力。

── 蕭伯納，愛爾蘭劇作家與作家

The trouble with her is that she lacks the power of conversation but not the power of speech.

─George Bernard Shaw, Irish playwright and author

在你批評一個人之前，先穿著他們的鞋子走上一哩。這樣子，當你批評他們的時候，你不但離他們一哩遠，你還擁有他們的鞋子。── 傑克・韓第，美國喜劇演員

Before you criticize someone, you should walk a mile in their shoes. That way, when you criticize them, you are a mile away from them and you have their shoes.

─Jack Handey, American comedian

他們在天安門廣場都是這樣開車的嗎？賤人。

── 艾瑞・戈德，出自美國電視影集《我家也有大明星》

Is that the way they drive in Tiananmen Square, bitch?

─Ari Gold, *Entourage*

我們要對蠢蛋心懷感激。要是沒有他們，我們無法獲得成功。
—— 馬克・吐溫，美國作家

Let us be thankful for the fools. But for them the rest of us could not succeed.
—Mark Twain

地球有它的界限，但人類的愚蠢沒有極限。
—— 古斯塔夫・福樓拜，法國小說家

Earth has its boundaries, but human stupidity is limitless.
—Gustave Flaubert, French novelist

　　沒有人會在早上醒來的時候想：「多麼美好的一天，我真希望可以在上班途中踩到充滿大爛人的地雷！」不過很不幸的是，這正是在前方等著你的東西。討厭同伴無損你的人格；但你抗拒內心想用掃街車輾過他們的衝動，這才應該受到讚揚。而且，你絕不孤單；因為有些坦率的王八蛋會無畏地讚揚你的易怒，或者至少能同情你。

通往真相的道路是漫長的，而且沿路排滿了煩人的混帳。
—— 亞歷山大・尤布拉科夫，美國作家

The road to truth is long, and lined the entire way with annoying bastards.
—Alexander Jablokov, American author

我只是覺得她是個卑鄙、醜陋、沒有任何可取之處的人。

—— 男扮女裝流行歌手喬治男孩對全方位藝人瑪丹娜的評論

I just think she's a vile, hideous human being with no redeeming qualities.

—Boy George on Madonna

我愛人類，令我無法忍受的是人群。

—— 查爾斯·舒茲，美國漫畫家與漫畫《花生》❼的創作者

I love mankind. It's people I can't stand.

—Charles Schulz, American cartoonist and creator of the "peanuts" comics

傻瓜多到數不清。　—— 德西德里烏斯·伊拉斯謨，荷蘭神學家

Fools are without number.

—Desiderius Erasmus, Dutch theologian

常常覺得挪亞一行人沒錯過那條船真是很可惜。

—— 馬克·吐溫，美國作家

Often it does seem a pity that Noah and his party did not miss the boat.

—Mark Twain

---

❼《花生》是走紅全球的漫畫，史努比與查理·布朗就是漫畫裡的核心人物。

有些人就像翻轉彈簧❽：沒什麼實際用處，但你看到它摔下樓梯的時候，還是會忍不住笑出來。——來源不詳

Some people are like Slinkies: not really good for anything, but you still can't help but smile when you see one tumble down the stairs.

—Unknown

混蛋跟小孩有許多共通點：他們幼稚、自我中心而且極容易分心。跟小孩一樣，在所有事物中，混蛋最痛恨的就是被忽視。所以當一個混蛋大吼、戳你、惹你或是跺腳的時候，你要嘛走開，再不就是跟這些更機車的傢伙學著點，你就會沒事。

被你侮辱就像是戴上百合做的花環一樣。
——阿里斯托芬，古希臘喜劇作家

To be insulted by you is to be garlanded with lilies.

—Aristophanes

紳士不會侮辱我，而且沒有任何一個不是紳士的人可以侮辱我。
——弗雷德里克·道格拉斯，曾為奴隸，美國廢奴主義領導人，美國第一位黑人外交使節

A gentleman will not insult me, and no man not a gentleman can insult me.

—Frederick Douglass, American abolitionist leader and former slave

❽ Slinky 為一種由 Slinky 公司設計出來的玩具，外觀即為一巨大彈簧。

多聽少說。

──威廉・莎士比亞，英國戲劇家

Listen to many, speak to a few.

—William Shakespeare

如果你無法說服他們，就攪亂他們。

──哈瑞・S・杜魯門，美國第34任副總統

If you can't convince them, confuse them.

—Harry S. Truman

如果你無法忽視某個侮辱，就超越它；如果你無法超越它，就一笑置之；如果你連一笑置之都做不到，那麼這個侮辱大概是你應得的。 ──J・羅素・萊恩斯，美國歷史學家與作家

If you can't ignore an insult, top it; if you can't top it, laugh it off; and if you can't laugh it off, it's probably deserved.

—J. Russell Lynes, American historian and author

你的話傷透我的心。我一路哭著去銀行。

──列勃拉斯，美國演員、鋼琴家

What you said hurt me very much. I cried all the way to the bank.

—Liberace

規矩一，別想拍我馬屁。我已經很討厭你了，而且這件事不會改變。——米蘭達‧貝莉，出自美國電視影集《實習醫生》

Rule number one, don't bother sucking up. I already hate you; that's not gonna change.

—Miranda Bailey, *Grey's Anatomy*

一個睿智的男人會超越任何施加在他身上的羞辱，對不禮貌的行為最好的回應就是耐心與溫和。——莫里哀，法國劇作家與演員

A wise man is superior to any insults which can be put upon him, and the best reply to unseemly behavior is patience and moderation.

—Molière, French playwright and actor

我認為你冒犯公眾，而每個人都該揍你一頓。
——威廉‧莎士比亞，英國戲劇家

Me think'st thou art a general offence and every man should beat thee.

—William Shakespeare

無益之言少開口。——佛陀

Do not speak, unless it improves upon silence.

—Buddha

雖然有些混蛋很容易被忽視，但有些卻不是那麼好打發。你的本能可能是逃走並像個小孩縮成一團，不過，有些人可不是好惹的，他們會用以下這些可貴的話來反擊。

你的無知妨礙了我的談話。 ──安東尼‧霍普，英國小說家
Your ignorance cramps my conversation.
—Anthony Hope, British novelist

去找讀心術的人時，他有算你半價嗎？
── 大衛‧萊特曼，美國電視節目主持人
When you go to the mind reader, do you get half price?
—David Letterman

我敢打賭，你爸在你生命中的第一年都把時間拿來用石頭丟送子鳥。 ──厄文‧布雷赫爾，美國編劇
I'll bet your father spent the first year of your life throwing rocks at the stork.
—Irving Brecher, American screenwriter

人生很艱難，如果你是個笨蛋，會更艱難。
── 約翰‧韋恩，美國電影演員

Life's tough. It's tougher if you're stupid.

—John Wayne

我一點也不了解這個人。不過不管怎樣，我知道他的兩件事：一是他沒吃過牢飯，另一件是我不知道為什麼。

—— 馬克‧吐溫，美國作家

I don't know anything about this man. Anyhow, I only know two things about him. One is, he has never been in jail, and the other is, I don't know why.

—Mark Twain

他就跟他的文字一樣好，不過他的文字很差。

—— 蘇馬斯‧麥克馬努斯，愛爾蘭作家

He is as good as his word—and his word is no good.

—Seamus MacManus, Irish author

有兩種侮辱是人類無法忍受的：一個是他沒有幽默感，另一個是他從不知道什麼是麻煩。 —— 辛克萊‧路易斯，美國小說家

There are two insults no human being will endure: that he has no sense of humor, and that he has never known trouble.

—Sinclair Lewis

我無法相信你是十萬個精子裡面最快的那個。
—— 史蒂芬・波爾，美國喜劇演員

I can't believe that out of 100,000 sperm, you were the quickest.
—Steven Pearl, American comedian

　　一天之中，你經歷了被混蛋比中指、被爛咖逼車、最後還被不太友善的服務生毀了一頓午餐，也許你會好奇這些每天都會出現的該死傢伙究竟來自何方。好吧，如果你想了解這些無禮、輕率、給社會帶來困擾的混蛋為何會如此猖狂，就必須將歷史往前翻回幾頁。當清教徒在普利茅斯岩上岸，展開驅逐原住民的工作（另一個說法叫「種族滅絕」），我們都為了這塊突然出現、任我們處置的富庶大地歡欣鼓舞。當我們為了大量生產機動馬車而開始過度消耗地球自然資源時，我們都豎起了大拇指還立刻跳上車。我們把那些腦殘、只熱中自己出現在哪個頻道的電視「明星」當神來崇拜，而不是嘲笑他們，希望他們消失在電視上。所以，當街頭巷尾的小混混認為用糖灌滿你的油箱沒什麼大不了，這有什麼好驚訝的？如果你不覺得驚訝，那下面的王八蛋也跟你有同感。

這個世界的問題就是笨蛋都很有自信，而聰明的人卻充滿疑問。
—— 伯特蘭・羅素，英國哲學家

The trouble with the world is that the stupid are cocksure and the intelligent are full of doubt.
—Bertrand Russell, British philosopher

人們以為當超級天才一定很有趣，但他們不了解的是，要忍受世上所有的白癡有多麼痛苦。 ──卡爾文，出自漫畫《卡爾文與霍布斯》

People think it must be fun to be a super genius, but they don't realize how hard it is to put up with all the idiots in the world.

—Calvin, *Calvin and Hobbes*

如果你因為自己很好就期待世界會公平地對待你，這就像是期望公牛不會攻擊你，只因為你是個素食主義者。

──丹尼斯‧何利，美國電視主持人

Expecting the world to treat you fairly because you are good is like expecting the bull not to charge because you are a vegetarian.

—Dennis Wholey, American television host

你掌握了自己的人生，然後呢？這可麻煩了，因為你不能怪任何人。 ──埃麗卡‧容，美國作家

You take your life in your own hands, and what happens? A terrible thing: no one to blame.

—Erica Jong, American author

我們放棄的那些人，其實我們跟他們沒兩樣，真悲哀啊。

──佛瑞德‧羅傑斯，美國電視主持人

How sad it is that we give up on people who are just like us.

—Fred Rogers

千萬別在大熱天踢一坨新鮮的屎。

——哈瑞·S·杜魯門，美國第34任副總統。

Never kick a fresh turd on a hot day.

—Harry S. Truman

大自然只製造不會說話的動物，傻瓜的存在必須歸功於這個社

會。——奧諾雷·德·巴爾扎克，法國小說家

Nature makes only dumb animals. We owe the fools to society.

—Honoré de Balzac, French novelist

認為自己什麼都懂的人，對我們這些真的什麼都懂的人來說是很

煩的。——艾薩克·艾西莫夫，美國科幻作家

People who think they know everything are a great annoyance to those
of us who do.

—Isaac Asimov, American science-fiction author

要在爭論中打敗無知的人是不可能的。

——威廉·G·麥卡杜，美國參議院議員

It is impossible to defeat an ignorant man in argument.

—William G. McAdoo, United States senator

當你邀請全世界參加你的派對時，難免會有人尿在啤酒裡。
—— 潔妮・賈丁，美國科技記者

When you invite the whole world to your party, inevitably someone pees in the beer.

—Xeni Jardin, American tech journalist

　　每天遇到這些混蛋其實有個好處，就是你終於可以明白，跟他們比起來你有多好。事實上，不論狀況有多糟，永遠會有一堆蠢貨、王八蛋與爛咖提醒你：你真棒！如果你巴不得來場瘟疫把世上所有無可救藥的混蛋都給消滅掉的話，那麼請想像一下：要是沒有他們，你的感覺會有多糟？正因如此，你不必告訴這些傻瓜他們有多失敗，以下這些王八蛋已經替你說了。

要是除掉世上所有的傻瓜，活在這世上就沒那麼有趣了，也沒那麼多好處。—— 亨利・威勒・蕭，美國幽默作家

Take all the fools out of this world and there wouldn't be any fun living in it, or profit.

—Henry Wheeler Shaw, American humorist

他很清楚自己有多無知。—— 埃倫・格拉斯哥，美國幽默作家

He knows so little and knows it so fluently.

—Ellen Glasgow, American novelist

不用那麼謙虛，你沒那麼好。 ——果爾達‧梅厄，前以色列總理

Don't be so humble—you are not that great.

—Golda Meir, former Israeli prime minister

有些人從黑猩猩進化而來的時間似乎比其他人更晚。

——法蘭克‧麥金尼‧哈伯德，以「金‧哈伯」為筆名，美國漫畫家

Some folks seem to have descended from the chimpanzee later than others.

—Frank McKinney "Kin" Hubbard, American cartoonist

他的注意力維持的時間跟閃電不相上下。 ——勞勃‧瑞福

He has the attention span of a lightning bolt.

—Robert Redford

理智的最大勝利，就是它讓我們可以跟沒有理智的人好好相處。

——伏爾泰，法國哲學家

The true triumph of reason is that it enables us to get along with those who do not possess it.

—Voltaire, French philosopher

請自備酒瓶

溫斯頓・邱吉爾曾詢問阿斯特子爵夫人,他該穿什麼出席她的化妝舞會。她回答:「首相先生,您何不清醒著過來?」

Winston Churchill asked Lady Astor what disguise he should wear to her masquerade ball. She said, "Why don't you come sober, Mr. Prime Minister?"

第五章

喝酒

　　沒有人知道我們的祖先究竟是如何與酒精相遇的，當他們發現它具有神奇療效而且能夠增加個人魅力時，他們就花了比製作長矛更多時間在玩倒立喝酒遊戲上。過了幾千年，這情況沒什麼改變，人們還是很愛喝酒。對某些人來說，住在離酒館近的地方遠比緊鄰功能完善的公立學校重要的多。不過只要你找得到酒精，就找得到王八蛋。這是美國人最愛的消遣，它們和自我放縱如影隨形，因而帶出人性最醜陋的一面。

敬酒精！所有人生問題的根源及解決之道。
—— 荷馬・J・辛普森，出自《辛普森家庭》
To alcohol! The cause of, and solution to, all of life's problems.
—Homer J. Simpson, *The Simpsons*

為什麼他們只在房間裡放聖經，而不是放在樓下的酒吧？通常等到了房間時已經太遲了。—— 克里斯多福・莫爾利，美國作家。
Why do they put the Gideon Bibles only in the bedrooms, where it's

usually too late, and not in the barroom downstairs?
—Christopher Morley, American writer

只要一杯酒就可以讓我醉倒，但問題是，我不記得那究竟是第
十三杯還是第十四杯。 ——喬治‧伯恩斯，美國喜劇演員與演員
It takes only one drink to get me drunk. The trouble is, I can't
remember if it's the thirteenth or the fourteenth.
—George Burns, American comedian and actor

指定一個人保持清醒開車送大家回家的問題在於，不會有人喜歡
這檔事；如果不幸輪到你，就好好享受它的樂趣吧。一夜狂歡之
後，把這些酒鬼丟錯家。 ——傑夫‧法克斯渥西，美國喜劇演員
The problem with the designated driver program, it's not a desirable
job, but if you ever get sucked into doing it, have fun with it. At the
end of the night, drop them off at the wrong house.
—Jeff Foxworthy, American comedian

我寧願相信上帝沒死，只是醉了。
　　——約翰‧休斯頓，美國演員與導演
I prefer to think that God is not dead, just drunk.
—John Huston, American actor and director

醉鬼沒有朋友，只有共犯。——梅森‧庫利，英國教授與作家

Drunks do not have friends, but accomplices.

—Mason Cooley, English professor and writer

我有個重大的發現……只要攝取足夠的酒精，就會產生各種陶醉的效果。——奧斯卡‧王爾德，愛爾蘭作家

I have made an important discovery ... that alcohol, taken in sufficient quantities, produces all the effects of intoxication.

—Oscar Wilde

如果你們沒喝酒，那麼彼此之間的長談可能會考驗兄弟情誼。——P‧J‧歐羅克，美國政治諷刺作家

Long conversations with pals when neither you nor they have had a drink can be a test of palship.

—P. J. O'Rourke, American political satirist

我認為一個男人原則上一年應該至少要喝醉兩次，這樣他才不會讓他自己對這件事顯得太自大。——雷蒙‧錢德勒，美國小說家

I think a man ought to get drunk at least twice a year just on principle, so he won't let himself get snotty about it.

—Raymond Chandler, American novelist

我喝故我在。——Ｗ·Ｃ·菲爾茲，美國喜劇演員

I drink, therefore I am.

—W. C. Fields, American comedian

我從酒精得到的東西比酒精從我這得到的還多。

—— 溫斯頓·邱吉爾，前英國首相

I have taken more out of alcohol than alcohol has taken out of me.

—Winston Churchill

　　在所有可以讓你喝醉的選項中，沒有任何一種酒可以讓極為誘人的老式啤酒黯然失色。它冰冰涼涼的、很便宜、很好喝，而且可以讓你喝醉。不幸地，它也可以把你喜歡與他們為伴的正常人，轉變成憤怒、過度自信、沒人想跟他們在一起的混球。也難怪，有些歷史上著名的大人物可以跟那些名不見經傳的酒醉混蛋一樣，把酒瓶從他們的嘴巴裡拿出來的時間足以頌讚上帝賜與人類的聖禮。

啤酒是上帝愛我們且希望我們快樂的活生生證據。

—— 班傑明·富蘭克林，美國政治家

Beer is living proof that God loves us and wants us to be happy.

—Benjamin Franklin

毫無疑問地，人類歷史上最偉大的發明是啤酒。噢，我保證汽車也是很好的發明，但是汽車一點也不適合搭配披薩。

—— 戴夫‧貝瑞，美國作家與專欄作家

Without question, the greatest invention in the history of mankind is beer. Oh, I grant you that the wheel was also a fine invention, but the wheel does not go nearly as well with pizza.

—Dave Barry, American author and columnist

如果你沒有一種啤酒或一家航空公司，根本無法成為一個真正的國家。如果你有足球隊或一些核子武器可能會有點幫助，但至少還是要有一種啤酒。—— 法蘭克‧札帕，美國搖滾音樂家

You can't be a real country unless you have a beer and an airline—it helps if you have some kind of a football team, or some nuclear weapons, but at the very least you need a beer.

—Frank Zappa, American rock musician

光啜飲一口也許能斷定啤酒好不好，不過還是喝光確認比較好。

—— 捷克諺語

A fine beer may be judged with only one sip, but it's better to be thoroughly sure.

—Czech proverb

給我一個愛啤酒的女人，我就可以征服全世界。

—— 威廉大帝，德國皇帝

Give me a woman who loves beer and I will conquer the world.

—Kaiser Wilhelm, German emperor

他是個聰明人，他發明啤酒。

—— 柏拉圖，古希臘哲學家

He was a wise man who invented beer.

—Plato

發薪日到了，終於可以跟啤酒為伍。

—— 魯德亞德・吉卜林，生於孟買的英國作家

Payday came and with it beer.

—Rudyard Kipling

科學家在研究中指出，喝啤酒對肝臟有益。抱歉，我說了科學家嗎？我想說的是愛爾蘭人。 —— 蒂娜・菲，美國女演員與喜劇演員

In a study, scientists report that drinking beer can be good for the liver.
I'm sorry, did I say scientists? I meant Irish people.

—Tina Fey, American actress and comedian

當我用油溫暖我的房子時，一年平均要用掉八百加侖。後來我發現我只需要超過那個量的一半再多一點的啤酒，就可以讓我整個冬天保持溫暖舒適。 ── 戴夫‧貝瑞，美國作家與專欄作家。

When I heated my home with oil, I used an average of 800 gallons a year. I have found that I can keep comfortably warm for an entire winter with slightly over half that quantity of beer.
—Dave Barry, American author and columnist

肥胖、酒醉跟愚蠢，在人生的道路上是死路一條。
── 迪恩‧弗農‧沃瑪，出自電影《動物屋》
Fat, drunk, and stupid is no way to go through life, son.
—Dean Vernon Wormer, *Animal House*

　　對那些沒有時間與心力喝啤酒喝到醉的人來說，烈酒是個好選擇。不過，有些話得說在前頭，如果你喝完整瓶，很有可能你會一命嗚呼，而且因為它比啤酒烈，你可以在某些禁止酒精的場合謹慎地攜帶少量烈酒。但烈酒的問題在於，有些喝了啤酒還可以保持低調的人，卻會在喝威士忌或長島冰茶後變成一個臭王八蛋……尤其如果他們把酒藏在外套口袋裡的隨身酒瓶，還在執行陪審團任務時拿出來啜飲幾口。那些混蛋可能會說出和以下很像的話：

威士忌治不好的，別的東西也治不好。 ——愛爾蘭諺語

What whiskey will not cure, there is no cure for.

—Irish proverb

我還是繼續喝琴酒吧，香檳不過是炫耀人脈的薑汁啤酒。

—— 鷹眼，出自美國電視影集《外科醫師》

I'll stick with gin. Champagne is just ginger ale that knows somebody.

—Hawkeye, *M*A*S*H*

世界上最糟的事就是喝到爛威士忌。但是好喝的威士忌實在少之又少。不過，一個男人在五十歲之前實在不該跟酒精搞在一起；但如果不這樣，他一定是個白癡。 ——威廉·福克納，美國小說家

There is no such thing as bad whiskey. Some whiskeys just happen to be better than others. But a man shouldn't fool with booze until he's fifty; then he's a damn fool if he doesn't.

—William Faulkner, American novelist

我需要大量健康營養的酒精。化學能量可以讓我的燃料電池維持足夠的電量。 ——班德，出自美國喜劇動畫《飛出個未來》

I need plenty of wholesome nutritious alcohol. The chemical energy keeps my fuel cells charged.

—Bender, *Futurama*

我的奶奶已經八十多歲了，卻還不需要戴眼鏡，直接拿酒瓶灌著喝。——漢尼‧楊曼，英國喜劇演員

My grandmother is over eighty and still doesn't need glasses. Drinks right out of the bottle.

—Henny Youngman, British comedian

我不該從威士忌換喝馬丁尼的。——亨弗萊‧鮑嘉，美國演員

I should never have switched from Scotch to martinis.

—Humphrey Bogart, American actor

　　的確沒有任何東西比一杯好的葡萄酒更能傳達豐富與優雅的氛圍。不過，這些特質並不等同於禮貌。喝葡萄酒的人不見得比社會上其他人更好；只是他們更有錢、更聰明、更有品味而已，至少他們自己這樣覺得。從喝葡萄酒的人身上可以找到一種喝其他酒類的人所沒有的自我優越感……而那份自我優越感孕育出了令人難以忍受的高級混蛋，以下這些高傲的言論就是證據。

有個喜愛葡萄酒的男人，發現晚餐後上的甜點是葡萄，他表達謝意，一邊卻推開盤子，說他還不習慣吞葡萄酒做的藥丸。

——尚‧安瑟瑪‧布西亞－薩維亨，法國律師與政治家

A man who was fond of wine was offered some grapes at dessert after dinner. Much obliged, said he, pushing the plate aside, I am not accustomed to take my wine in pills.

—Jean Anthelme Brillat-Savarin, French lawyer and politician

葡萄酒一喝下，怪事就來了。

──約翰‧克里斯多福‧弗里德里希‧馮‧席勒，德國詩人

When the wine goes in, strange things come out.

—Johann Christoph Friedrich von Schiller, German poet

有些人整天抱怨頭痛、又花整晚喝下讓他頭痛的葡萄酒，我跟他們不一樣。──約翰‧沃爾夫岡‧馮‧歌德，德國作家

I will not be as those who spend the day in complaining of headache, and the night in drinking the wine that gives it.

—Johann Wolfgang von Goethe, German author

有些黃鼠狼偷走了我午餐的軟木塞。──Ｗ‧Ｃ‧菲爾茲，美國喜劇演員

Some weasel took the cork out of my lunch.

—W. C. Fields, American comedian

葡萄酒喝著喝著，友誼就出現了！──約翰‧蓋伊，英國詩人

From wine what sudden friendship springs!

—John Gay, British poet

繼上帝之後，葡萄酒萬歲。
——羅薩莉亞·卡斯特羅，西班牙加里西亞作家
After God, long live wine.
—Rosalia de Castro, Galician writer

葡萄酒的缺點之一就是，它讓人不小心把腦袋裡的想法給說了出
來。——塞繆爾·詹森，英國作家
This is one of the disadvantages of wine: it makes a man mistake words
for thought.
—Samuel Johnson, British author

葡萄酒的一大缺點是它一開始就直衝腳底，而且是個狡猾的摔角
手。——提圖斯·馬丘斯·普勞圖斯，古羅馬劇作家
This is the great fault of wine; it first trips up the feet: it is a cunning
wrestler.
—Titus Maccius Plautus, Roman playwright

我用葡萄酒做飯，有時候我甚至把它當食物。
——W·C·菲爾茲，美國喜劇演員
I cook with wine, sometimes I even add it to the food.
—W. C. Fields, American comedian

對有些人來說，喝酒是種消遣。對其他人來說則是志業。但對特定少數人來說，喝酒是一種生活方式。當然，你可以認為他們是可悲的墮落傢伙，但也許你該停下來想想，這些可憐蟲為你做出多大的犧牲。要是沒有他們，你要從哪得到優越感的錯覺？

我本來有慢跑的習慣，但冰塊一直從我的威士忌杯子裡掉出來。
──大衛‧李‧羅斯，美國搖滾歌手

I used to jog, but the ice cubes kept falling out of my glass.
─David Lee Roth

喝醉是個很好的偽裝。我喝醉才能跟王八蛋講話，包括我自己。
──吉姆‧莫里森，美國創作歌手、詩人

Being drunk is a good disguise. I drink so I can talk to a**holes. This includes me.
─Jim Morrison

如果你不用任何支撐就能躺在地上，那表示你還沒醉。
──迪恩‧馬丁，美國演員、歌手

You're not drunk if you can lie on the floor without holding on.
─Dean Martin

清醒的時候去做那些你說你喝醉時會做的事，這可以讓你閉嘴。

——厄尼斯特·海明威，美國作家

Always do sober what you said you'd do drunk. That will teach you to keep your mouth shut.

—Ernest Hemingway

一個充滿陽光的美麗午後，有著鳥鳴與風吹過樹葉的窸窣聲，這些會讓你想喝醉嗎？ ——傑克·韓第，美國喜劇演員

What is it about a beautiful sunny afternoon, with the birds singing and the wind rustling through the leaves, that makes you want to get drunk?

—Jack Handey, American comedian

雖然已經有人試過了，但還是沒人找到可以靠喝酒為生的方法。

——琴·柯爾，美國作家與劇作家

Even though a number of people have tried, no one has ever found a way to drink for a living.

—Jean Kerr, American author and playwright

每當有人問我要不要在威士忌裡加水，我會說我是口渴，不是身上髒了。 ——喬·E·路易斯，美國喜劇演員與歌手

Whenever someone asks me if I want water with my scotch, I say I'm thirsty, not dirty.

—Joe E. Lewis, American comedian and singer

人，因為清醒，所以要喝醉；人生還有什麼事比酒醉更美妙？

—— 拜倫勳爵，英國詩人

Man, being reasonable, must get drunk; the best of life is but intoxication.

—Lord Byron

生活就是宿醉與酒吧營業之間這段無聊的時間。

—— 麥克・奧布萊恩，美國詩人

Life is the boring bit between the hangover and the opening time.

—Michael O'Brien, American poet

　　如果能夠謹慎節制地喝酒，酒精可以讓你從忙碌的生活裡放鬆。但如果你無法控制自己，飲酒過量，酒精帶來的後果就不只是這樣了。經歷一夜放縱狂飲後，通常隔天早上都會讓你痛不欲生，不過，還是有很多人認為飲酒有數不完的好處，遠遠超過那些不好的後果。此外，酒精可以讓你更聰明、更有趣、更性感、反應更快而且更猛。雖然這些能力的提升通常只存在於酒鬼的腦袋裡，但我們永遠別低估正面思考的力量。

只有愛爾蘭咖啡能在一杯飲料中就提供了四大類基本食物：酒精、咖啡因、糖與脂肪。——亞歷克斯‧萊文，愛爾蘭演員與音樂家

Only Irish coffee provides in a single glass all four essential food groups: alcohol, caffeine, sugar, and fat.
—Alex Levine, Irish actor and musician

並非所有的化學物質都是不好的。舉例來說，要是沒有氫和氧，就沒有辦法製造出啤酒的重要成分之一：水。
——戴夫‧貝瑞，美國作家與專欄作家

Not all chemicals are bad. Without chemicals such as hydrogen and oxygen, for example, there would be no way to make water, a vital ingredient in beer.
—Dave Barry, American author and columnist

比起用前腦葉白質切除術來治療精神病❾，我寧可要一瓶酒。
——桃樂絲‧帕克，美國詩人

I'd rather have a bottle in front of me than a frontal lobotomy.
—Dorothy Parker, American poet

---

❾ 1930 至 1950 年代盛行治療多種精神疾病的腦外科手術。

不論是什麼情況，對一個男人來說，酒精是必要的，因為這有助於他正面看待自己。── 法利・彼得・德昂，美國幽默作家

Alcohol is necessary for a man so that he can have a good opinion of himself, undisturbed by the facts.
—Finley Peter Dunne, American humorist

酒是男人最糟糕的敵人，不過，聖經也說了，要愛你的敵人。
── 法蘭克・辛納屈，美國演員、歌手

Alcohol may be man's worst enemy, but the Bible says love your enemy.
—Frank Sinatra

有時回想起我喝掉的啤酒，我覺得很羞愧。我看著杯子，想著那些在啤酒廠的工人們以及他們的希望與夢想。如果我不喝掉這杯酒，他們可能會失業，夢想也會破碎，於是我告訴自己：「比起自私地擔心我的肝，我還是喝掉這杯啤酒，讓他們夢想成真比較好。」── 傑克・韓第，美國喜劇演員

Sometimes when I reflect back on all the beer I drink, I feel ashamed. Then I look into the glass and think about the workers in the brewery and all of their hopes and dreams. If I didn't drink this beer, they might be out of work and their dreams would be shattered. Then I say to myself, "It is better that I drink this beer and let their dreams come true than to be selfish and worry about my liver."
—Jack Handey, American comedian

有個女人開車載我去喝酒，而我居然連謝謝她的禮貌都沒做到。
——Ｗ・Ｃ・菲爾茲，美國喜劇演員

A woman drove me to drink, and I never even had the courtesy to thank her.
—W. C. Fields, American comedian

　　儘管所有證據都顯示，酒是烈酒杯之後最偉大的發明，仍有少數特定的混蛋不這麼認為。反對酒精的人用了一些巧妙的欺瞞手法，例如援引事實與詳細研究，來證明長期飲用會導致肝病、酒精成癮甚至引發心臟問題。至於要不要相信這些尖酸刻薄的王八蛋，你自己決定。

應該要有人提醒那些想借酒澆愁的人，悲傷不會因此消失。
——安・蘭德斯，美國專欄作家

People who drink to drown their sorrow should be told that sorrow knows how to swim.
—Ann Landers

在我的經驗裡，要一群喝茫的男人好好點根菸，別把火點在濾嘴上，可能還容易些，但如果要他們做出比這更複雜的事，你就頭大了。——戴夫・貝瑞，美國作家與專欄作家

In my experience, you run into trouble when you ask a group of beer-drinking men to perform any task more complex than remembering not to light the filter ends of cigarettes.

—Dave Barry, American author and columnist

酒精飲料上的警語都太平淡了，應該要更生動點。我會建議這樣寫：酒精會把你變得跟你爸一樣混蛋。 ——喬治‧卡林，美國喜劇演員

I think the warning labels on alcoholic beverages are too bland. They should be more vivid. Here are a few I would suggest: Alcohol will turn you into the same a**hole your father was.

—George Carlin, American comedian

喝酒是因為有件事想要做，然後可以把一切歸咎給酒精。

——蜜妮翁‧麥克勞克林，美國作家

The chief reason for drinking is the desire to behave in a certain way, and to be able to blame it on alcohol.

—Mignon McLaughlin, American writer

真正重要的事情都是在喝雞尾酒時說的，而且從沒做出來。

——彼得‧F‧杜拉克，美國社會經濟學家

The really important things are said over cocktails and are never done.

—Peter F. Drucker, American social ecologist

在我朋友喝醉摔倒前，他們總是舉杯敬健康。
—— 菲莉絲・狄樂，美國喜劇演員與女演員

Health—what my friends are always drinking to before they fall down.
—Phyllis Diller, American comedian and actress

有些得天獨厚的幸運傢伙擁有強壯的肚子及濃醇的血液，讓他們幾乎不需要愛惜自己的身體。才喝第二杯蘋果馬丁尼便頭昏眼花的人，就沒有這種變態的幸運，他們很清楚「適量」有多重要。

所以，當朋友建議你把酒吧裡所有種類的酒混進兩個酒杯，看誰能先喝完的時候，如果你可以冷靜從容地說：「你先喝，再告訴我味道如何？」你可要好好讚美一下自己。最好先聽聽經驗豐富的酒鬼怎麼說，絕對比你先喝再發問更好。

在雞尾酒派對上喝啤酒不是很好，尤其是在一個你搞不清楚浴室在哪兒的房子裡。
—— 比利・卡特，美國商人、卡特總統的弟弟

Beer is not a good cocktail-party drink, especially in a home where you don't know where the bathroom is.
—Billy Carter, American businessman and younger brother to President Jimmy Carter

酒後別駕車，也別推桿。 ── 迪恩・馬丁，美國演員、歌手

If you drink, don't drive. Don't even putt.

──Dean Martin

永遠別接受泌尿科醫生給你的飲料。

── 爾瑪・龐貝克，美國幽默作家

Never accept a drink from a urologist.

──Erma Bombeck, American humorist

與其警告孕婦不要喝酒，我覺得應該叫女性酗酒者不要做愛。

── 喬治・卡林，美國喜劇演員

Instead of warning pregnant women not to drink, I think female alcoholics should be told not to fuck.

──George Carlin, American comedian

沒有價值的人活著只為了吃喝，有價值的人吃喝只為了活著。

── 蘇格拉底，古希臘哲學家

Worthless people live only to eat and drink; people of worth eat and drink only to live.

──Socrates

小心烈酒。它會讓你對收稅人員開槍，而且還射不中。
── 羅伯特・A・海萊因，美國科幻作家

Be wary of strong drink. It can make you shoot at tax collectors—and miss.
—Robert A. Heinlein, American science fiction author

　　某些一心想喝醉的酒鬼可能會驚訝地發現，有些人不需要從喉嚨灌入大量龍舌蘭就可以有段愉快的時光。例如，長途散步或是讀一本好書，都是簡單的快樂；但對酒鬼來說，這就跟喝到吐翻之前看看能自己灌入多少啤酒一樣刺激。這種生活方式可能還滿適合某些人的，就在你打算嘗試之前，不妨先聽聽看世上最惡名昭彰的酒徒是怎麼看待這件事的，這樣會比較明智一些。

很久以前，我曾經清醒長達五年之久，但無聊到爆。
── 查理・辛，美國演員

I was sober for five years a long time ago and was just bored out of my tree.
—Charlie Sheen

我替那些不喝酒的人感到惋惜，早上醒來那種不怎樣的感覺會持續一整天。── 法蘭克・辛納屈，美國演員、歌手
I feel sorry for people who don't drink. When they wake up in the morning, that's as good as they're going to feel all day.
—Frank Sinatra

一九六九年，我放棄了女人和酒，那是我人生最糟的二十分鐘。
——喬治·貝斯特，愛爾蘭足球員

In 1969 I gave up women and alcohol and it was the worst 20 minutes of my life.
—George Best, Irish footballer

節制，是有權選擇的人才有的美德。 ——亨利·季辛吉，美國外交官

Moderation is a virtue only in those who are thought to have an alternative.
—Henry Kissinger, American diplomat

我不信任駱駝，也不相信那些不喝一杯酒就能過完一週的人。
——喬·E·路易斯，美國喜劇演員與歌手

I distrust camels, and anyone else who can go a week without a drink.
—Joe E. Lewis, American comedian and singer

酗酒是一種病，也是唯一一種你得到時還會被臭罵的病。他媽的，奧托，你真是個酒鬼。他媽的，奧托，你有狼瘡……其中一個聽起來果真不太妙。 ——米奇·赫貝格，美國喜劇演員

Alcoholism is a disease, but it's the only one you can get yelled at for having. Goddamn it, Otto, you are an alcoholic. Goddamn it, Otto, you have lupus ... one of those two doesn't sound right.
—Mitch Hedberg, American comedian

我不是個重度酒鬼，因為有時候我可以好幾個小時不沾一滴酒。

——諾爾‧寇威爾，英國劇作家

I am not a heavy drinker. I can sometimes go for hours without touching a drop.

—Noel Coward, British playwright

我開始注意飲食，發誓戒酒，也不再大吃大喝。十四天後，我發現人生整整失去了兩週。

——喬‧E‧路易斯，美國喜劇演員與歌手

I went on a diet, swore off drinking and heavy eating, and after 14 days I'd lost exactly two weeks.

—Joe E. Lewis, American comedian and singer

戒酒之後，我了解到我依然是過去那個王八蛋，只是車上少了些凹痕。——羅賓‧威廉斯，美國演員

After I quit drinking, I realized I am the same a**hole I always was; I just have fewer dents in my car.

—Robin Williams

第六章
藥物、毒品

　　當我們還是小孩的時候，大人跟我們提出三個毋庸置疑的真理。第一個也是最重要的一個，聖誕老人絕對是真的。第二個，吞西瓜子絕對會從肚子裡長出西瓜。最後一個，但不是最不重要，藥物不是好東西。

　　我們的哥哥跟科學已經分別反駁了前面兩項真理，這讓我們開始質疑第三個的有效性。首先，據我們所知，我們的父母沒有試過毒品，所以他們絕對沒資格在這件事上做出明智的決定。其次，還有個偽善的事實就是，不管他們有多堅持藥物不好，每當我們咳嗽的時候，他們還是會直接去拿諾比舒冒止咳糖漿。

　　經過了這些年，藥物這麼重要的事，以及不知怎麼搞得，每個家裡都出現快樂的男胖子，但願你已經有了自己的看法。如果你還沒有定論，很多坦率的王八蛋可以幫你形成自己的意見。

在歷史的洪流中，死於喝酒與迷幻藥的人比為了信仰和國家而死的人要多得多。——奧爾德斯‧赫胥黎，英國作家

In the course of history, many more people have died for their drink and their dope than have died for their religion or their country.
—Aldous Huxley, British author

我從七克的冰毒裡獲得快感，而且我吸光了它們。因為那就是驅使我的動力，我有安非他命，就有動力❿。上吧！
——查理‧辛，美國演員

I was banging sevengram rocks and finishing them. Because that's how I roll. I have one speed, I have one gear: Go!
—Charlie Sheen

我嚐試過各種東西。我可以很有自信地告訴你，我很了解迷幻藥。我從沒因為社交需求而使用這些東西，但好奇心帶我去過很多有趣的領域。——丹‧拉瑟，美國記者、新聞主播

I've tried everything. I can say to you with confidence, I know a fair amount about LSD. I've never been a social user of any of these things, but my curiosity has carried me into a lot of interesting areas.
—Dan Rather

我以前有毒品問題，不過現在我賺的錢夠多了。
——大衛‧李‧羅斯，美國搖滾歌手

I used to have a drug problem; now I make enough money.
—David Lee Roth

---

❿ speed 可指變速箱，gear 則是排檔。在這裡被用來當做雙關語使用。Speed 在俗語中亦有安非他命的意思。

為什麼會有這麼多關於藥物測試的爭議呢？我認識一堆傢伙願意試用任何他們能提供的藥物。

——喬治‧卡林，美國喜劇演員

Why is there so much controversy about drug testing? I know plenty of guys who would be willing to test any drug they could come up with.

—George Carlin, American comedian

我不會建議任何人縱慾、吸毒或幹些荒唐事，不過它們對我很有用。——亨特‧S‧湯普森，美國作家與記者

I wouldn't recommend sex, drugs, or insanity for everyone, but they've always worked for me.

—Hunter S. Thompson, American author and journalist

有個基本問題從來沒有人提過，就是為什麼人們要使用各種毒品？為什麼我們在日常生活中會擁有這些東西？我的意思是，這個社會究竟出了什麼問題，讓我們的壓力大到如果不保護自己、對抗社會，我們就無法生存？

——約翰‧藍儂，英國音樂人，以披頭四創團團員揚名全球

The basic thing nobody asks is why do people take drugs of any sort? Why do we have these accessories to normal living to live? I mean, is there something wrong with society that's making us so pressurized that we cannot live without guarding ourselves against it?

—John Lennon

我以前會吸毒，我現在還在吸，不過我以前也吸。
——米奇‧赫貝格，美國喜劇演員
I used to do drugs. I still do, but I used to, too.
—Mitch Hedberg, American comedian

我不會像某些郵輪上的廉價魔術師一樣，把吸毒當成逃脫的把戲。我吸毒的目的跟在窮鄉僻壤的探勘師一樣，是為了尋找黃金。——理查‧克拉克，出自《非洲狩獵旅行日記》
I don't take drugs as an escape trick, like some cheap magician on a cruise ship. I take drugs to find gold, like a greedy prospector in the backcountry.
—Richard Clark, *The African Safari Papers*

　　世界上少有東西可以跟這小小不起眼、被稱為大麻的植物一樣如此兩極化。有些人認為這是來自上天的贈禮，為了幫助人類應付地球上生命的各種考驗與磨難。也有人認為，如果讓大麻掌控我們的人民，這個邪惡物質將會摧毀社會。就像多數情況一樣，如果你走入兩個極端陣營中的任何一方，那你就錯了。不過這從來也沒阻止過任何人向任何願意傾聽的人鼓吹他們的論點。

我認為大麻應該要合法。雖然我不抽大麻，但我喜歡它的香味。——安迪‧沃荷，美國藝術家，普普藝術開創者

I think pot should be legal. I don't smoke it, but I like the smell of it.
—Andy Warhol

當我還是孩子的時候，我就常吸菸。那才是重點。

—— 巴拉克‧歐巴馬，美國總統

When I was a kid, I inhaled frequently. That was the point.
—Barack Obama

大麻不是毒品。我以前會為了古柯鹼吸別人老二，那才叫成癮。
你曾經為了大麻吸別人老二嗎？ —— 鮑伯‧西格，美國喜劇演員

Marijuana is not a drug. I used to suck dick for coke. Now that's an addiction. You ever suck some dick for marijuana?
—Bob Saget, American comedian

人們說你可以濫用大麻，你當然也可以濫用起司漢堡。我們不是
小孩了，我們是成人，而我們只能在有限的時間內掌控自己的身
體，所以我們應該要好好在身上實驗一番。

—— 喬‧羅根，美國喜劇演員、武術家與電視明星

People say you can abuse pot. You can abuse cheeseburgers, too. We're not children. We're adults, and we are in control of our bodies for a limited period of time only, and we should experiment with it.
—Joe Rogan, American comedian, martial artist, and television personality

我抽過這麼多迷幻藥，很幸運地沒變成一棵灌木。

——喬·史特拉默，音樂家與樂團《The Clash》的共同創辦人

I smoked so much dope, I'm lucky I didn't turn into a bush.

—Joe Strummer, British musician and cofounder of The Clash

我以前會抽大麻。不過我告訴你，我只在夜深的時候抽。噢，偶爾會在傍晚抽，不過通常是深夜或晚上。只在傍晚、晚上跟深夜的時候抽。偶爾，剛過中午抽，下午稍早抽，或者下午稍晚抽。噢，有時候會在清晨的任何時候抽……不過絕不在黃昏的時候抽。——史提夫·馬丁，美國電影演員、喜劇演員

I used to smoke marijuana. But I'll tell you something: I would only smoke it in the late evening. Oh, occasionally the early evening, but usually the late evening—or the midevening. Just the early evening, midevening and late evening. Occasionally, early afternoon, early midafternoon, or perhaps the late-midafternoon. Oh, sometimes the early-mid-lateearly morning ... But never at dusk.

—Steve Martin

其實藥物只分兩種：一種會毀了你的人生，另一種可以讓你的人生更美好。像是咖啡因、消炎止痛的安舒疼與避孕藥就被歸在後者。如果你不知道哪些藥會被歸在前者，那它們很可能已經摧毀你了。

不過就像大多數的事一樣，一旦告訴人們要遠離毒品，我打

賭百分之百反而讓他們想試試看。畢竟人類是充滿好奇心的物種，有些人非得親自試試看不可。

古柯鹼會放大你的個性。沒錯，但如果你本來就是個王八蛋呢？
——比爾・寇司比，美國諧星

Cocaine magnifies your personality. Yeah, but what if you're an a**hole?
—Bill Cosby

鴉片只教我們一件事，就是除了身體所受的折磨之外，沒有什麼是真的。 ——安德烈・馬爾羅，法國作家與冒險家，曾被提名諾貝爾文學獎

Opium teaches only one thing, which is that aside from physical suffering, there is nothing real.
—André Malraux, French author and adventurer

我聽過推銷古柯鹼最厲害的方法是八〇年代初，有個街頭販毒者沿著人行道跟著我說：「我這裡有些好貨。我有那種害死美國當紅喜劇演員約翰・貝魯西的東西。」
——丹尼斯・利里，美國電視演員

The best pitch I ever heard about cocaine was back in the early eighties when a street dealer followed me down the sidewalk going, "I got some great blow, man. I got the stuff that killed Belushi."
—Denis Leary

小時候我吸了很多膠。我一直對強力膠很有興趣，後來我開始喝啤酒、吸安非他命，接著投向海洛因的懷抱，因為在成長過程中，每個人都跟我說：「別抽大麻，那會害死你……」
—— 歐文・威爾許，蘇格蘭小說家，電影《猜火車》原著作者

I'd always done a lot of [sniffing] glue as a kid. I was very interested in glue, and then I went to lager and speed, and I drifted into heroin because as a kid growing up everybody told me, "Don't smoke marijuana, it will kill you ... "
—Irvine Welsh, Scottish novelist and author of *Trainspotting*

對無法負擔毒品的人，現實是他們賴以行走的拐杖。
—— 莉莉・湯姆琳，美國女演員、作家

Reality is a crutch for people who can't cope with drugs.
—Lily Tomlin

上帝用古柯鹼跟你說：你錢賺太多了。
—— 羅賓・威廉斯，美國演員。

Cocaine is God's way of telling you that you make too much money.
—Robin Williams

我不吸毒，我就是毒品。
—— 薩爾瓦多・達利，西班牙超現實主義畫家。

I don't do drugs. I am drugs.

—Salvador Dalí, Spanish surrealist painter

　　石油、金錢以及復活節彩蛋裡那些不知名的東西，都是來自地球的邪惡物質，毒品只不過是為了炒熱氣氛，兩相比較，卻嚴重地被誤解，甚至被妖魔化。不過，世界上成千上萬的擁護者才不搭理毒品被加諸的負面形象，盡情地吸、抽、注射甚至吃下它。不管再怎麼混亂，世界依然持續轉動，但是，這並不意謂毒品不該被謹慎看待。任何一種可以讓人相信自己是快樂綠巨人的物質，我們都應該要敬畏。但也許，只是也許，毒品並沒有讓我們的社會充滿混蛋。或許一直以來，我們大部分的人一直都是爛人。

毒品為我們做了很多好事。如果你不相信？幫我個忙，把你所有的專輯、錄音帶跟CD都拿去燒掉。你知道嗎？寫出那些偉大的音樂並在這些年讓你生活過得更好的音樂家們……都他媽的嗨爆了。 ——比爾·希克斯，美國喜劇演員。

Drugs have done good things for us. If you don't believe they have, do me a favor: Take all your albums, tapes, CDs, and burn 'em. Because you know what? The musicians who made that great music that has enhanced your lives throughout the years ... real fucking high.

—Bill Hicks, American comedian

我認為宗教不好，而毒品是好的。
──比爾・馬厄，美國喜劇演員與政治評論家

I think religion is bad and drugs are good.
—Bill Maher, American comedian and political commentator

藥物既不道德，也沒有不道德，它就只是種化合物。化合物對社會並不是個威脅，只有當人類把它當成是可以幹些狗屁倒灶之事的臨時許可證時，它才會有問題。
──法蘭克・札帕，美國搖滾音樂家

A drug is neither moral nor immoral—it's a chemical compound. The compound itself is not a menace to society until a human being treats it as if consumption bestowed a temporary license to act like an a**hole.
—Frank Zappa, American rock musician

緝毒警察的權力真大。可以無端把一個人拖回監獄六個月，但他對社會又沒有危害。
──戴爾・吉倫葛，加州NORML（全國大麻改革組織）州協調員

The arms of the drug police state are awesomely long. To drag a man back to jail for six months for nothing? He's not a danger to society.
—Dale Gieringer, the state coordinator of NORML (National Organization for the Reform of Marijuana Laws) in California

我從沒有毒品問題，跟我有問題的是警察。

——基思・理查茲，英國搖滾樂歌手

I've never had a problem with drugs. I've had problems with the police.

—Keith Richards

你知道美國的教育程度排名最低，但用藥排名最高嗎？雖然說第一名的感覺很好，不過我們可以改變這個狀況。就像反毒一樣，我們只需要對教育全面宣戰；如果反毒可以有點績效，那麼我們也都會很快迷上讀音法。——蓮恩・羅爾德，美國喜劇演員

Did you know America ranks the lowest in education but the highest in drug use? It's nice to be number one, but we can fix that. All we need to do is start the war on education. If it's anywhere near as successful as our war on drugs, in no time we'll all be hooked on phonics.

—Leighann Lord, American comedian

總之，導致社會根本弊病的既非毒品也不是酒精。如果我們想要尋找問題根源，就不該檢測人們有沒有吸毒；而是檢測他們是否愚蠢、無知、貪婪又熱愛權力。——P・J・歐羅克，美國政治諷刺作家

Anyway, no drug, not even alcohol, causes the fundamental ills of society. If we're looking for the source of our troubles, we shouldn't test people for drugs; we should test them for stupidity, ignorance, greed, and love of power.

—P. J. O'Rourke, American poltical satirist

毒品當然很好玩，這也是那些反毒活動愚蠢的地方，他們死不肯承認這件事。根據我的吸毒經驗，我說不出來我有驚嚇到或感覺體力衰退。毒品的名聲已經夠糟了。
——安傑麗卡‧休斯頓，美國演員。

Of course, drugs were fun. And that's what's so stupid about antidrug campaigns: They don't admit that. I can't say I feel particularly scarred or lessened by my experimentation with drugs. They've gotten a very bad name.

—Anjelica Huston

雖然可能有點難以置信，但還是有些人認為現實生活滿不錯的，維持原樣就好。他們寧願捨棄毒品帶來感官上悲喜的感受，而選擇繼續用老派無聊的方式來使用他們的五感。給他們力量吧！堅強的人，可以每天早上醒來決定要撐過整天，不吸一口膠來緩和一下。

藥物對老鼠來說很危險，對人類則是非常安全的東西，所以老鼠們不該用藥。——J‧W‧D‧韓德森，加拿大藥物、健康與福利管理局局長

The drug is really quite a remarkably safe one for humans, although it is really quite a dangerous one for mice and they should not use it.

—J. W. D. Henderson, director of the Canadian Bureau of Human Drugs, Health and Welfare

任何形式的成癮都不好，不管上癮的是酒精、嗎啡還是理想主義。——卡爾・榮格，瑞士心理學家

Every form of addiction is bad, no matter whether the narcotic be alcohol or morphine or idealism.

—Carl Jung

別吸毒，因為吸毒會讓你進監獄，而且監獄裡毒品真的很貴。——約翰・哈德威克，英國導演

Don't do drugs because if you do drugs, you'll go to prison, and drugs are really expensive in prison.

—John Hardwick, British director

我不吸毒，我的夢已經夠可怕了。——Ｍ・Ｃ・艾雪，荷蘭圖像藝術家

I don't use drugs; my dreams are frightening enough.

—M. C. Escher, Dutch graphic artist

你可以不理一個人，但你永遠不可以不理毒品，尤其當它在你眼裡揮舞著鋒利的獵刀時。——亨特・Ｓ・湯普森，美國作家與記者

You can turn your back on a person, but never turn your back on a drug, especially when it's waving a razor-sharp hunting knife in your eye.

—Hunter S. Thompson, American author and journalist

乍看之下，點燃一根白色小管子、吸入致癌的煙霧，似乎有點怪，尤其考慮到節節高升的菸價。進一步來看，其實有很多更加危險的事，像是高空跳傘、與鯊魚搏鬥或是為了科學而測試未受管制的藥物。聽聽以下這些傢伙的話，他們說出了你永遠不會知道的事。

我試著用告訴自己「我不想抽菸」的方式來戒菸，但我根本不相信自己。 ── 芭芭拉‧凱莉，加拿大女演員

I tried to stop smoking cigarettes by telling myself I just didn't want to smoke, but I didn't believe myself.

─Barbara Kelly, Canadian actress

如果香菸真的不是好東西，那就不會到處都有人在賣了。

── 迪克‧所羅門，出自美國電視劇《歪星撞地球》

If cigarettes were bad, they wouldn't sell them everywhere.

─Dick Solomon, *3rd Rock from the Sun*

就跟多數老菸槍一樣，我只有在抽第一根時可以品味。接下來再抽的，味道都沒有比燒錢的煙霧好，因為這純粹只是慣性使然。

── 克萊夫‧詹姆斯，出自小說《倒向英國》

Like most people who smoked umpteen cigarettes a day, I tasted only the first one. The succeeding umpteen minus one were a compulsive

ritual that had no greater savor than the fumes of burning money.
—Clive James, *Falling Towards England*

抽菸是促成統計學發展的重要成因。

—— 弗萊徹・內貝爾，美國作家

Smoking is one of the leading causes of statistics.
—Fletcher Knebel, American author

抽根菸是多麼幸福啊！或許這是發現美洲新大陸帶來的最偉大貢
獻。—— 亞瑟・海爾普斯，英國歷史學家與小說家

What a blessing this smoking is! Perhaps the greatest that we owe to the
discovery of America.
—Arthur Helps, British historian and novelist

在美國某些社交圈裡，帶把手槍似乎比帶包菸更能被接受。

—— 凱薩琳・懷特洪恩，英國專欄作家

There are some circles in America where it seems to be more socially
acceptable to carry a handgun than a packet of cigarettes.
—Katharine Whitehorn, British columnist

一根好的雪茄就像是一個有好身材的漂亮小妞，她還知道美國聯盟的積分。 —— 克林格，出自美國電視影集《外科醫師》

A good cigar is like a beautiful chick with a great body who also knows the American League box scores.
—Klinger, *M*A*S*H*

戒菸很簡單，我已經戒了幾百次。
—— 馬克·吐溫，美國作家

It's easy to quit smoking. I've done it hundreds of times.
—Mark Twain

如果天堂不能抽菸，那我不去了。
—— 馬克·吐溫，美國作家

If I cannot smoke in heaven, then I shall not go.
—Mark Twain

我很高興我不用跟火星來的人解釋為什麼每天我要點燃一堆小紙片，並把它們塞進我嘴裡。 —— 蜜妮翁·麥克勞克林，美國作家

I'm glad I don't have to explain to a man from Mars why each day I set fire to dozens of little pieces of paper, and then put them in my mouth.
—Mignon McLaughlin, American writer

關於毒品有個認識很重要，就是不會有老毒蟲。用藥過量的生活終究是要付出代價，即使是玩性堅強的派對咖，最終也會被迫放棄搖滾明星的生活方式，換成不那麼具有傷害性的嗜好，像是舞蛇之類的。

雖然要保持戒毒成功後不回頭碰毒品不是件容易的事，不過在你之前已經有很多人身體力行了，這應該可以讓你鬆口氣。而且有些人還更成功。

我說過不要碰古柯鹼，到現在我還是認為這是個很好的建議，除非你可以有節制地使用。如果你可以，那就用吧，但你知道嗎？沒有太多人辦得到。——查理‧辛，美國演員

I said stay off the crack, and I still think that's pretty good advice, unless you can manage it socially. If you can manage it socially, then go for it, but not a lot of people can, you know?
—Charlie Sheen

避免施打任何毒品，唯一該注射的，只有尼克森總統❶。
——艾比‧霍夫曼，青年國際黨共同創辦人

Avoid all needle drugs—the only dope worth shooting is Richard Nixon.
—Abbie Hoffman, cofounder of the Youth International Party

---

❶ 艾比‧霍夫曼是知名的反尼克森人士，尼克森對當時盛行的反主流文化嗤之以鼻。霍夫曼這裡使用了shooting的雙關，並指尼克森爲毒品。

如果我們可以讓他們了解，拒絕毒品就是對父母與過去世代的反叛，我們就成功了。

—— 約翰．范．坎普，美國政治家

If we can get them to understand that saying no to drugs is rebelling against their parents and the generations of the past, we'd make it an enormous success.

—John Van de Kamp, American politician

所有讓擁有一般智力的美國人感興趣的藥物，在今天都變成禁藥。—— 湯瑪斯．薩斯，匈牙利精神病學家與教授

All drugs of any interest to any moderately intelligent person in America are now illegal.

—Thomas Szasz, Hungarian psychiatrist and professor

沒什麼比適當的教養、完善的價值觀更容易讓人抵抗誘惑，重點是見證這是所言不虛的人。

—— 富蘭克林．P．瓊斯，美國作家

Nothing makes it easier to resist temptation than a proper bringingup, a sound set of values—and witnesses.

—Franklin P. Jones, American author

我只有在放棄藥物的時候才會生病。

── 基思・理查茲，英國搖滾樂歌手

I only get ill when I give up drugs.

—Keith Richards

逃避誘惑的人走的時候通常都會留下轉寄信的地址。

── 連恩・歐林豪斯，美國作家

Those who flee temptation generally leave a forwarding address.

—Lane Olinghouse, American author

第七章
一夜風流

一定是某種特定類型的人，才會縱情於派對狂歡。首要條件是，你完全不管安全與什麼好的服務，一聽到城裡有間酒吧標榜有機械公牛被毒蛇坑包圍，你就會亢奮得不得了，一心想著「我得去那裡！」

其次，雖然不是必要的，但如果你有扭曲的是非觀念，這也會很有幫助。跑趴專家很清楚酩酊大醉時偷推土機去釋放動物園裡全部的猴子，可能不是世界上最好的點子，但他們也很清楚，如果你想舉辦一場全是猴子的時裝秀，你得走些捷徑。

幸運的是，你不必搞一場通宵達旦飲酒作樂的派對就可以一窺那種生活方式的吸引力。如果有什麼事是歷史上跑趴專家們的最愛，那就是吹噓跟其他人比起來，自己在派對上是多麼放浪地搖擺著身體。

雜亂無序的好處之一，就是可以持續有令人興奮的發現。
　　——A・A・米恩，英國作家，以《小熊維尼》聞名

One of the advantages of being disorderly is that one is constantly making exciting discoveries.
—A. A. Milne

把燈光調暗一點，派對才開始嗨呢！

——丹‧拉瑟美國記者、新聞主播

Turn the lights down; the party just got wilder.

—Dan Rather

在正式的晚宴中，最接近死亡的人永遠都該被安排坐在最靠近廁所的位置。——喬治‧卡林，美國喜劇演員

At a formal dinner party, the person nearest death should always be seated closest to the bathroom.

—George Carlin, American comedian

讓我們對所有事都發懶吧，除了愛情與喝酒，除了懶惰。

——戈特霍爾德‧埃夫萊姆‧萊辛，德國啟蒙運動哲學家

Let us be lazy in everything, except in loving and drinking, except in being lazy.

—Gotthold Ephraim Lessing, German Enlightenment philosopher

我有過一個完美精采的夜晚，但今晚不是那樣。

——格魯喬‧馬克斯，美國電影與喜劇演員

I've had a perfectly wonderful evening. Butthis wasn't it.

—Groucho Marx

麻煩違反了萬有引力定律，撿起它比放掉它容易得多。
——喬納森·拉班，英國旅遊作家

Trouble defies the law of gravity. It's easier to pick up than to drop.
—Jonathan Raban, British travel writer

我跟你說，我們在地球上就是為了鬼混，而且別讓任何人跟你說
沒這回事。——庫爾特·馮內果，美國黑色幽默文學作家

I tell you, we are here on earth to fart around, and don't let anyone tell
you different.
—Kurt Vonnegut

對我而言，參加一場派對就像是在課堂裡上課，學個經驗，你知
道的。——娜塔莉·波曼，以色列裔美國女星

Going to a party, for me, is as much a learning experience as,you know,
sitting in a lecture.
—Natalie Portman

　　我不否認，搭乘豪華轎車四處遊覽時被一群半裸的追星族包
圍，讓你看起來真像個搖滾明星，但真正的跑趴專家很清楚你在
此刻也得看起來很體面。不過，時尚產業的潮流就是來來去去，
毫無章法、一團混亂，要判斷某個特定時間點到底流行什麼，其
實滿難的。這可以解釋為什麼某些時尚達人可以憑著把生肉釘在

身上並稱之為藝術而僥倖成功。任何有真知灼見的混蛋都會跟你說，時尚的第一條規則就是沒有規則。

有人曾跟我提過時尚產業中組織犯罪的事，不過我不能談論這個話題。我還想活命。
——卡爾文・克雷恩，美國時裝設計師，打造同名品牌「CK」

People have told me about organized crime in the fashion industry, but I can't talk about that. I'm looking to stay alive.
—Calvin Klein

時尚就像國王，有時是個非常愚蠢的統治者。
——E・T・貝爾，科幻小說家

Fashion as King is sometimes a very stupid ruler.
—E. T. Bell, science fiction novelist

我的時尚品味多半要看什麼東西不會讓我發癢。
——吉爾達・拉德納，美國喜劇演員

I base most of my fashion taste on what doesn't itch.
—Gilda Radner, American comedian

時尚是一種要求，為了控制自由。

—— 果爾達・梅厄，前以色列總理，比柴契爾夫人更早被認定是「鐵娘子」

Fashion is an imposition, a reign on freedom.

—Golda Meir, former Israeli prime minister

每個時代都會嘲笑過往的流行，卻如信仰般追隨新潮流。

—— 亨利・大衛・梭羅，美國自然主義思想家

Every generation laughs at the old fashions, but follows religiously the new.

—Henry David Thoreau

多數情況下，時尚不過是有錢人炫富的手段。

—— 約翰・洛克，英國哲學家

Fashion for the most part is nothing but the ostentation of riches.

—John Locke, British philosopher

時尚是讓人難以忍受的醜陋形式，以至於我們每六個月就要改變它一次。—— 奧斯卡・王爾德，愛爾蘭作家

Fashion is a form of ugliness so intolerable that we have to alter it every six months.

—Oscar Wilde

我買昂貴的西裝，但它們在我身上看起來就很廉價。

—— 華倫·巴菲特，美國商人

I buy expensive suits. They just look cheap on me.

—Warren Buffett, American businessman

看到膚淺的男人一身華服，我會感到很難過，為那身衣服。

—— 亨利·威勒·蕭，美國幽默作家

When I see a man of shallow understanding extravagantly clothed, I feel sorry—for the clothes.

—Henry Wheeler Shaw, American humorist

　　沒有人有十足把握怎樣可以開起一個趴，但一般的看法是，為了炒熱氣氛，超過五個人聚集在一起的場合就算是。不過要是有酒精的話，人數可以降至四人；如果有毒品，則可降至三人；如果兩者都有，那一個人也可以。既然標準如此寬鬆，也難怪「派對」這個字，從靠汽水提神的電玩馬拉松到公司強制參加的冰淇淋社交活動都看得到。但不論是哪種類型的派對，你都可以確定，多數參加派對的人都寧可自己在別的地方。

雞尾酒派對可輕易登上自蓖麻油之後最糟糕的發明寶座。

—— 艾爾莎·馬克士威，美國社交名媛

The cocktail party is easily the worst invention since castor oil.

—Elsa Maxwell, American socialite

沒有任何方式能讓你容忍鄰居的吵雜派對，除非你就在那裡面。——富蘭克林·P·瓊斯，美國作家

Nothing makes you more tolerant of a neighbor's noisy party than being there.

—Franklin P. Jones, American author

雞尾酒派對是為了讓四十歲的人能夠順便談談自己的事所舉辦的聚會。在酒精飲料都喝完後，還會留下的人，就是主辦人。
——佛瑞德·亞倫，美國喜劇演員

Cocktail party: A gathering held to enable forty people to talk about themselves at the same time. The man who remains after the liquor is gone is the host.

—Fred Allen, American comedian

她擔心如果她離開了，就會變成派對的核心人物。
——格魯喬·馬克斯，美國電影與喜劇演員

She's afraid that if she leaves, she'll become the life of the party.

—Groucho Marx

每當我在派對裡想要好好研究蠢蛋到底是怎麼一回事時，我就會去找一名大美女，因為他們通常都會圍繞在她身邊，就跟水果攤上的蒼蠅一樣。——讓·保羅·里克特，德國作家

Whenever, at a party, I have been in the mood to study fools, I have always looked for a great beauty: They always gather round her like flies around a fruit stall.

—Jean Paul Richter, German author

我喜歡參加我認識所有人的派對，不然你要怎麼跟不認識的人一起玩？——瑪麗-凱特·歐森，美國女演員

I like to go to parties where I know everyone. How are you going to have fun with people you don't know?

—Mary-Kate Olsen, American actress

晚上來訪的客人們，如果你們不會看時鐘，也應該在我臉上看到時間。——拉爾夫·沃爾多·愛默生，美國文學家

My evening visitors, if they cannot see the clock, should find the time in my face.

—Ralph Waldo Emerson

雖說你壓根不想參加那場派對，但如果連受邀都沒有，沒什麼比這更讓人咬牙切齒了。——威廉·E·「比爾」·渥恩，美國專欄作家

Nothing is more irritating than not being invited to a party you wouldn't be seen dead at.

—William E. "Bill" Vaughan, American columnist

甜點應該是一頓飯裡最重要的階段，因為甜點會是你的賓客在餐桌上昏過去前最後記得的東西。——威廉·鮑威爾，美國演員

Dessert is probably the most important stage of the meal, since it will be the last thing your guests remember before they pass out all over the table.
—William Powell, American actor

受歡迎是件累人的事。派對的靈魂人物最後通常都是以倒在角落、身上蓋件大衣收場。——威爾森·米茲納，美國劇作家

Popularity is exhausting. The life of the party almost always winds up in a corner with an overcoat over him.
—Wilson Mizner, American playwright

在時間早與晚之間的模糊地帶，縱情享受的跑趴專家總是能找到各種各樣的樂子，沒有什麼迷戀或慾望太黑暗或古怪。如果你真的很喜歡邊吃草莓鬆餅邊看一個獨臂、長鬍子的女人做開合跳，放心吧，會有某間酒吧很樂意提供這種服務。不過，當你早上醒來發現全身塗滿奶油且開始痛恨自己的時候，別去跟他們哭。

所有我很喜歡的東西，不是不道德的、違法的，就是會讓人發胖的。——亞歷山大·伍爾科特，美國評論家

All the things I really like are either immoral, illegal, or fattening.
—Alexander Woollcott, American critic

比起無聊的美德，我更喜歡有趣的邪惡。

—— 莫里哀，法國劇作家與演員

I prefer an interesting vice to a virtue that bores.

—Molière, French playwright and actor

你真的認為是因為軟弱才會屈服於誘惑嗎？我跟你說，有許多可怕的誘惑需要力量，是力量與勇氣才會向誘惑低頭。

—— 奧斯卡‧王爾德，愛爾蘭作家

Do you really think it is weakness that yields to temptation? I tell you that there are terrible temptations which it requires strength, strength, and courage to yield to.

—Oscar Wilde

不需帶我前往誘惑，我自己找得到路。

—— 麗塔‧梅‧布朗，美國作家

Lead me not into temptation; I can find the way myself.

—Rita Mae Brown, American author

向誘惑臣服，因為它可能不會出現第二次。

—— 羅伯特‧A‧海萊因，美國科幻作家

Yield to temptation. It may not pass your way again.

—Robert A. Heinlein, American science fiction author

為什麼良心不該有假期？── 塞繆爾·巴特勒，英國維多利亞時代小說家
Why should not Conscience have a vacation?
—Samuel Butler, Victorian novelist

壞事就像一早吃了鯡魚與洋蔥，整天徘徊不去。
── 塞繆爾·泰勒·柯勒律治，英國浪漫主義時期詩人
How like herrings and onions our vices are in the morning after we
have committed them.
—Samuel Taylor Coleridge

沒有邪惡是好事，但沒有誘惑就不好了。
── 沃爾特·白芝浩，英國作家
It is good to be without vices, but it is not good to be without
temptations.
—Walter Bagehot, British writer

他擁有所有我討厭的美德，卻沒有任何我推崇的邪惡。
── 溫斯頓·邱吉爾，前英國首相
He has all the virtues I dislike and none of the vices I admire.
—Winston Churchill

這世上每個人時時刻刻都在賭博；只是大多數的人沒有了解到這點。當你站在車輪後面，你拿自己的生命去賭你的駕駛同伴不會害你搞丟小命；你去上班，是用一天的工作去賭那天不會被炒魷魚；那麼，為什麼有人下注一萬元美金、賭一顆小白球會落進一個小紅洞的時候，突然間他就成了墮落的傢伙。對於賭錢你可以發表任何意見，但你能輸的也只是些美鈔，那多少還有一點尊嚴。

你不可能贏得了輪盤賭桌，除非你從那兒偷錢。
——阿爾伯特·愛因斯坦，物理哲學家
You cannot beat a roulette table unless you steal money from it.
—Albert Einstein

我的運氣背到如果我買了一塊墓地，大家就會停止死亡。
——艾德·法戈爾，美國高爾夫球選手
My luck is so bad that if I bought a cemetery, people would stop dying.
—Ed Furgol, American golfer

唯一能靠賽馬賺錢的，是拿著掃把跟鏟子的人。
——艾爾伯特·哈伯德，美國作家
The only man who makes money following the races is one who does it with a broom and shovel.
—Elbert Hubbard, American writer

贏來的一塊錢比賺來的一塊錢要甜美兩倍。

——快槍手艾迪‧費爾森，出自《金錢本色》

A dollar won is twice as sweet as a dollar earned.

—Fast Eddie Felson, *The Color of Money*

除了賭場擁有者之外，輪盤桌不會付錢給任何人。雖然熱愛賭博是很稀鬆平常的事，但是否熱愛到去擁有一個輪盤桌，就不得而知了。——蕭伯納，愛爾蘭劇作家與作家

The roulette table pays nobody except him that keeps it. Nevertheless a passion for gaming is common, though a passion for keeping roulette tables is unknown.

—George Bernard Shaw, Irish playwright and author

想賭博的衝動是很平常的，而實踐起來又這麼愉快，所以我認為它一定是邪惡的。

——海伍德‧布魯恩，美國記者

The urge to gamble is so universal and its practice so pleasurable that I assume it must be evil.

—Heywood Broun, American journalist

我對那些還沒出生的人建議是，別生來就有賭博的本能，除非你對機率有很敏銳的概念。——傑克・德雷福斯，美國商人

My advice to the unborn is, don't be born with a gambling instinct unless you have a good sense of probabilities.

—Jack Dreyfus, American businessman

讓你的錢變成兩倍最安全方式就是把它對摺一次後放進你的口袋。——法蘭克・麥金尼・哈伯德，以「金・哈伯」為筆名，美國漫畫家

The safest way to double your money is to fold it over once and put it in your pocket.

—Frank McKinney "Kin" Hubbard, American cartoonist

你玩撲克牌贏來的錢，幾乎都不是因為你玩得有多好，而是因為你的對手很沒用。——盧・克里格，職業撲克牌選手

Most of the money you'll win at poker comes not from the brilliance of your own play, but from the ineptitude of your opponents.

—Lou Krieger, professional poker player

命運女神如果發現她無法讓蠢蛋變得睿智，她就會給他們好運。——米歇爾・埃康・蒙田，法國文藝復興時期作家

Fortune, seeing that she could not make fools wise, has made them lucky.

—Michel Eyquem De Montaigne, French Renaissance writer

我算過，你中樂透的機率跟買不買是一樣的。

——法蘭・列白維茲，美國作家

I've done the calculation and your chances of winning the lottery are identical whether you play or not.

—Fran Lebowitz, American author

　　如果你對狂野星期五之夜的想像是喝著熱可可，然後舒服地與魔戒三部曲依偎在一起，那麼你不是個壞蛋。不是說托爾金的傑作不夠刺激，而是以「……然後我把偷來的藍寶堅尼撞進麥克・泰森的游泳池裡，飛奔躲過了KGB探員」為結尾的故事，開頭通常都不會是「所以我講到了佛羅多抵達瑞文戴爾的部分……」

　　不過別擔心，你永遠都可以透過一些壞蛋來體會當一個壞蛋的感受。

我已經厭倦假裝我不特別。我已經厭倦假裝我不是個來自火星、真他媽酷斃了的搖滾巨星。—— 查理・辛，美國演員

I'm tired of pretending like I'm not special. I'm tired of pretending like I'm not bitchin', a total freakin' rock star from Mars.

—Charlie Sheen

七罐啤酒之後，再喝兩瓶威士忌跟抽一些大麻，睡意自己就來了，真有意思。——大衛·塞達里斯，美國幽默作家與廣播名人

Seven beers followed by two scotches and a thimble of marijuana and it's funny how sleep comes all on its own.

—David Sedaris, American humorist and radio personality

在派對進行的過程裡，總會有一定程度的破壞，逐漸、慢慢地延燒開來。——蓋文·迪克羅，美國音樂家

There's always some amount of gradual, slow-burning destruction over the course of partying.

—Gavin DeGraw, American musician

如果你要參加老闆家舉辦的變裝派對，你不覺得打扮成老闆的老婆會是個好主意嗎？相信我，它不是。——傑克·韓第，美國喜劇演員

If you go to a costume party at your boss's house, wouldn't you think a good costume would be to dress up like the boss's wife? Trust me, it's not.

—Jack Handey, American comedian

我從不覺得我喝醉了，但我大概是醉了。
——基思·理查茲，英國搖滾樂歌手

I never thought I was wasted, but I probably was.

—Keith Richards

我吸過的毒會讓辛納屈、弗林、傑格跟理查茲看起來像是眼睛下垂、無害的小孩。──查理·辛，美國演員

The run I was on made Sinatra, Flynn, Jagger, and Richards look like droopy-eyed, armless children.

—Charlie Sheen

如果出去玩一晚就很棒了，那計算假期樂趣的方程式應該長這樣：（休息的天數 × 很棒）^{2}。話雖如此，但這簡單的方程式沒有計算到某些會改變相對樂趣程度的因素，像是出現在旅途中的小孩數量、抽水馬桶的相對距離，以及一旦你離開渡假村會被射殺的可能性。下面這些人的毒舌能夠證明，你還不如把時間花在放火燒掉那些原本你規畫的旅費，然後在一張舒服的椅子上坐上兩個星期可能還會好一些。

我痛恨假期。如果你可以蓋房子，為什麼要去坐在海灘上？
──菲力普·強森，美國建築師

I hate vacations. If you can build buildings, why sit on the beach?
—Philip Johnson, American architect

嬰兒不需要假期，但我還是會在海灘上看到他們。我會走過去跟他們說：「你們在這裡幹嘛？你從來沒在你的人生裡工作過一天！」──史蒂芬·萊特，美國喜劇演員

Babies don't need a vacation, but I still see them at the beach. I'll go over to them and say, "What are you doing here? You've never worked a day in your life!"

—Steven Wright, American comedian

渡假，就是當你再也無法忍受一直在做的事情時會做的事。

──厄爾‧威爾森，美國專欄作家

A vacation is what you take when you can no longer take what you've been taking.

—Earl Wilson, American columnist

假期就是無事可做，整天無所事事。

──羅伯特‧奧本，美國魔術師與作家

A vacation is having nothing to do and all day to do it in.

—Robert Orben, American magician and writer

大致上來說，母親與家庭主婦是沒有固定休息時間的勞工。她們是偉大的無假階級。

──安‧莫洛‧林白，美國飛行員、作家、探險家查爾斯‧林白之妻

By and large, mothers and housewives are the only workers who do not have regular time off. They are the great vacationless class.

—Anne Morrow Lindbergh, American aviator and wife of Charles Lindbergh

渡假是要付出代價的。

──卡爾‧哈卡瑞能，美國作家

No vacation goes unpunished.

─Karl Hakkarainen, American writer

渡假就是在充滿陽光的沙灘上兩個星期，接著一年裡剩下的日子
都在經濟的礁石上捱著。

──山姆‧艾溫，退役多倫多藍鳥外野手

Vacation: Two weeks on the sunny sands—and the rest of the year on
the financial rocks.

─Sam Ewing, retired Blue Jays outfielder

第三篇

被企業接管的人生

我的父親教我工作，卻沒教我要愛工作。我不否認，我從未喜歡
過工作。我寧可看書、說故事、講笑話、說話、笑，做任何事，
就是不想工作。　　　　　　　　── 亞伯拉罕・林肯，美國第16任總統

My father taught me to work; he did not teach me to love it. I never
did like to work, and I don't deny it. I'd rather read, tell stories, crack
jokes, talk, laugh—anything but work.
—Abraham Lincoln

第八章

找一份你必然痛恨的工作

　　在我還是個孩子的時候，我的父母買給我一套把小木樁放進小圓洞的玩具。買這玩具，不是因為他們樂於看我可以把木樁插進我鼻子多深；相反地，他們是希望我可以提升運動能力，好讓我在學校跟其他孩子玩的時候不會受傷。根據他們的計畫，我在中學會避開性、毒品、搖滾樂以及各種誘惑，好好用功以便能夠進入頂尖私立大學就讀。經過四年花掉數十萬美金後，我終於準備好實現人類文明最重要的事，就是覓得一份朝九晚五的工作。如果我可以早點知道現在我懂的這些事，我會叫老爸把那套木樁遊戲塞進他的屁股。

　　真相就是沒有什麼工作是有趣的。想想替專門生產冰品的班傑利公司品嚐新冰淇淋口味的傢伙。一開始很有趣，但現在他體重重達一百八十公斤而且想不起來他自己的腳長什麼樣子。不過，別聽我的話。另外有一堆王八蛋寧可在自己身上塗滿花生醬後出去獵狼獾，也不要在斗室大小的辦公室裡待上五分鐘。

所有拿薪水的工作都會消耗人的心靈，降低人的心智。
—— 亞里斯多德，古希臘哲學家

All paid jobs absorb and degrade the mind.

—Aristotle

如果我們確保某些人的工作，那就是在危害每個人的工作。
—— 阿爾伯特・鄧拉普，美國企業縮編專家

If we guarantee employment for some, we jeopardize employment for everyone.

—Albert Dunlap, American corporate downsizer

當你不知道要罵什麼髒話的時候，會更難承受生活中不如意的事。—— 卡爾文，出自漫畫《卡爾文與霍布斯》

Life's disappointments are harder to take when you don't know any swear words.

—Calvin, *Calvin and Hobbes*

布希總統試圖把最近悲慘的經濟數據逆轉勝，今天，他宣布戰勝「就業戰爭」。—— 克雷格・基爾伯恩，美國演員

President Bush is trying to put a positive spin on the latest bad economic numbers. Today he declared victory in the "War on Jobs."

—Craig Kilborn, American actor

千萬別在面試時反戴棒球帽，除非你面試的工作是棒球裁判。

　　——丹·澤文，美國幽默作家

Never wear a backward baseball cap to an interview unless applying for the job of umpire.

—Dan Zevin, American humor author

如果你沒在一開始就成功，就消滅所有你嘗試過的證據。

　　——大衛·布蘭特，出自美國電視劇《辦公室瘋雲》

If at first you don't succeed, remove all evidence you ever tried.

—David Brent, *The Office*

千萬別找個冬天寒風可以灌進你褲子的工作。

　　——傑拉多·里維拉，美國律師、記者

Never take a job where winter winds can blow up your pants.

—Geraldo Rivera

給一個女人工作，她就會長出蛋蛋。

　　——傑克·蓋爾伯，美國劇作家

Give a woman a job and she grows balls.

—Jack Gelber, American playwright

大人總愛問小孩長大之後想做什麼，因為他們想找些點子。
── 寶拉‧龐德史東，美國喜劇演員

Adults are always asking little kids what they want to be when they grow up because they're looking for ideas.
—Paula Poundstone, American comedian

我想要的是，老老實實工作一天，就可以賺到一個星期的薪水。
── 史提夫‧馬丁，美國電影演員、喜劇演員

All I've ever wanted was an honest week's pay for an honest day's work.
—Steve Martin

　　拜某些高等教育延續下來的聰明宣傳之賜，在你考慮找尋第一份工作前，有幾件事你一定得做。第一，你要想辦法借到你欠缺的幾十萬美金。第二，你得拿那些錢與你四年的人生光陰，去交換一張價值大約六十美分的紙。最後，你必須假裝花了四年用功向學，而不是試用各種毒品跟酒精。如果你覺得你已經有點看透這個過程，你絕不孤單。

我認為每個人都該進大學並拿到文憑，接著花六個月當酒保，再花六個月當計程車司機。那時候，他們就可以說是受過教育的。── 艾爾‧麥奎爾，馬凱特大學男子籃球隊主教練

I think everyone should go to college and get a degree and then spend six months as a bartender and six months as a cabdriver. Then they would really be educated.

—Al McGuire, head coach for the Marquette University men's basketball team

如果你覺得教育很昂貴，試試看無知吧！

——德瑞克‧包克，前哈佛大學校長

If you think education is expensive, try ignorance!

—Derek Bok, former president of Harvard University

已經學過、又被遺忘之後還留存著的，就是教育。

——B‧F‧斯金納，美國行為主義心理學家

Education is what survives when what has been learned has been forgotten.

—B. F. Skinner, American behaviorist

人生不是學期制，你沒有暑假可以放，也沒有雇主有興趣幫你找到自我。——比爾‧蓋茲，微軟公司創辦人

Life is not divided into semesters. You don't get summers off and very few employers are interested in helping you find yourself.

—Bill Gates

大部分的人要花上五年的時間才能從大學教育恢復過來。

——布魯克斯‧愛金生，美國戲劇評論家

It takes most men five years to recover from a college education.

—Brooks Atkinson, American theater critic

教育是件值得尊崇的事，但請牢牢記住，沒有什麼值得知曉的事情是能夠被教導的。 ——奧斯卡‧王爾德，愛爾蘭作家

Education is an admirable thing, but it is well to remember from time to time that nothing worth knowing can be taught.

—Oscar Wilde

這聽起來可能很怪，再多的學習都無法治療愚蠢，而正規教育證明了這一點。 ——史蒂芬‧維經茲，匈牙利作家

Strange as it may seem, no amount of learning can cure stupidity, and formal education positively fortifies it.

—Stephen Vizinczey, Hungarian writer

沒上過學的人可能會從貨車偷東西，但如果他受過大學教育，他可能會偷走整條鐵路。 ——狄奧多‧羅斯福，前美國總統

A man who has never gone to school may steal from a freight car; but if he has a university education, he may steal the whole railroad.

—Theodore Roosevelt

通才教育的目的就是讓你能夠達觀地接受你永遠也賺不了大錢的事實。——來源不詳

The purpose of a liberal education is to make you philosophical enough to accept the fact that you will never make much money.

—Unknown

打從父母第一次叫我們收拾玩具的那一刻起，我們大部分的人就對工作產生反感。不管眼前的工作看起來有多麼令人興奮，但總是有更好的事可做，例如咬指甲或是默數到十億之類的。有些人可能會說這叫懶惰，但事實上，真正的混球對每天坐在辦公室隔間八小時一點也不會猶豫，他們反而會假裝喜歡這件事。

無所事事是件很困難的事……你永遠不知道何時會完成它。
——萊斯里·尼爾森，加拿大演員與喜劇演員

Doing nothing is very hard to do ... you never know when you're finished.

—Leslie Nielsen, Canadian actor and comedian

我不想工作，就是這麼簡單。我不信任工作，也不喜歡工作。我覺得它真的是人類不幸為自己發明出來、很糟糕的東西。
——阿嘉莎·克莉絲蒂，英國推理小說家

I didn't want to work. It was as simple as that. I distrusted work,

disliked it. I thought it was a very bad thing that the human race had
unfortunately invented for itself.
—Agatha Christie

當人們去工作時，他們不該把心留在家裡。
—— 貝蒂‧班德，美國作家
When people go to work, they shouldn't have to leave their hearts at
home.
—Betty Bender, American author

多數人錯過機會，是因為機會身穿工作服，而且看起來像工作。
—— 湯瑪斯‧愛迪生
Opportunity is missed by most people because it is dressed in overalls
and looks like work.
—Thomas Edison

玩樂總是出於自願。如果是被迫，就不是玩樂而是工作。
—— 鮑伯‧布萊克，美國無政府主義者
Play is always voluntary. What might otherwise be play is work if it's
forced.
—Bob Black, American anarchist

為什麼我得工作才可以獲得？這就像是在說，我不值得擁有這一切！──卡爾文，出自漫畫《卡爾文與霍布斯》

Why should I have to WORK for everything?! It's like saying I don't deserve it!

—Calvin, *Calvin and Hobbes*

我是工作者的朋友，我寧可當他的朋友，也不想變成他。

── 克萊倫斯・蘇厄德・丹諾，美國律師，為教授演化論的高中生物老師約翰・T・斯科普斯辯護，也是後來著名的「斯科普斯猴子審判」

I am a friend of the working man, and I would rather be his friend than be one.

—Clarence Seward Darrow, American lawyer famous for his defense of John T. Scopes in the "Scopes Monkey Trial"

我需要很多時間來無所事事，所以我根本沒時間工作。

── 皮埃・勒維迪，法國詩人

I need so much time for doing nothing that I have no time for work.

—Pierre Reverdy, French poet

這個世界充滿了有意願的人。有的人很願意工作，其他人則願意讓他們工作。── 羅伯特・佛洛斯特，美國詩人，四度獲普立茲獎

The world is full of willing people. Some willing to work, the rest willing to let them.

—Robert Frost

死於過勞的人遠遠超過這個世界的重要性能被合理化的程度。

——魯德亞德‧吉卜林，生於孟買的英國作家

More men are killed by overwork than the importance of this world justifies.

—Rudyard Kipling

如果你能夠馬馬虎虎只做一半的工作，那你就是個身處盲人國度的獨眼龍。 ——庫爾特‧馮內果，美國黑色幽默文學作家

If you can do a half-assed job of anything, you're a one-eyed man in a kingdom of the blind.

—Kurt Vonnegut

　　能夠讓自己有吃飽穿暖的能力，是在企業生活裡值得擁有的副作用，但這交易真的划得來嗎？任何一個在找工作的人都該問問自己是否寧可去盡陪審團的義務。如果答案是肯定的，那你也許就不該繼續找工作。但這些人也無法怪別人，畢竟是他們自己要去應徵的，又不是被強制徵召。或許，依照這些傢伙的中肯建議，工作危機的真正解答就是別再汲汲營營尋覓一份好工作。我們也許會破產，但至少會很快樂。

工作是一種危險的病症，它會讓想去釣魚的高官跑回來工作。
——安布羅斯·比爾斯，美國作家與《魔鬼辭典》的作者

Work: a dangerous disorder affecting high public functionaries who want to go fishing.

—Ambrose Bierce, American writer and author of *The Devil's Dictionary*

工作是世上所有痛苦的根源。幾乎任何你叫得出名的邪惡都來自於工作或是來自於為工作而生的世界裡，為了不再受折磨，我們應該要停止工作。——鮑伯·布萊克，美國無政府主義者。

Work is the source of nearly all the misery in the world. Almost any evil you'd care to name comes from working or from living in a world designed for work. In order to stop suffering, we have to stop working.

—Bob Black, American anarchist

工作是個該避免的必要之惡。——馬克·吐溫，美國作家

Work is a necessary evil to be avoided.

—Mark Twain

工作是那些沒更好的事可做的人的避難所。
——奧斯卡·王爾德，愛爾蘭作家

Work is a refuge of people who have nothing better to do.

—Oscar Wilde

腦子生不出好想法，無可避免就用打扮來代替。那些沒有專業技術卻又西裝筆挺的老闆或經理人，他們一身打扮可不是湊巧而已。──保羅‧格雷厄姆，英國攝影師與藝術家

Dressing up is inevitably a substitute for good ideas. It is no coincidence that technically inept business types are known as suits.
—Paul Graham, British photographer and artist

我們在地球上沒有多少時間了！我們不該用這種方式度過時間。我們不該整天坐在辦公室小隔間裡盯著電腦、填沒用的表格以及被八個老闆輪番疲勞轟炸。
──彼得‧吉本斯，出自電影《上班一條蟲》

We don't have a lot of time on this earth! We weren't meant to spend it this way. Human beings were not meant to sit in little cubicles staring at computer screens all day, filling out useless forms, and listening to eight different bosses drone on about mission statements.
—Peter Gibbons, *Office Space*

企業不再試圖把方柱放進圓洞裡了，他們把方柱放進方形辦公室隔間裡。──羅伯特‧布勞特，美國部落客與作家

Corporations no longer try to fit square pegs into round holes; they just fit them into square cubicles.
—Robert Brault, American blogger and writer

困難的工作可以突顯人的個性，有的人會捲起袖子，有的人會嗤之以鼻，有的人則毫無反應。——山姆・艾溫，退役多倫多藍鳥外野手
Hard work spotlights the character of people: Some turn up their sleeves, some turn up their noses, and some don't turn up at all.
—Sam Ewing, retired Blue Jays outfielder

　　沒有方法可以確保你一定找得到工作，但多數專家同意應徵是有用的。根據不同的公司，這個過程可能會包含將你所有的成就編輯成一份條理分明的履歷表，並可能需要一封詳盡的推薦函來說明為什麼你會是有史以來最好的人選。跟所得稅很像，對於這兩種文件裡所填的資訊是否屬實，其實沒人抱著期望。但在你用求職表覆蓋整個就業市場前，先聽聽看這些討厭鬼的想法可能會好些。

一個人最接近完美的狀態，就是在他填求職表的時候。
——史丹利・J・藍道，加拿大商人
The closest to perfection a person ever comes is when he fills out a job application form.
—Stanley J. Randall, Canadian Businessman

避免僱用倒楣的人：把一半的履歷丟進垃圾桶，讀都別讀。
——大衛・布蘭特，出自美國電視劇《辦公室瘋雲》

Avoid employing unlucky people. Throw half of the pile of CV's in the bin without reading them.

—David Brent, *The Office*

每一件我正在做的事都是自毀前途，不過就是「恐懼成功」這檔
小事罷了。 ──喬恩‧史都華，美國政治諷刺作家

I'm doing everything I can to sabotage my career. It's a little thing called "fear of success."

—Jon Stewart, American political satirist

如果在一開始你沒成功，試試看，再試一次。然後就別幹了。沒
必要在這件事上當個該死的傻瓜。

──W‧C‧菲爾茲，美國喜劇演員

If at first you don't succeed, try, try again. Then quit. There's no point in being a damn fool about it.

—W. C. Fields, American comedian

現在有很多傢伙擁有學士學位、碩士學位或博士學位。不幸地，
他們就是沒有工作。 ──胖子多明諾，美國節奏藍調與搖滾鋼琴家

A lot of fellows nowadays have a BA, MD, or PhD. Unfortunately, they don't have a J.O.B.

—Fats Domino, American R&B and rock and roll pianist

去面試工作時，我認為有個問題很值得問，就是他們有沒有告過人。——傑克・韓第，美國喜劇演員

When you go in for a job interview, I think a good thing to ask is if they ever press charges.

—Jack Handey, American comedian

每當被問起長大後想做什麼的時候，很多小孩目標都很遠大，總統、太空人以及海洋生物學家都是很常見的抱負。時間快轉個十五到二十年，標準就會降低一些，總統變校長，太空人變電工，海洋生物學家變成水族館清潔人員。依據實際就業市場需求，你可能得把工作目標訂在清理路上被撞死的動物或是更不想要的職位，就像下面這些沮喪的可憐蟲一樣。

替政府工作就像是試著從上顎取出梅子皮。因為企業提供的工作量遠超過就業市場的合理需求。——卡斯齊・史提內特，美國作家

Working for a federal agency was like trying to dislodge a prune skin from the roof of the mouth. More enterprise went into the job than could be justified by the results.

—Caskie Stinnett, American author

目前以閱讀與寫作為生的人，換成養兔子可能更容易找到工作。——伊迪絲・希特維爾，英國詩人

A great many people now reading and writing would be better employed keeping rabbits.
—Edith Sitwell, British poet

把時間花在不停勞動的人生根本就是浪費人生，只有傻子會把一份討人厭的訃聞當成豐富的報酬。
——喬治·讓·納森，美國作家與編輯

A life spent in constant labor is a life wasted, save a man be such a fool as to regard a fulsome obituary notice as ample reward.
—George Jean Nathan, American writer and editor

老鼠賽跑的問題是，就算你贏了，你還是隻老鼠。
——莉莉·湯姆琳，美國女演員、作家

The trouble with the rat race is that even if you win, you're still a rat.
—Lily Tomlin

工作，是男人唯一可以一天做上八小時的事，這聽來真是遺憾。他不能吃八個小時，不能喝八個小時，也不能做愛八個小時。而工作是唯一一件男人可以做上八小時的事。
——威廉·福克納，美國小說家

It's a shame that the only thing a man can do for eight hours a day is work. He can't eat for eight hours; he can't drink for eight hours; he

can't make love for eight hours. The only thing a man can do for eight hours is work.
—William Faulkner

替大公司工作就像是搭上一列火車。究竟是你以一小時六十英哩的速度在移動，還是火車以一小時六十英哩的速度移動，而你只是呆坐在上面？——J‧保羅‧蓋蒂，美國商人
Going to work for a large company is like getting on a train. Are you going sixty miles an hour or is the train going sixty miles an hour and you're just sitting still?
—J. Paul Getty, American businessman

　　男人，花點時間感謝你的老二。要是沒有他，你賺的錢會比你現在賺的少18.2%。（女人，男人目前正忙著誇獎他們的小兄弟，這是個發動政變的好時機。）不過除了長距離尿尿之外，女人在很多工作上是可以表現得跟男人一樣好，甚至更好。社會可以繼續假裝沒任何問題，不過，或許傾聽女人想法的時候到了。因為只要認為女性生殖器是錯失某些就業機會的原因，沒有女人聽了會高興。

為什麼男人可以被允許著迷於他們的工作，女人卻只能被允許著迷於男人？——芭芭拉‧史翠珊，猶太裔美國歌手與演員

Why is it men are permitted to be obsessed about their work, but women are only permitted to be obsessed about men?
—Barbra Streisand

女人如果要贏得男人一半的信譽，她必須加倍努力而且加倍聰明。幸好那不是很難的事。

—— 夏洛特・惠頓，前渥太華市長

For a woman to get half as much credit as a man, she has to work twice as hard and be twice as smart. Fortunately, that isn't difficult.
—Charlotte Whitton, former mayor of Ottawa

實際上，只有少數幾種工作需要老二或陰道，其他所有職業都該開放給所有人。

—— 佛羅倫絲・甘迺迪，美國律師與平權提倡者

There are few jobs that actually require a penis or vagina. All other jobs should be open to everybody.
—Florynce Kennedy, American lawyer and equal rights advocate

定義女人的工作，本身就是件爛事。

—— 葛羅莉亞・斯坦能，美國女性主義者

The definition of women's work is shitwork.
—Gloria Steinem, American feminist

男人只有生小孩跟奶媽無法勝任，同樣的，女人唯一無法勝任的工作就是捐贈精子。——威爾瑪·史考特·海德，美國作家與社會運動家。

The only jobs for which no man is qualified are human incubators and wet nurse. Likewise, the only job for which no woman is or can be qualified is sperm donor.

—Wilma Scott Heide, American author and social activist

第九章

工作，就這麼回事

　　擁有一份工作代表你已經獲得某些公司的信任，用美金跟你交換每週四十個小時，之後你可以用那些紙鈔購買各種商品或服務。這戲碼會每週不停地重複，直到你老到無法理解你的工作變得有多卑微，或是直到你倒下死掉為止，就看哪個先發生。

　　不過先別急著開始做橡皮筋絞索，一切還是有希望的。現在你已經找到一份工作，困難的部分已經結束了。如果你能精通打嘴炮與拍馬屁的藝術，整個職涯中，很有可能你都不會被要求去做一些實質的工作。當然，除非你是少數以整天辛勤工作為傲的笨蛋之一。

　　跟你一樣，許多出現在這章的蠢貨也是天真爛漫、懷抱著野心展開他們的職業生涯。他們早早上班，加班到很晚，然後把每件出現在他們辦公桌上的工作做好。但他們逐漸接受了一個事實，就是例行工作絕大多數都是毫無意義的，唯有解放可以振奮人心。

精神快要崩潰的症狀之一，就是相信某個人的工作非常重要。
—— 伯特蘭・羅素，英國哲學家

One of the symptoms of an approaching nervous breakdown is the belief that one's work is terribly important.
—Bertrand Russell, British philosopher

問一個職業作家對於評論家有什麼想法，就像是問一根燈柱對狗的感覺如何。
—— 克里斯多福・漢普頓，英國劇作家

Asking a working writer what he thinks about critics is like asking a lamppost how it feels about dogs.
—Christopher Hampton, British playwright

工作可以是有趣或是無聊，一切取決於你的態度。而我喜歡有趣。—— 柯琳・C・巴雷特，西南航空公司企業秘書

Work is either fun or drudgery. It depends on your attitude. I like fun.
—Colleen C. Barrett, corporate secretary of Southwest Airlines

一個永不過時的經驗法則就是，如果你已經活到三十五歲，而你的工作仍然要求你要別名牌，你的職涯已經犯了一個大錯。
—— 丹尼斯・米勒，美國喜劇演員

A good rule of thumb is if you've made it to thirty-five and your job still requires you to wear a name tag, you've made a serious vocational error.

—Dennis Miller, American comedian

早睡早起意謂著這份工作可能沒什麼技術含量。

—— 約翰・西亞迪，美國詩人

Early to bed and early to rise probably indicates unskilled labor.

—John Ciardi, American poet

工作有兩種：第一種，改變事物的位置，或改變靠近地球表面的事物與其他事物的關聯性；第二種，叫別人這樣做。

—— 伯特蘭・羅素，英國哲學家

Work is of two kinds: first, altering the position of matter at or near the earth's surface relative to other matter; second, telling other people to do so.

—Bertrand Russell, British philosopher

星期三就像是在一星期中間的星期一。

—— 李・福克斯・威廉斯，英國演員

Wednesdays are like Mondays in the middle of the week!

—Lee Fox Williams, British actor

古羅馬有一種傳統：每當一名工程師完成一座圓拱後，當頂石被吊到它的位置時，工程師會用最令人印象深刻的方式為他的工作承擔起責任，就是站在圓拱的下方。

——麥克・阿姆斯壯，美國商人與美國電信公司 AT&T 前執行長

The ancient Romans had a tradition: Whenever one of their engineers constructed an arch, as the capstone was hoisted into place, the engineer assumed accountability for his work in the most profound way possible—he stood under the arch.

—Michael Armstrong, American businessman and former CEO of AT&T

你上班穿的衣服很自然地會吸引各種有顏色的液體，這種吸引力在重要會議之前最為強烈。

——史考特・亞當斯，美國漫畫家與漫畫《呆伯特》的創作者

Your business clothes are naturally attracted to staining liquids. This attraction is strongest just before an important meeting.

—Scott Adams, American cartoonist and creater of the *Dilbert comics*

光是站在場邊啜泣跟抱怨不會讓你有任何進展，進步是透過實踐想法而來的。——雪莉・赫夫斯特德勒，美國前教育部長

You don't make progress by standing on the sidelines, whimpering and complaining. You make progress by implementing ideas.

—Shirley Hufstedler, former secretary of education

如果你喜歡你的工作，那麼在你的人生中，你沒有一天是在工作。──湯米‧拉索達，美國職棒大聯盟棒球選手與經理

If you love your job, you haven't worked a day in your life.
—Tommy Lasorda, American major league baseball player and manager

記得那個聰明、能言善道、僱用你的人嗎？他可能看起來很像是你的老闆，但他絕對不是。因為你在面試時遇到的那個人絕對會使用電腦，但你現在正在看著你的老闆用一台傳真機試著搜尋「收益來源」。每個管理者都不太一樣，但通常只需要幾個星期，你那無畏的領導者就會洩漏出他們原來是個會毀了周遭所有事物的粗心笨蛋。不相信嗎？有點耐心，你會看到的。

這個世界分成做事的人，跟得到功勞的人。
──德懷特‧莫羅，美國參議員

The world is divided into people who do things—and people who get the credit.
—Dwight Morrow, United States senator

頭銜越長，這職位越不重要。
──喬治‧麥戈文，美國歷史學家，曾任參眾議員

The longer the title, the less important the job.
—George McGovern

如果你覺得老闆很笨，記住，如果他比現在更聰明，你就不會有工作。 ── 約翰・高蒂，美國黑手

If you think your boss is stupid, remember: You wouldn't have a job if he was any smarter.

—John Gotti, American mobster

要騙自己很簡單，也可能可以騙過你的上司，要騙你的同事就比較難了，但要騙過你的下屬幾乎是不可能的。
── 哈利・B・塞耶，美國商人

It is easy to fool yourself. It is possible to fool the people you work for. It is more difficult to fool the people you work with. But it is almost impossible to fool the people who work under you.

—Harry B. Thayer, American businessman

不用擔心別人剽竊你的想法，如果你的想法真的很好，你就得強迫其他人接受。 ── 霍華德・H・艾肯，美國電腦工程師

Don't worry about people stealing your ideas. If your ideas are any good, you'll have to ram them down people's throats.

—Howard H. Aiken, American computer engineer

發出批評比做得對要簡單得多了。 ── 班傑明・迪斯雷利，前英國首相

How much easier it is to be critical than to be correct.

—Benjamin Disraeli, former British prime minister

我們所說的管理，絕大多數都是讓工作變得更困難。
—— 彼得‧F‧杜拉克，美國社會生態學家
So much of what we call management consists in making it difficult for people to work.
—Peter F. Drucker, American social ecologist

她對一切問題都有答案，卻解決不了任何事情。
—— 奧斯卡‧萊文特，美國音樂家與演員
She has the answer to everything and the solution to nothing.
—Oscar Levant, American musician and actor

　　雖然世上有些重要的工作被完成，但可能不是由你辦公室裡的任何人完成的，尤其不會是你。大體而言，這是因為多數在任何特定時間完成的工作，都是個徹頭徹尾的騙局。有個很簡單的測試方法可以確認你的工作是否屬於這一類，第一步：停止做你的工作；第二步：等兩個星期；假如結果是都沒人發現，那麼你的工作就是場騙局。只要接受這個事實，你就可以在許多前輩一步一腳印踏出來的平庸小徑上自由漫步。

只要有人會接受爛東西，這在經濟上就是有利可圖的事。

——迪克・卡維特，美國電視脫口秀主持人

As long as people will accept crap, it will be financially profitable to dispense it.

—Dick Cavett, American television talk show host

如果每次有人帶著的不只是問題本身，還有可能的解決方案來找我時，我就可以獲得一塊美金的話，那我會有六塊美金。

——布萊恩・瓦斯基利，美國勵志作家

If I had $1 for every time someone came to me with not only a problem but also a possible solution to that problem, I'd have $6.

—Brian Vaszily, American motivational author

如果你必須用一個字確定為什麼人類尚未、也永遠無法實現所有的潛能，那個字就是「會議」。 ——戴夫・貝瑞，美國作家與專欄作家

If you had to identify, in one word, the reason why the human race has not achieved, and never will achieve, its full potential, that word would be meetings .

—Dave Barry, American author and columnist

顧問之所以可信，就是因為他們沒有笨到在你公司工作。

——史考特・亞當斯，美國漫畫家與漫畫《呆伯特》的創作者

Consultants have credibility because they are not dumb enough to work at your company.
—Scott Adams, American cartoonist and creater of the *Dilbert comics*

商業，很容易定義，商業就是別人的錢。——大仲馬，法國作家
Business, that's easily defined; it's other people's money.
—Alexandre Dumas, French author

世上最簡單的工作應該是驗屍官。在死人身上動手術，最糟可以發生什麼事？如果所有事都出錯了，說不定你還會測到脈搏。
——丹尼斯・米勒，美國喜劇演員
The easiest job in the world has to be coroner. Surgery on dead people. What's the worst thing that could happen? If everything went wrong, maybe you'd get a pulse.
—Dennis Miller, American comedian

專家就是在非常狹小的領域裡，犯過所有能犯的錯。
——尼爾斯・波爾，丹麥物理學家
An expert is a man who has made all the mistakes which can be made in a very narrow field.
—Niels Bohr, Danish physicist

我知道那只是個他們非做不可的工作，但有時我真的希望他們別做。——黛安娜王妃，英國親王查爾斯的第一任妻子

I know it's just a job they have to do, but sometimes I do wish they wouldn't.

—Princess Diana

企業宗旨是一塊版子上寫了字，笨呆了的點子，是大型組織用來叮嚀員工不能只是整天坐在辦公桌前下載網路色情影片。

——戴夫・貝瑞，美國作家與專欄作家

A Mission Statement is a dense slab of words that a large organization produces when it needs to establish that its workers are not just sitting around downloading Internet porn.

—Dave Barry, American author and columnist

　　如果你想了解一個人的工作狀態，從他第一次坐到辦公桌前到第一次喝咖啡休息的這段時間，就可以看到很多蛛絲馬跡。這段時間平均是三十分鐘，但對有些人來說，這時間差是如此微小，小到你可能只是眨個眼就錯過了。

　　但這些工作不是當老闆的應聲蟲，就是卑微到連受過訓練的倉鼠都會做，誰能怪他們只要有任何機會就逃避責任呢？或許我們應該少花一點時間關注他們差強人意的表現，而是多花點時間關注他們的工作到底有多爛。

沒有工作，生命會腐朽。但工作沒有靈魂，生命就會窒息而亡。

── 阿爾貝·卡繆，法國作家

Without work, all life goes rotten. But when work is soulless, life stifles and dies.

—Albert Camus, French author

我以為我看到了隧道盡頭的光明，但那只是某個混帳舉著火把，帶來更多工作給我。── 大衛·布蘭特，出自美國電視劇《辦公室瘋雲》

I thought I could see the light at the end of the tunnel, but it was just some bastard with a torch, bringing me more work.

—David Brent, *The Office*

喔，你討厭你的工作？怎麼不早說？有個針對討厭工作的支援團體叫做「所有人」，他們都在酒吧聚會。

── 德魯·加利，美國喜劇演員、演員與遊戲節目主持人

Oh, you hate your job? Why didn't you say so? There's a support group for that. It's called EVERYBODY, and they meet at the bar.

—Drew Carey, American comedian, actor, and game show host

為什麼大家總希望每天都是星期五？如果每天都是星期五，那我們就會嚇死人地每天都在這耶。── 艾德·貝爾納，美國演員

Why do people say they wish every day was Friday? If it was always Friday, we'd be here every freakin' day.

—Ed Bernard, American actor

我這樣說會侮辱整個產業，但電視節目真的像是給沒辦法拍電影的人來玩的。我不是指女演員；我指的是燈光師。電視節目的燈光真的是……罪孽深重，真的是這樣。

——凱文・奧庫安，美國彩妝藝術家

I'm going to insult a whole industry here, but it seems like TV is for people who can't do film. I'm not talking about actresses; I'm talking about lighting people. Lighting on TV is just so ... it's sinful, it really is.

—Kevyn Aucoin, American makeup artist

今天，我坐在小小的辦公室隔間裡，終於了解，打從我開始工作起，我人生中每一天都比前一天還要糟糕。這意謂著，你見到我的每一天，都是我人生中最糟糕的那一天。

——彼得・吉本斯，出自電影《上班一條蟲》

So I was sitting in my cubicle today, and I realized, ever since I started working, every single day of my life has been worse than the day before it. So that means that every single day that you see me, that's on the worst day of my life.

—Peter Gibbons, *Office Space*

職場上最悲慘的現實就是，成功的不一定是最有生產力或最稱職的員工，而是誰最會拍馬屁。所以你可以繼續埋頭苦幹並希望你微薄的成就會獲得回報，但如果你把時間花在記住你的老闆喜歡怎樣的咖啡，你會好過很多。

所謂的每月最佳員工，是指一個人如何可以同時身兼勝利者與失敗者的最佳範例。──狄米崔‧馬丁，美國喜劇演員

Employee of the month is a good example of how somebody can be both a winner and a loser at the same time.

—Demetri Martin, American comedian

工作比玩笑還要有趣。

──諾爾‧寇威爾，英國劇作家

Work is much more fun than fun.

—Noel Coward,British playwright

享受開會的人不該負責任何事。

──托馬斯‧索維爾，美國經濟學家與作家

People who enjoy meetings should not be in charge of anything.

—Thomas Sowell, American economist and author

太努力工作的人都不會值得信任。——愛德嘉‧華生‧浩威，美國小說家

It's no credit to anyone to work too hard.

—Edgar Watson Howe, American novelist

工作是由尚未達到無能水準的員工所完成的。

——勞倫斯‧J‧彼得，加拿大作家

Work is accomplished by those employees who have not yet reached their level of incompetence.

—Laurence J. Peter, Canadian author

　　如果你把一件緊急任務交給一個每天認真工作八小時、積極進取的員工，那很有可能工作可以順利完成；把同樣的工作分配給懶惰的員工，還不如要他們在下午五點前拆掉柏林圍牆。

　　並不是說那工作特別困難，事實是，喜歡拖拖拉拉的人寧可跳進一座活火山，也不願意跑下樓、問行銷部新的標示該用什麼顏色。所以你當然可以繼續把工作分配給這些懶惰的雜碎，只是當工作只完成一半或是根本沒動的時候，你就別太驚訝了。

拖延就像是信用卡，直到你收到帳單前，都會非常開心。

——克里斯多福‧帕克，英國演員

Procrastination is like a credit card; it's a lot of fun until you get the bill.

—Christopher Parker, British actor

完成不可能的任務，意味著老闆會把這項工作加進你的例行工作裡。 ──道格・拉森，美國專欄作家

Accomplishing the impossible means only the boss will add it to your regular duties.

—Doug Larson, American columnist

努力工作快跟一夫一妻制一樣，都名不符實。

──休伊・朗，前路易斯安那州州長

Hard work is damn near as overrated as monogamy.

—Huey Long, former Louisiana governor

我不是在睡覺，我只是在用心觀察我的眼皮內部。

──喬納森・拉班，英國旅遊作家

I ain't sleeping. I'm just taking a good look at the insides of my eyelids.

—Jonathan Raban, British travel writer

不管有多少事，都是可以做的，只要不是那個時間他該做的事。

──羅伯特・本奇利，美國幽默作家與作家

Anyone can do any amount of work provided it isn't the work he is supposed to be doing at the moment.

—Robert Benchley, American humorist and writer

死於操心的人多於死於工作的人，因為操心的人多於工作的人。
　　——羅伯特・佛洛斯特，美國詩人，四度獲普立茲獎

The reason why worry kills more people than work is that more people worry than work.

—Robert Frost

大腦是個神奇的器官，它從你早上醒來的那一刻開始工作，直到你進辦公室前，它都不會停止運作。
　　——羅伯特・佛洛斯特，美國詩人，四度獲普立茲獎

The brain is a wonderful organ; it starts working the moment you get up in the morning and does not stop until you get into the office.

—Robert Frost

有史以來，唯一一個坐著就可以成功的是母雞。
　　——莎拉・布朗，美國女演員

The only thing that ever sat its way to success was a hen.

—Sarah Brown, American actress

每當有困難的工作需要完成時，我都會把它分配給懶惰的人，因為他一定會找到簡單的方式去完成它。
　　——華特・克萊斯勒，美國商人與克萊斯勒企業創始人

Whenever there is a hard job to be done, I assign it to a lazy man; he is

sure to find an easy way of doing it.
—Walter Chrysler, American businessman and founder of the Chrysler Corporation

　　在難以忍受的馬屁精與墮落懶惰的混帳之間，還是有理想的員工。他知道何時該說好，也知道何時該閉上嘴巴；他可以準時完成任何出現在他辦公桌上的工作，一旦完成，他也不會追求更好的表現。他那禪意般的平庸是美麗的，如果你在辦公室裡可以找到這樣的一個人，你最好多學著點。如果你能設法做剛好的工作量，同時讓自己看起來很忙，但實際上並沒有那麼忙，那麼你的工作絕對可以好過些，也許。

我要跟你分享這三個短短的句子，絕對可以讓你撐過你的人生：第一，罩我一下；第二，噢，好主意，老闆！第三，我來的時候，這裡就是這樣了。 —— 荷馬・J・辛普森，出自《辛普森家庭》
I want to share something with you: The three little sentences that will get you through life. Number 1: Cover for me. Number 2: Oh, good idea, Boss! Number 3: It was like that when I got here.
—Homer J. Simpson, *The Simpsons*

如果A等於成功，那方程式就是A等於X加上Y跟Z，X是工作，Y是玩，而Z是閉上你的嘴巴。 —— 阿爾伯特・愛因斯坦，物理哲學家

If A equals success, then the formula is A equals X plus Y and Z, with X being work, Y play, and Z keeping your mouth shut.

—Albert Einstein

每天老老實實地工作八個小時，最終你可能可以變成老闆，然後每天工作十二小時。——羅伯特‧佛洛斯特，美國詩人，四度獲普立茲獎

By working faithfully eight hours a day, you may eventually get to be boss and work twelve hours a day.

—Robert Frost

每當你被問到是否可以做某件事時，告訴他們：「當然，我可以！」然後趕快去找出解決方法。——狄奧多‧羅斯福，前美國總統

Whenever you are asked if you can do a job, tell 'em, "Certainly, I can!" Then get busy and find out how to do it.

—Theodore Roosevelt

每個與我共事的人都比我懂某件事。我的工作就是花時間好好聆聽，然後我就可以了解並運用它們。

——傑克‧尼可斯，美國同性戀權利社會運動家

Every person I work with knows something better than me. My job is to listen long enough to find it and use it.

—Jack Nichols, American gay rights activist

工作上難免會出錯，所謂適當的處置方式，意味著被開除或是升職這兩種截然不同的結果。事實上，一天工作結束時，根本沒人想知道要怎麼解決問題，他們只想知道可以把錯怪到誰的頭上。

在這種處境下，員工只有兩個選擇：方案一，勇敢站出來承擔責任；你還有方案二可選，推卸給任何一個離你最近的同事。這傢伙或許是個討厭鬼，但至少他是個仍有工作的討厭鬼。

對不需要親自去做的人來說，沒什麼是不可能的。
——A‧H‧威勒，紐約時報電影編輯

Nothing is impossible for the man who doesn't have to do it himself.
—A. H. Weiler, *New York Times* film editor

明明是我播了種，卻由別人收成，不過我不打算抱怨。
——查爾斯‧固特異，美國發明家

I am not disposed to complain that I have planted and others have gathered the fruits.
—Charles Goodyear, American inventor

老鷹或許可以在高空翱翔，但黃鼠狼絕不會被吸進飛機引擎裡。——約翰‧班菲爾德，英國演員

Eagles may soar high, but weasels don't get sucked into jet engines.
—John Benfield, British acto

事情出錯時還在微笑的人，已經想好要把責任推給誰了。

——羅伯特‧布洛克，美國小說家

The man who smiles when things go wrong has thought of someone to blame it on.

—Robert Bloch, American novelist

經營管理能力就是快速下決定，讓別人來做。

——厄爾‧南丁格爾，美國作家與勵志演說家

Executive ability is deciding quickly and getting somebody else to do the work.

—Earl Nightingale, American author and motivational speaker

如果工作真的這麼棒，那有錢人就會多留些工作給他們自己。

——大衛‧布蘭特，出自美國電視劇《辦公室瘋雲》

If work was so good, the rich would have kept more of it for themselves.

—David Brent, *The Office*

我的工作內容基本上包括掩飾我對混蛋上司的輕蔑，以及每天至少躲進男廁一次，邊打手槍邊幻想一個沒那麼接近地獄的人生。

——萊斯特‧伯納姆，出自電影《美國心玫瑰情》

My job consists of basically masking my contempt for the a**holes in

charge and, at least once a day, retiring to the men's room so I can jerk off while I fantasize about a life that doesn't so closely resemble hell.
—Lester Burnham, *American Beauty*

我上班總是遲到，不過我會用早退離開來彌補。
—— 查爾斯·蘭姆，英國作家

I always arrive late at the office, but I make up for it by leaving early.
—Charles Lamb, British author

如果你要遲到了，那就遲到吧，而且別只是遲到兩分鐘，乾脆遲到個一小時，然後好好享受你的早餐。
—— 大衛·布蘭特，出自美國電視劇《辦公室瘋雲》

If you're gonna be late, then be late and not just two minutes— make it an hour and enjoy your breakfast.
—David Brent, *The Office*

我喜歡工作，它令我著迷。我可以坐在那兒盯著它好幾個小時。
—— 傑羅姆·K·傑羅姆，英國作家

I like work; it fascinates me. I can sit and look at it for hours.
—Jerome K. Jerome,

工作是世上最偉大的事，所以我們該把一些工作留給明天。

── 唐‧赫羅德，美國幽默作家

Work is the greatest thing in the world, so we should always save some
of it for tomorrow.

—Don Herold, American humorist

如果老闆讓你不開心，就從叉子的縫隙間看他，並想像他在監獄
裡的樣子。 ── 大衛‧布蘭特，出自美國電視劇《辦公室瘋雲》

If your boss is getting you down, look at him through the prongs of a
fork and imagine him in jail.

—David Brent, *The Office*

第十章
被炒魷魚

　　幾乎沒什麼事會比把人生耗費在讓人憂鬱的工作上還糟，如果有，大概只有一件事可以讓你更崩潰，就是在你拖著沉重的步伐踱進辦公室準備上班時，卻在信箱裡發現一封醒目的解僱通知書[12]。不過，跟其他驚天動地消息需要經歷五種階段不一樣，被開除通常只有兩個階段：震驚與憤怒，接著而來的是一種難以描述的冷淡。就好像是發現你的狗死掉了，但馬上又想起牠一輩子都在咬你的腳踝跟大便在地毯上那樣。不過不管你如何看待這件事，被開除真的是爛透了……貫穿這整章的苦澀白癡語錄可以證明這件事。

我的意思是，沒有爭議，什麼也沒有，也沒有拐彎抹角。「你被開除了」是很強烈的字眼。　——唐納・川普，美國第45任總統；商業大亨
I mean, there's no arguing. There is no anything. There is no beating around the bush. *You're fired* is a very strong term.
—Donald Trump

---

❷ Pink slip 為解僱通知書的意思。在美國的慣例裡，許多表格是一式三份，而其中一份通常是粉紅色。

多數人只努力工作到剛好不會被開除的程度，然後也只拿到剛好讓人不會想辭職的薪水。——喬治·卡林，美國喜劇演員

Most people work just hard enough not to get fired and get paid just enough money not to quit.

—George Carlin, American comedian

我不知道還有什麼經費是可以刪減的，有我們現在所需要的技能的人，我們都已經把他們資遣了。

——葛雷格·梅費特，卡崔娜颶風期間紐奧良代理市長

I don't know what else we can cut when we've already laid off all these people whose skills we could use right now.

—Greg Meffert, deputy mayor of New Orleans during Hurricane Katrina

我們失業時，被說成是懶惰；白人失業時，他們說是不景氣。

——傑西·傑克遜，美國公民權利社會運動家

When we're unemployed, we're called lazy; when the whites are unemployed, it's called a depression.

—Jesse Jackson, American civil rights activist

在你往上爬的時候，對其他人好一點，因為你走下坡的時候會遇見他們。——吉米·杜蘭特，美國演員與音樂家

Be nice to people on your way up because you meet them on your way down.

—Jimmy Durante, American actor and musician

你被開除了！沒有任何其他字眼可以如此輕易簡潔地把一個充滿自信的主管大卸八塊成不安、卑躬屈膝的碎片。

—— 法蘭克·P·勞屈海姆，美國商人

You're fired! No other words can so easily and succinctly reduce a confident, self-assured executive to an insecure, groveling shred of his former self.

—Frank P. Louchheim, American businessman

自一九九八年起，自殺案件年齡成長最大的區段就是那些被遣散或生意失敗的中年人或年紀更大的人。—— 山田昌弘，日本社會學家

The bulk of the increase since 1998 is suicides by men who are middle-aged or older and have either been laid off or whose businesses have failed.

—Masahiro Yamada, Japanese sociologist

我還處於被開除的驚恐之中。—— 彼得·阿奈特，紐西蘭記者

I am still in shock and awe at being fired.

—Peter Arnett, New Zealander journalist

鄰居失業是經濟不景氣，你失業就是大蕭條了。
── 羅納德·雷根，美國第40任總統

Recession is when a neighbor loses his job. Depression is when you lose yours.
──Ronald Reagan

如果你沒被熱情激發，那你會被熱情地開除。
── 文斯·隆巴迪，美式足球教練

If you aren't fired up with enthusiasm, you will be fired with enthusiasm.
──Vince Lombardi, American football coach

　　得知自己被開除後，試著想搞清楚是哪裡做錯了，是很正常的反應。究竟是因為你不修邊幅的外型、缺乏幹勁、還是經常無法控制的啜泣？也許是這三項的結合？

　　不論你的老闆給你哪種藉口，想當然爾，你一定是做了些什麼才會得到如此下場，就跟下面這些笨蛋一樣。也許真的有些老闆只是憑著射飛鏢到靶上，看射中誰就開除誰。因此，與其搞清楚狀況，或許最好的作法是聳聳肩放下它，然後下次找間有工會的公司。

我曾經是個洗窗工人，我被開除是因為我偶爾喜歡喝一些會起泡的水。　── 潔米莉亞，英國歌手與模特兒

I used to be a window cleaner. I got fired because I sometimes liked to drink the soapy water.

—Jamelia, British singer and model

多數人對待辦公室手冊的方式就像對待軟體手冊一樣，從不看它一眼。——詹姆斯‧李汶，美國指揮家與鋼琴家

Most people treat the office manual the way they treat a software manual. They never look at it.

—James Levine, American conductor and pianist

你在辦公室派對上搞錯露屁股❸的對象，突然間你就不再「專業」了。——傑夫‧法克斯渥西，美國喜劇演員

You moon the wrong person at an office party and suddenly you're not "professional" anymore.

—Jeff Foxworthy, American comedian

如果你在上班時間看棒球賽，會加倍有趣。

——威廉‧斐勒，美國作家

A baseball game is twice as much fun if you're seeing it on the company's time.

—William Feather, American author

---

❸ Moon 為月亮。非正式用法裡有躬身對人露出屁股的意思。

哈佛大學的研究指出，下午睡一小時可以讓你完全重振精神。他們說當你醒來的時候，你的感覺會好到可以開始找新工作了。

——傑‧雷諾，美國脫口秀節目主持人

Researchers at Harvard say that taking a power nap for an hour in the afternoon can totally refresh you. They say that by the time you wake up, you'll feel so good, you'll be able to start looking for a new job.

—Jay Leno

千萬別問你被開除的原因，因為如果你問了，他們就有義務要告訴你。——傑里‧科爾曼，棒球分析專家

You never ask why you've been fired because if you do, they're liable to tell you.

—Jerry Coleman, baseball analyst

為了週薪一千元美金的薪水，我去那裡上班，星期一報到，星期三就被開除。僱用我的傢伙星期二就出城不在了。

——納爾遜‧艾格林，美國作家

I went out there for a thousand a week, and I worked Monday, and I got fired Wednesday. The guy that hired me was out of town Tuesday.

—Nelson Algren, American author

有時我會在半夜醒著躺在床上想：「我到底是哪裡做錯？」然後有個聲音跟我說：「這得花上不只一個晚上的時間。」

──查爾斯・舒茲，美國漫畫家與漫畫《花生》的創作者

Sometimes I lie awake at night and ask, "Where have I gone wrong?" Then a voice says to me, "This is going to take more than one night."
—Charles Schulz, American cartoonist and creator of the "Peanuts" comics

沒有人會在下班時間之前離開，除非老闆提早走。
──格魯喬・馬克斯，美國電影與喜劇演員

No man goes before his time—unless the boss leaves early.
—Groucho Marx

要被政府開除很困難，就像你得殺人一樣。
──旺達・塞克絲，美國喜劇演員

It's hard to get fired from the government. You have to, like, kill people.
—Wanda Sykes, American comedian

感謝幾個有遠見的傢伙，美國有個替怠忽職守的員工準備好的安全措施。願意吞下他們驕傲的人，就能夠以失業保險形式從納稅人那接受施捨。以前，這樣的人必須忍受眾人皆知的恥辱並排隊領取他們的支票，但現代科技讓你在自己的躺椅上就可以領到失業補助。所以現在的問題已經不是「你什麼時候要找新工作？」而是「你為什麼要找新工作？」

失業保險是給白吃白喝的人的假期，而且薪水還預付。

——羅納德‧雷根，美國第40任總統

Unemployment insurance is a prepaid vacation for freeloaders.

—Ronald Reagan

以前每個人都說要有更多閒暇時間，現在他們卻在抱怨失業了。——菲利普親王，英國女王伊莉莎白二世夫婿

Everybody was saying we must have more leisure. Now they are complaining they are unemployed.

—Prince Philip

我希望我的兄弟可以學會某種謀生技能，這樣我就知道他在哪個行業失業了。——漢尼‧楊曼，英國喜劇演員

I wish my brother would learn a trade so I would know what kind of work he's out of.

—Henny Youngman, British comedian

現在找不到工作的不只是主修哲學的人了。

——肯特‧布羅克曼，出自《辛普森家庭》

Now joblessness isn't just for philosophy majors.

—Kent Brockman, *The Simpsons*

我是個鋼琴演奏家，那是種「我現在失業中」的做作說法。
——奧斯卡‧萊文特，美國音樂家與演員

I'm a concert pianist. That's a pretentious way of saying "I'm unemployed at the moment."
—Oscar Levant, American musician and actor

失業的問題就是，當你早上醒來的瞬間，你就在工作了。
——史萊皮‧懷特，美國喜劇演員與演員

The trouble with unemployment is that the minute you wake up in the morning, you're on the job.
—Slappy White, American comedian and actor

失業就像是頭痛或發燒，令人不愉快又筋疲力盡，但它卻沒有任何原因可以解釋。——威廉‧亨利‧卑弗列治，英國經濟學家

Unemployment is like a headache or a high temperature—unpleasant and exhausting but not carrying in itself any explanation of its cause.
—William Henry Beveridge, British economist

　　等你度過失去工作的震驚，接著就是評估狀況的時候了。你不必每天早起，不必應付無能的同事，你唯一要負的責任，只有每週打一次電話給失業救濟部門，並記得把自己餵飽。這是中大獎！與其羞愧低頭收拾你的辦公桌，你應該要衝進老闆的辦公室

給他來個大熊抱才對。他也許幫了你人生中最大的一個忙。

我曾經與許多快死的人相處，從來沒有一個人說：「我唯一的遺憾就是沒多花點時間在辦公室裡。」
──丹尼斯‧普拉格，保守主義廣播脫口秀主持人

I have been with many men approaching death, and not one has ever said, "I only regret that I didn't spend more time at the office."
—Dennis Prager, conservative radio talk show host

可以用點創意看待被炒魷魚這件事，丟了的工作是他根本就不想做的，這下終於可以實際體驗如釋重負的感覺。
──法蘭克‧P‧勞屈海姆，美國商人

Handled creatively, getting fired allows an executive to actually experience a sense of relief that he never wanted the job he has lost.
—Frank P. Louchheim, American businessman

被開除可以是種解放，讓你了解到世界沒有因此結束，還有其他賺錢的方法與更好的工作等著你。──羅恩‧利文斯頓，美國演員

It can be liberating to get fired because you realize the world doesn't end. There's other ways to make money, better jobs.
—Ron Livingston, American actor

過多的工作與精力跟過多的惡習或酗酒一樣，可以有效地殺死一個人。——魯德亞德·吉卜林，生於孟買的英國作家

Too much work and too much energy kill a man just as effectively as too much assorted vice or too much drink.

—Rudyard Kipling

它就只是個工作。青草生長，鳥兒飛，海浪拍打著沙灘。我揍人。——穆罕默德·阿里，美國拳擊手

It's just a job. Grass grows, birds fly, waves pound the sand. I beat people up.

—Muhammad Ali

對許多人來說，被開除不只是失去一份穩定的收入來源，它也意味著失去所有自我認同。當被問到：「你從事哪一行？」時，以前他們能夠不加思索地把自己的經歷說得無比流利，儼然一場極佳的自我推銷演說；而現在面對同樣的問題，他們的反應變成兩眼無神並開始緊張地大口喘氣。幸好這些可悲的人們還是有希望。如果他們可以從這些厚臉皮的傢伙獲得一些提醒並學著擁抱平凡，他們就能學會一件事：無法讓人印象深刻，其實也沒什麼關係。

為了繼續活下去，一個人得試圖避免與完美主義有關的死亡。
──漢娜‧鄂蘭，德國政治理論家

In order to go on living, one must try to escape the death involved in perfectionism.
—Hannah Arendt, German political theorist

二十年前被解僱是個污點，現在則是常態。
──麥克‧沃辛頓，人力網站 RESUMEDOCTOR.COM 的共同創辦人

Twenty years ago there was a stigma about being laid off; now it's the norm.
—Michael Worthington, co-founder of ResumeDoctor.com

被開除沒什麼不對。──泰德‧透納，美國透納廣播公司創辦人

There's nothing wrong with being fired.
—Ted Turner, American businessman and founder of Turner Broadcasting System, Inc.

接受有些時候你是鴿子，有些時候你是雕像吧。
──呆伯特，出自《呆伯特》

Accept that some days you are the pigeon, and some days you are the statue.
—Dilbert, *Dilbert*

現在我跟風一樣自由，還有大致上一樣的收入。

——吉恩‧佩雷，美國喜劇作家

I'm now as free as the breeze—with roughly the same income.

—Gene Perret, American comedy writer

雖然新工作可能是你目前生活中最不想要的東西，但你如果想讓自己往後可以吃飽穿暖，可能還是得找個新工作。你可能需要把自己用力搖醒，去想想上次丟履歷是多久以前的事。首先，工作不會像過去一樣從天上掉下來；其次，你一九九二年畢業時給人印象深刻的那張大學文憑，現在就跟你小時候買的尪仔標❹一樣不值錢。不過別擔心，只要你能好好鑽研拍馬屁的能力並隨時複習以下的語錄，一定沒問題的。

男人就是這樣，他只能藉由從一種勞動換成另一種勞動中尋求放鬆。——阿納托爾‧法郎士，法國詩人

Man is so made that he can only find relaxation from one kind of labor by taking up another.

—Anatole France, French poet

❹ Pogs 是一種流行於90年代的圓形卡牌遊戲。不論牌的造型跟玩法，都跟我們的尪仔標類似。

很多人有了一份職業，就不再找工作做了。

—— 吉格・金克拉，美國勵志演說家

A lot of people quit looking for work as soon as they find a job.

—Zig Ziglar, American motivational speaker

我以為我想要事業，但其實我只想要一份薪水。

—— 來源不詳

I thought I wanted a career; turns out I just wanted a salary.

—Unknown

我很想僱用所有的美國勞工，但沒有人要來為我們工作，因為知道他們會在六、七個月後被解僱。 —— 克里斯・海耶斯，企業家

I'd like to hire all American workers, but nobody will come to work for us knowing they'll be laid off in six or seven months.

—Chris Hayes, vice president of Groundmasters

如果我說我是因為性醜聞在國會山莊被開除，他們絕對會僱用我。 —— 潔西卡・卡特勒，美國作家與前國會助理人員

They'll totally hire me if I say I got fired from my job on the Hill because of a sex scandal.

—Jessica Cutler, American author and former congressional staff assistant

在好萊塢有句話是說，你永遠都該原諒你的敵人，因為你不知道什麼時候得跟他們一起工作。──拉娜·透納，美國女演員

It's said in Hollywood that you should always forgive your enemies—because you never know when you'll have to work with them.

—Lana Turner, American actress

　　在戰爭裡，為了避免將來流血，有時先發制人的襲擊是必要的。同樣的話也適用於職場。當你有預感老闆快要開除你的時候，或許那是個考慮辭職的好時機。有些人可能會覺得「我要帶我的球回家去」的作法有點幼稚，但這作法是對的。當你可以扭轉局勢、搶先開除你的老闆時，為什麼要給老闆機會，讓他滿足炒你魷魚的成就感呢？

弱勢的人唯一可以珍視的自由，就是辭職，在太陽底下伸懶腰並抓癢的自由。

──H·L·曼肯，美國記者

The only liberty an inferior man really cherishes is the liberty to quit work, stretch out in the sun, and scratch himself.

—H. L. Mencken, American journalist

有人問如何才能成為一個成功的搖滾樂團。我總是說，就他媽的辭掉你的工作然後在街上生活。當你真的很餓的時候，你就會寫

出些好東西。

——保羅·利里，樂團「屁眼衝浪客」的吉他手

People ask what it takes to become a successful rock band. I always say just fucking quit your job and live on the street. And when you get really hungry, you'll come up with something good.

—Paul Leary, guitarist for the Butthole Surfers

是我閃到一邊的時候了，把位置讓給那些沒經驗也更無能的人。

——史考特·伊利治，美國作家與康乃大學退休教授

It is time I stepped aside for less experienced and less able men.

—Scott Elladge, American author and professor on his retirement from Cornell

我沒有放棄電影，是他們放棄我。 ——珍·鮑威爾，美國歌手與女演員

I didn't quit movies. They quit me.

—Jane Powell, American singer and actress

我是為了辭職而辭職，我不是為了寫小說而辭職，我只是不想再工作了。 ——唐·德里羅，美國小說家

I quit my job just to quit. I didn't quit my job to write fiction. I just didn't want to work anymore.

—Don DeLillo, American novelist

如果感覺好像所有底線都往上跑時，所有球員都該辭職不幹。
　　──貝比·魯斯，洋基隊球員

All ballplayers should quit when it starts to feel as if all the baselines run uphill.
─Babe Ruth

　　如果你保持低調而且沒惹火太多人，也許可以避免被開除的命運，然後一直抵達你的應許之地：退休。跟不新鮮的咖啡與午餐會議說再見，同時也跟早鳥優惠與日間電視節目打聲招呼吧。也因此，你一生最偉大的成就是沒被開除過。這好像有點悲哀，不過至少你不必在職業介紹所裡排隊等工作。

當一個男人退休時，他的妻子獲得了雙倍的丈夫，卻只有一半的收入。　　──奇奇·羅德里格茲，波多黎各職業高爾夫球選手

When a man retires, his wife gets twice the husband but only half the income.
─Chi Chi Rodriguez, Puerto Rican professional golfer

退休很美妙，可以無所事事，不用擔心被逮到。
　　──吉恩·佩雷，美國喜劇作家

Retirement is wonderful. It's doing nothing without worrying about getting caught at it.
─Gene Perret, American comedy writer

六十五歲退休有夠荒謬。我六十五歲的時候，還會長青春痘呢。

——喬治・伯恩斯，美國喜劇演員與演員

Retirement at sixty-five is ridiculous. When I was sixty-five, I still had pimples.

—George Burns, American comedian and actor

公司的會計很害羞而且要退休了，他的帳短少了二十五萬美金，這就是他退休的原因。 ——米爾頓・伯利，美國喜劇演員與演員

The company accountant is shy and retiring. He's shy a quarter of a million dollars. That's why he's retiring.

—Milton Berle, American comedian and actor

如果你有一份不發怒的工作，那表示你根本沒有工作。

——邁爾康・富比士，美國出版商

If you have a job without any aggravations, you don't have a job.

—Malcolm S. Forbes, American publisher

退休就像是在拉斯維加斯渡長假，目標是徹底地享受它。但如果你把錢花光，就沒那麼享受了。 ——喬納森・克萊門茨，英國作家

Retirement is like a long vacation in Las Vegas. The goal is to enjoy it the fullest, but not so fully that you run out of money.

—Jonathan Clements, British author

第十一章
金錢

　　只要不一味地把錢視為萬惡淵藪，就可以發現它在現代社會裡有多實用。撇除它可以用來交換各種商品與服務這再明顯不過的事實，錢還可以讓你打炮、幫你交朋友、提高你的自尊，甚至只要操作得當，它還會自我複製。既然如此，為什麼它仍是歷史上最受詆毀的東西呢？

　　有許多理論解釋為什麼人們如此痛恨金錢，但大部分理論都很冗長、複雜且大錯特錯。因為真相是，人們一點都不痛恨金錢。他們只是痛恨有錢的王八蛋們而已。但誰能怪他們？當你分類垃圾一小時只能賺七塊五毛美金，而華爾街的主管光拉個屎就賺到了你的一百倍，你當然非常容易就會覺得不爽。但不論你是戶頭裡的錢多到要從存摺流出來，還是你的畢生積蓄都在一個咖啡罐裡，你都可以從下面這些人身上學到一兩件關於錢的事，不論他們是貧富貴賤哪一種。

快離開！貧窮正在逮人。　——阿芙拉・貝恩，英國作家
Come away! Poverty's catching.
—Aphra Behn, British writer

如果這是個好劇本，我就演。如果這是個爛劇本，而他們付我夠多的錢，我還是會演。——喬治‧伯恩斯，美國喜劇演員與演員

If it's a good script, I'll do it. If it's a bad script, and they pay me enough, I'll do it.

—George Burns, American comedian and actor

一個成功的男人就是賺的比他老婆能花的還多。一個成功的女人就是找到一個這樣的男人。——拉娜‧透納，美國女演員

A successful man is one who makes more money than his wife can spend. A successful woman is one who can find such a man.

—Lana Turner, American actress

每天早上起床，我就看一遍富比士雜誌列出的美國富豪名單。如果我不在上面，我就會去工作。——羅伯特‧奧本，美國魔術師與作家

Every morning, I get up and look through the Forbes list of the richest people in America. If I'm not there, I go to work.

—Robert Orben, American magician and writer

你可以年輕沒有錢，但你不能老了還沒有錢。
——田納西‧威廉斯，美國劇作家與作家

You can be young without money, but you can't be old without it.

—Tennessee Williams, American playwright and author

母性就是這樣，她真的一點兒都不在乎你是哪個經濟階層。

—— 琥碧・戈柏，美國演員、作家、歌手

That's the thing about Mother Nature: She really doesn't care what economic bracket you're in.

—Whoopi Goldberg

郵局寄送帳單的速度比支票快兩倍。

—— J・史蒂芬・萊特，美國喜劇演員

Bills travel through the mail at twice the speed of checks.

—J. Steven Wright, American comedian

如果你可以數得出你有多少錢，那表示你沒有十億美金。

—— 保羅・蓋蒂，美國商人

If you can count your money, you don't have a billion dollars.

—Paul Getty, American businessman

我們從來都不清楚我們的財務狀況。

—— 艾希莉・歐森，美國女演員

We were never aware of our financial situation.

—Ashley Olsen, American actress

唯一一個不為錢的事傷腦筋的方法就是擁有很多錢。
——伊迪絲·華頓，美國小說家

The only way not to think about money is to have a great deal of it.
—Edith Wharton, American novelist

如果有人跟你說他靠辛勤工作致富，繼續問他：「是靠誰的辛勤
工作？」——唐·馬奎斯，美國記者

When a man tells you that he got rich through hard work, ask him:
"Whose?"
—Don Marquis, American journalist

有錢人的笑話總是很好笑。——托馬斯·布朗，英國作家

A rich man's joke is always funny.
—Thomas Browne, British author

據我所知，沒什麼事比得上一個人把他所有清醒的時間都花在為
了錢而賺錢還要更卑劣、更可悲的。
——約翰·D·洛克菲勒

I know of nothing more despicable and pathetic than a man who
devotes all of the hours of the waking day to the making of money for
money's sake.
—John D. Rockefeller

霸子，有了一萬元美金，我們就是百萬富翁了！我們可以買各種有用的東西，像是……愛！—— 荷馬．Ｊ．辛普森，出自《辛普森家庭》

Bart, with $10,000, we'd be millionaires! We could buy all kinds of useful things like ... love!

—Homer J. Simpson, *The Simpsons*

總有一天，我要變得很有錢。有些人有錢到失去所有對人性的尊重。我就是要變那麼有錢。—— 麗塔．魯德納，美國女演員與喜劇演員

Someday I want to be rich. Some people get so rich they lose all respect for humanity. That's how rich I want to be.

—Rita Rudner, American actress and comedian

　　如果你認為錢沒有掌控你，我得很遺憾地告訴你，你大錯特錯了！需要證據嗎？如果你在地上發現二十元美金，你會興奮地撿起來嗎？這樣就夠了。

　　不過你不必因為金錢束縛你的心靈而感到難過。根據以下語錄顯示，錢可以說是人類文明最重要的事。如果你同樣著迷於其他沒有價值的東西像是愛、友誼與健康，那你可能有麻煩了。

酒能使人快活，錢能教萬事應心。—— 聖經，傳道書，10:19

Wine maketh merry: but money answereth all things.

—Bible, Ecclesiastes, 10:19

錢買不到快樂，但錢可以拿來支付一個龐大研究團隊的薪水，讓他們研究問題所在。——威廉·E·「比爾」·渥恩，美國專欄作家

Money won't buy happiness, but it will pay the salaries of a large research staff to study the problem.

—William E. "Bill" Vaughan, American columnist

當人們說「我們不能感情用事」的時候，你就知道他們打算要做什麼殘忍的事情。如果他們還加上「我們要實際點」，那表示他們要利用那件事賺錢。——布莉吉德·布洛菲，英國小說家

Whenever people say, "We mustn't be sentimental," you can take it they are about to do something cruel. And if they add, "We must be realistic," they mean they are going to make money out of it.

—Brigid Brophy, British novelist

我們美國有一句話是這麼說的：「我們相信上帝。」上帝就出現在耶穌想要的地方：在我們的鈔票上面。
——史蒂芬·荷伯，美國政治諷刺作家

There's a phrase we live by in America: "In God We Trust." It's right there where Jesus would want it: on our money.

—Stephen Colbert, American political satirist

金錢買不到你的幸福，但它的確可以讓你的苦難有一種更愉快的

形式。——史派克‧米利根，愛爾蘭喜劇演員

Money can't buy you happiness, but it does bring you a more pleasant form of misery.
—Spike Milligan, Irish comedian

幸福快樂有什麼用？它又不能買錢給你。
——漢尼‧楊曼，英國喜劇演員

What's the use of happiness? It can't buy you money.
—Henny Youngman, British comedian

豐厚的收入是我聽過最好的幸福祕訣。
——珍‧奧斯汀，英國女性文學家

A large income is the best recipe for happiness I ever heard of.
—Jane Austen

　　有些人不認為錢有那麼偉大，哪怕所有的證據都否定這種看法，但他們依舊這麼相信。的確，這種人大多都很窮，根本不知道自己在說什麼，但也有少數幾個有錢人這麼認為。雖然對那些「我討厭錢俱樂部」的貧窮會員沒什麼好說的，不過那些隸屬這個陣營的有錢混蛋真的該停止發牢騷。畢竟，有很多人會盡一切所能讓有錢混蛋從他們的重擔中解脫。

想要一次拿到這隻鵝所能給的黃金，他殺了牠並剖開牠，結果什麼也沒有。—— 伊索寓言

Thinking to get at once all the gold the goose could give, he killed it and opened it only to find—nothing.

—Aesop

如果你想知道上帝對錢的看法，只需要看看那些祂給他們錢的人就知道了。—— 桃樂絲·帕克，美國詩人

If you want to know what God thinks of money, just look at the people he gave it to.

—Dorothy Parker, American poet

我認識的大多數有錢人都過得很慘。
—— 阿嘉莎·克莉絲蒂，英國推理小說家

Most of the rich people I've known have been fairly miserable.

—Agatha Christie

對金錢適度成癮不一定有害，但攝取過量的話，對健康可就不好了。—— 克勞倫斯·戴伊，美國作家

A moderate addiction to money may not always be hurtful, but when taken in excess, it is nearly always bad for the health.

—Clarence Day, American author

把錢當成你的上帝，它就會像鬼一樣替你帶來厄運。
—— 亨利‧菲爾丁，英國小說家

Make money your god and it will plague you like the devil.
—Henry Fielding, British novelist

一個只會賺錢的企業是個貧乏的企業。
—— 亨利‧福特，美國企業家，建立福特汽車

A business that makes nothing but money is a poor business.
—Henry Ford

要向朋友借錢之前，先決定你最需要哪一個。
—— 諺語

Before borrowing money from a friend, decide which you need most.
—Proverb

所有的進步都奠基於一種共通的天生慾望，就是每個生物都想過
一種超過收入的優渥生活。
—— 塞繆爾‧巴特勒，英國維多利亞時代小說家

All progress is based upon a universal innate desire on the part of every
organism to live beyond its income.
—Samuel Butler, Victorian novelist

雖然錢不能替你買到快樂是真的，毫無疑問地，貧窮當然也沒辦法。沒有任何事比完全沒錢這狀況更能提醒我們：錢真的很重要。在你抱怨自己有多窮之前，記住你已經比下面某些混帳好上太多。

如果你曾必須偷自己小孩的錢，之後還被他發現錢不見了，我覺得最好的辦法就是把這事算在聖誕老人頭上。
——傑克‧韓第，美國喜劇演員

If you ever have to steal money from your kid, and later on he discovers it's gone, I think a good thing to do is to blame it on Santa Claus.
—Jack Handey, American comedian

你似乎沒有意識到一個不快樂的窮人其實比一個不快樂的有錢人還要好。因為窮人還抱有希望，他認為錢可以解決問題。
——琴‧柯爾，美國作家與劇作家

You don't seem to realize that a poor person who is unhappy is in a better position than a rich person who is unhappy. Because the poor person has hope. He thinks money would help.
—Jean Kerr, American author and playwright

我以前覺得我很窮，但他們說我不是窮，是貧困。然後，他們說認為自己貧困是種自我失敗的想法，我是被剝奪了。（噢，也不是被剝奪，應該說社經地位低下。）然後他們說「社經地位低下」這個詞太超過，我是弱勢。我現在還是一毛錢都沒有；不過我懂很多字彙。——吉爾斯·菲佛，連環漫畫《菲佛》的創作者

I used to think I was poor. Then they told me I wasn't poor, I was needy. Then they told me it was self-defeating to think of myself as needy. I was deprived. (Oh not deprived but rather underprivileged.) Then they told me that underprivileged was overused. I was disadvantaged. I still don't have a dime. But I have a great vocabulary.

—Jules Feiffer, creator of the comic strip *Feiffer*

讓你的小孩學著認識金錢，最簡單的方法就是你沒有任何錢。
——凱薩琳·懷特洪恩，英國專欄作家

The easiest way for your children to learn about money is for you not to have any.

—Katharine Whitehorn, British columnist

我之前靠賣傢俱為生。問題是，我賣的是我的傢俱。
——萊斯·道森，英國喜劇演員

I used to sell furniture for a living. The trouble was, it was my own.

—Les Dawson, British comedian

沒錢是萬惡淵藪。—— 馬克・吐溫，美國作家

The lack of money is the root of all evil.

—Mark Twain

他們說貧窮但快樂比有錢卻悽慘來的要好，但為什麼不折衷一下，像是普通有錢但只有一點點鬱鬱寡歡呢？—— 黛安娜王妃

They say it is better to be poor and happy than rich and miserable, but how about a compromise like moderately rich and just moody?

—Princess Diana

傻瓜留不住金錢。—— 諺語

A fool and his money are soon parted.

—Proverb

當屎變得值錢的時候，窮人就會生來沒屁眼。
—— 亨利・米勒，美國小說家

When shit becomes valuable, the poor will be born without a**holes.

—Henry Miller, American novelist

貧窮的另一個好處就是當你七十歲的時候，你的小孩不會在法律上宣稱你瘋了，就只為了掌控你的房產。

—— 伍迪・艾倫，美國電影導演

Another good thing about being poor is that when you are seventy, your children will not have declared you legally insane in order to gain control of your estate.

—Woody Allen

　　對於那些沒有賺大把鈔票所需的技術或能力的人來說，還有另一種方法可以獲得意外之財：慈善事業。的確，為了拿到錢，你得先過一段真的很辛苦的日子，不過有時候你必須衡量這樣的選擇。

人類進步的一大阻礙就是盲目施捨。

—— 安德魯・卡內基，蘇格蘭商人與卡內基鋼鐵公司創辦人

One of the serious obstacles to the improvement of our race is indiscriminate charity.

—Andrew Carnegie, Scottish businessman and founder of the Carnegie Steel Company

錢跟肥料很像：除了撒出去之外沒什麼用。

—— 法蘭西斯・培根，英國哲學家

Money is like manure: of very little use except it be spread.

—Francis Bacon, British philosopher

接受施捨的人總是痛恨他們的恩人。這是人性本質。

——喬治‧歐威爾，英國作家與記者

A man receiving charity always hates his benefactor—it is a fixed characteristic of human nature.

—George Orwell, British author and journalist

施捨讓接受的人墮落，讓給予的人更堅強。

——喬治‧桑，法國小說家

Charity degrades those who receive it and hardens those who dispense it.

—George Sand, French novelist

施捨是有害的，除非它能讓接受的人變得更加獨立自主。

——約翰‧D‧洛克菲勒，美國實業家、慈善家

Charity is injurious unless it helps the recipient to become independent of it.

—John D. Rockefeller

如果他只有好意的話，沒人會記得樂善好施的人。重點是，他有錢。 ——瑪格麗特‧柴契爾，前英國首相，也是至今為止唯一的女首相

No one would remember the Good Samaritan if he'd only had good intentions. He had money as well.

—Margaret Thatcher

這個世界需要的是正義，不是施捨。

——瑪莉‧雪萊，英國小說家

It is justice, not charity, that is wanting in the world.

—Mary Shelley, British novelist

永遠別站著乞討你有力量去賺取的東西。

——米格爾‧德‧賽凡提斯‧薩維德拉，西班牙小說家

Never stand begging for what you have the power to earn.

—Miguel de Cervantes Saavedra, Spanish novelist

很多人覺得他們捐出不要的舊衣物就是樂善好施。

——美特爾‧里德，美國作家

Lots of people think they're charitable if they give away their old clothes and things they don't want.

—Myrtle Reed, American author

慈善事業最糟糕的一點就是，他們要求你保護的那些生命，根本不值得保護。 ——拉爾夫‧沃爾多‧愛默生，美國文學家

The worst of charity is that the lives you are asked to preserve are not worth preserving.

—Ralph Waldo Emerson

仁慈的人就像是棵蘋果樹，他給予果實並保持沉默；而慈善家則像母雞。——來源不詳

A charitable man is like an apple tree—he gives his fruit and is silent; the philanthropist is like the hen.

—Unknown

　　沒幾個人可以像卡通《大力水手》裡那個財務上不負責任的朋友溫皮那麼適合解釋「信用」這概念。他最有名的一句話就是：「我很樂意在星期二時付你今天的漢堡錢。」把「星期二」代換成「永不」，再把「漢堡」代換成「所有東西」，基本上你就懂美國大眾的心態了。這不是說我們無法靠自己的財產度日，而是我們更喜歡靠別人的財產過活。

只有窮人才付現，但那不是出於美德，而是因為他們的信用不被接受。——阿納托爾·法郎士，法國詩人

It is only the poor who pay cash, and that not from virtue, but because they are refused credit.

—Anatole France, French poet

信貸這種制度的要義是，由一個付不出錢的人去找另一個付不出錢的人來保證他可以付錢。
——查爾斯·狄更斯，英國維多利亞時代文豪

Credit is a system whereby a person who cannot pay gets another person who cannot pay to guarantee that he can pay.

—Charles Dickens

現代人開著貸款買來的車，加滿了用信用卡付款的汽油，在公債蓋起來的高速公路上奔馳。

——厄爾·威爾森，美國專欄作家

Modern man drives a mortgaged car over a bond-financed highway on credit-card gas.

—Earl Wilson, American columnist

建立信用最可靠的方法就是努力讓你自己達到不需要證明任何信用的狀態。 ——莫里斯·史威哲，美國作家

The surest way to establish your credit is to work yourself into the position of not needing any.

—Maurice Switzer, American author

不要向人借錢，也別借錢給人；因為這常常會失掉了錢還失去朋友。 ——威廉·莎士比亞，英國戲劇家

Neither a borrower or a lender be/For Loan oft loses both itself and friend.

—William Shakespeare

如果你覺得沒人在乎你的死活，試試停繳幾次車貸看看。

——厄爾‧威爾森，美國專欄作家

If you think nobody cares if you're alive, try missing a couple of car payments.

—Earl Wilson, American columnist

銀行家是個在大晴天把他的傘借給你，一旦開始下雨，他就立刻把傘要回去的傢伙。——馬克‧吐溫，美國作家

A banker is a fellow who lends you his umbrella when the sun is shining and wants it back the minute it begins to rain.

—Mark Twain

　　這個事實跟錢有關，但鮮為人知。當把錢埋進銀行金庫黑暗的保險櫃裡時，錢會慢慢生長然後變成更多錢。雖然科學家不確定這是有性生殖還是無性，但結果都一樣。這個過程還要求藏錢的擁有者在這段期間不能使用任何一毛。由於這個令人遺憾的事實，多數人錯失了不方便卻有利可圖的機會。

五分鎳幣再也不值一角銀幣 ❶ 了。

——尤吉‧貝拉，美國棒球經理與前球員

---

❶ 美金 1 分是 cent, penny；nickel 為 5 分；dime 為 10 分，也就是 1 毛；quarter 則是 2 毛 5 分。

A nickel ain't worth a dime anymore.

—Yogi Berra, American baseball manager and former player

當銀行帳戶已經清清楚楚告訴你透支了，三十六計走為上策。

—— 桃樂絲‧帕克，美國詩人

When your bank account is so overdrawn that it is positively photographic, steps must be taken.

—Dorothy Parker, American poet

我已經擁有所有我需要的錢了，如果我四點就死掉的話。

—— 漢尼‧楊曼，英國喜劇演員

I've got all the money I'll ever need, if I die by four o'clock.

—Henny Youngman, British comedian

銀行是個會借錢給你的地方，如果你能證明你不需要錢。

—— 鮑伯‧霍伯，美國著名演員

A bank is a place that will lend you money if you can prove that you don't need it.

—Bob Hope

你看到那些圖表了嗎？上面說，如果你從二十歲起每年存五百元美金，到你五十歲時就會有一大筆錢。這一切只是要讓你因為沒這樣做而覺得不舒服。——詹姆斯・卡維爾，美國政治評論家

You see those charts that say if you put away $500 a year starting at age 20, by the time you're 50, you'd have a gazillion dollars? It just makes you ill that you didn't do it.

—James Carville, American political commentator

　　如果我們沒好好記帳，錢有種傾向，它會亂晃而且可以自己找到路，跑去陌生地方，像是珠寶店、酒店跟脫衣舞俱樂部之類的。這就是為什麼制定一個萬無一失的財務計畫很重要，這才能確保錢會好好待在它該待的地方。這項計畫進行方式可以從詳細的試算表與圖表，到沒那麼精緻、潦草寫在雞尾酒紙巾上的筆記都算，只要有盡力掌握錢的去處就好。

先生，當一個人用的是他自己的錢，且也沒有報帳的對象時，記帳是沒有用的。你不會因為已經寫下昨天花了多少錢，今天就少吃點牛肉。——塞繆爾・詹森，英國作家

Keeping accounts, sir, is of no use when a man is spending his own money and has nobody to whom he is to account. You won't eat less beef today, because you have written down what it cost yesterday.

—Samuel Johnson, British author

看支票簿存根就可以判斷自己的價值。

—— 葛羅莉亞‧斯坦能，美國女性主義者

We can tell our values by looking at our checkbook stubs.

—Gloria Steinem, American feminist

四月是報稅的月份。如果你有報稅上的困難，那你應該要僱用一名會計。他們會給你他們已經給過幾百間企業的相同建議：稅，是蠢蛋在繳的。 —— 艾德‧赫姆斯，美國演員

April is tax month. If you are having trouble filing your taxes, then you should hire an accountant. They'll give you the same advice that they've given hundreds of corporations—taxes are for douche bags.

—Ed Helms, American actor

我說我只有幾塊錢是開玩笑的，我可能還有好幾塊。

—— 詹姆斯‧布朗，非裔美國歌手

I'm kidding about having only a few dollars. I might have a few dollars more.

—James Brown

破產是個把你的錢放到褲子口袋裡，再把你的外套給債權人的合法程序。——喬伊·亞當斯，美國喜劇演員

Bankruptcy is a legal proceeding in which you put your money in your pants pocket and give your coat to your creditors.

—Joey Adams, American comedian

我是個作家，我寫支票，但它們實在不怎麼樣。
—— 溫蒂·利布曼，美國喜劇演員

I'm a writer. I write checks. They're not very good.

—Wendy Liebman, American comedian

第十二章
權力

　　沒有任何其他無形事物可以像權力這樣享有變身能力。你可能是地球上最宅、最溫順的人，然而一旦有人給你一枚徽章跟一套制服，你就會立刻變成超級混帳，偏執地把你的想法強加在半徑十英哩內的人身上。但真正令人驚訝的並不是你的改變，而是那些人居然開始聽你的話。

　　正因如此善變，權力通常會保留給那些知道自己在利用權力做些什麼的人。但有些時候，某些不配擁有權力的爛人還是會奪走一些來享用。不過放心吧，當那種事發生時，一定會有許多超級王八蛋表達他們的不爽。

限制媒體是侮辱國家；禁止閱讀某些特定書籍，是宣告那裡的居民不是傻瓜就是奴隸。 ──克勞德‧阿德里安‧艾爾維修斯，法國哲學家
To limit the press is to insult a nation; to prohibit reading of certain books is to declare the inhabitants to be either fools or slaves.
──Claude Adrien Helvétius, French philosopher

千萬別低估政府實現它們巨大幻想的能力。

——唐・德里羅，美國小說家

Never underestimate the power of the State to act out its own massive fantasies.

—Don DeLillo, American novelist

我不知道有什麼崇高的東西不是來自權力的變型。

——埃德蒙・伯克，英國政治家與哲學家。

I know of nothing sublime which is not some modification of power.

—Edmund Burke, British statesman and philosopher

權力跟內衣不一樣，不可以隨便拿來穿然後順手就丟。

——約翰・肯尼斯・加爾布雷斯，蘇格蘭裔美國經濟學家

Power is not something that can be assumed or discarded at will like underwear.

—John Kenneth Galbraith, Canadian-American economist

追求權力的人不值得擁有權力。

——柏拉圖，古希臘哲學家

Those who seek power are not worthy of that power.

—Plato

可惜啊，那些知道如何治理國家的人都在忙著開計程車跟剪頭髮。——喬治‧伯恩，美國喜劇演員與演員

Too bad all the people who know how to run the country are busy driving taxicabs and cutting hair.

—George Burns, American comedian and actor

唯一真正的權力來自於一把長步槍。

——約瑟夫‧史達林，前蘇聯領導人

The only real power comes out of a long rifle.

—Joseph Stalin

即使有十億人，中國成為不了一個超級強國。

——約翰‧盧卡克斯，美國歷史學家

Even one billion Chinese do not a superpower make.

—John Lukacs, American historian

如果你是自私、無知的公民，那你也會有自私、無知的領導者。

——喬治‧卡林，美國喜劇演員

If you have selfish, ignorant citizens, you're going to get selfish, ignorant leaders.

—George Carlin, American comedian

所有擁有權力的人想要什麼？更多權力。

——先知，出自電影《駭客任務：重裝上陣》

What do all men with power want? More power.

—The Oracle, The *Matrix Reloaded*

當人得到任何一種權力，很自然地會拚命想抓住它；很少會有掌權的人可以輕易退到一邊並放下它。更多時候，權力必須伴隨武力。雖然這個事實明顯地可以解釋渴望權力的獨裁者與執行長，它甚至可以往下延伸到學校糾察隊或組織社區守望相助計畫的怪傢伙。根據不同的情況，篡奪權力的方法也會不太一樣，但原則是相同的：猛烈並快速地攻擊。

多數人似乎沒有意識到從文明殘骸中能賺到的錢，跟從建立中的文明中能賺到的一樣多。

——白瑞德，出自《飄》

What most people don't seem to realize is that there is just as much money to be made out of the wreckage of a civilization as from the upbuilding of one.

—Rhett Butler, *Gone with the Wind*

說句好話再配把槍會比只單純說好話讓你走得更遠。

——艾爾·卡彭，美國黑幫老大

You can get much farther with a kind word and a gun than you can with a kind word alone.

—Al Capone

我聽說過麻煩有很多種。有的來自前方，有的來自後面。不過我已經買了支大球棒。你看，我準備好了。現在我的麻煩就快要遇上我這個大麻煩了！

—— 蘇斯博士，美國著名童書作家、漫畫家

I have heard there are troubles of more than one kind. Some come from ahead, and some come from behind. But I've bought a big bat. I'm all ready, you see. Now my troubles are going to have troubles with me!

—Dr. Seuss

槍桿子裡出政權。 —— 毛澤東，中華人民共和國創立者

Political power grows out of the barrel of a gun.

—Mao Tse-tung, Chinese revolutionary and founder of the People's Republic of China

我喜歡權力，而且我喜歡使用它。

—— 山姆‧雷伯恩，前美國眾議院議長

I like power and I like to use it.

—Sam Rayburn, former Speaker of the U.S. House of Representatives

我幹嘛在意法律？我不是有權力嗎？

——柯尼利厄斯・范德比爾特，美國實業家

What do I care about law? Ain't I got the power?

—Cornelius Vanderbilt, American businessman

外交是門藝術，在你確認摸到石頭並反擊前，要不停地說：「乖狗狗、狗狗乖。」——威爾・羅傑斯，美國喜劇演員與演員

Diplomacy is the art of saying "Nice doggie" until you can find a rock.

—Will Rogers, American comedian and actor

人們愈覺得你笨，當你殺死他們時，他們就會愈驚訝。

——威廉・克萊頓，摩門教牧師

The dumber people think you are, the more surprised they're going to be when you kill them.

—William Clayton, Mormon minister

你何不把臉湊上來讓我揍一下？然後你就可以告訴我（我是不是比較強）。——俠客・歐尼爾，美國籃球選手

Why don't you bring your face up here and let me punch it? Then you can tell me (if I'm stronger).

—Shaquille O'Neal, American basketball player

或許獲取權力最簡單的方法就是踩著比你弱小的人肩膀往上爬。不只是因為踩小傢伙是項歷史悠久的傳統，同時也遠比對付大傢伙安全許多。雖然那些小傢伙也有可能會反抗你的意圖，不過，他們縮成一團球並等待危險過去的機會更大。

當我還是個孩子的時候，我曾經每晚祈禱想要一輛新腳踏車。然後我了解到上帝不是這樣做的，所以我偷了一輛，然後請求祂原諒我。——伊默‧菲利普斯，美國喜劇演員

When I was a kid, I used to pray every night for a new bicycle. Then I realized that the Lord doesn't work that way, so I stole one and asked Him to forgive me.

—Emo Philips, American comedian

當我們擊潰一個人的精神時，對權力的感受會遠比贏得他的心更強烈。——艾力‧賀佛爾，美國哲學家

Our sense of power is more vivid when we break a man's spirit than when we win his heart.

—Eric Hoffer, American philosopher

如果你是用膽識[16]收服他們，他們的心與精神也都會跟隨。
——約翰‧韋恩，美國電影演員

---

[16] Balls 在此指男人的睪丸。意指有種、有膽識。（見下一頁原文）

If you've got them by the balls, their hearts and minds will follow.
—John Wayne

權力的祕密就在於知道別人比你更懦弱。
——卡爾・路德維奇・伯恩，德國政治作家
The secret of power is the knowledge that others are more cowardly than you are.
—Karl Ludwig Börne, German political writer

如果你撿到一隻餓壞了的狗並填飽牠的肚子，牠絕不會咬你。這就是狗跟人本質上的不同。——馬克・吐溫，美國作家
If you pick up a starving dog and make him prosperous, he will not bite you. This is the principal difference between a dog and a man.
—Mark Twain

不濫用權力就會失去它的魅力。——保羅・瓦勒里，法國詩人
Power without abuse loses its charm.
—Paul Valéry, French poet

殺一個人，你是兇手。殺幾百萬人，你就成為征服者。殺光他們全部，你就成了神。——尚・羅斯坦德，法國生物學家與哲學家
Kill one man, and you are a murderer. Kill millions of men, and you

are a conqueror. Kill them all, and you are a god.
—Jean Rostand, French biologist and philosopher

　　一般而言，無限的權力絕對沒有任何缺點。你可以做任何你想做的事，每個人都假裝愛你，你還可以在電影上映前就搶先看。話雖如此，偶爾也會在你遊行時煞風景地下起雨。有人會建議你別再為了個人利益濫用你的職權，或說你被權力沖昏了頭之類的蠢事。當然你可以讓他們走開（或是殺掉他們），但某些王八蛋似乎真的知道他們在說什麼。

結合智慧與權力的嘗試極少成功過，即使有，也只是一下子。
—— 阿爾伯特・愛因斯坦，物理哲學家
The attempt to combine wisdom and power has only rarely been successful and then only for a short while.
—Albert Einstein

都說權力會使人腐化，但其實更正確的是，權力吸引的是會腐化的人。頭腦清楚的人通常是被權力以外的東西所吸引。
—— 大衛・布林，美國科幻作家
It is said that power corrupts, but actually it's more true that power attracts the corruptible. The sane are usually attracted by other things than power.
—David Brin, American science fiction writer

所有有權力的人都不能信任。

──紐特‧金瑞契，前美國眾議院議長

You can't trust anybody with power.

──Newt Gingrich, former Speaker of the U.S. House of Representatives

過去那些愚蠢地想藉由騎在老虎背上追求權力的人，下場就是被老虎吃進肚子裡。 ──約翰‧F‧甘迺迪，美國第35任總統

In the past, those who foolishly sought power by riding on the back of the tiger ended up inside.

──John F. Kennedy

權力使人腐化，絕對的權力使人絕對地腐化。

──阿克頓男爵，出自1887年給曼戴爾‧克雷頓主教的信

Power corrupts and absolute power corrupts absolutely.

──Lord Acton, letter to Bishop Mandell Creighton, 1887

一個有權力的朋友就不再是朋友。

──亨利‧亞當斯，美國記者，美國第六任總統亞當斯的孫子

A friend in power is a friend lost.

──Henry Adams, American journalist and grandson to John Quincy Adams

所有文字記錄下來的歷史裡，不是工人，而是強盜，一直掌控著世界。—— 史考特・尼爾林，美國天然資源保護論者

During the whole period of written history, it is not the workers but the robbers who have been in control of the world.

—Scott Nearing, American conservationist

　　一旦你征服了所有能征服的、得到了所有能得到的，也踐踏了每個你能踐踏的人，差不多是反省你那強大權力欲望的時候了。首先，你可能會注意到自己為了達到目的，已經搞砸了所有朋友的關係。人啊，在高處是相當寂寞的。其次，底下有一群憤怒的群眾、被剝奪權力的人正在集結並蠢蠢欲動著發起一場叛亂。最後，你可能會發現，擁有權力似乎沒有他們所說的那麼好。如果你早點聽到以下這些王八蛋的建議，你可能會更早明白這些狀況。

人生沒有所謂的勝利者，只有擁有瑞士銀行帳戶的混球。—— 馬修・洛蒂，美國作家

In life there are no winners, only a**holes with Swiss bank accounts.

—Matthew Lotti, American author

如果我早知道擁有一切是什麼感覺，我可能會願意退而求其次。

——莉莉·湯姆琳，美國女演員、作家

If I had known what it would be like to have it all—I might have been willing to settle for less.

—Lily Tomlin

你不能擁有一切……你要把一切放在哪？

——史蒂芬·萊特，美國喜劇演員

You can't have everything ... where would you put it?

—Steven Wright, American comedian

幾乎所有人都能承受逆境，但如果你想測試一個人的人格，給他權力。——亞伯拉罕·林肯，美國第 16 任總統

Nearly all men can stand adversity, but if you want to test a man's character, give him power.

—Abraham Lincoln

成功並沒有寵壞我，我一向就是這麼難搞。

——法蘭·列白維茲，美國作家

Success didn't spoil me; I've always been insufferable.

—Fran Lebowitz, American author

唯一一件比看著某人逐漸爬上權力的位置還要愉悅的，就是目睹他們迅速且無可避免的失寵。說它嫉妒或叫它羨慕都行，你喜歡就好，但無法否認的是，為了有點變化，目睹他人的失敗有種奇妙的滿足感。這解釋了為什麼每個人總是知道事情該怎樣做，卻沒人有遠見可以提早說出來，除了幾個你能在這本書裡找到的王八蛋以外。

美國永遠不會被外部擊敗，如果我們衰退並失去自由，一定是因為我們自我毀滅。
—— 亞伯拉罕・林肯，美國第 16 任總統
America will never be destroyed from the outside. If we falter and lose our freedoms, it will be because we destroyed ourselves.
—Abraham Lincoln

專制的權力就像大多數堅硬的東西一樣，非常容易被破壞。
—— 艾碧該・亞當斯，美國第 2 任總統約翰・亞當斯之妻
Arbitrary power is like most other things which are very hard, very liable to be broken.
—Abigail Adams

人們放棄權力最普遍的方式就是認為他們沒有任何權力。
—— 愛麗絲・華克，美國作家

The most common way people give up their power is by thinking they don't have any.

—Alice Walker, American author

權力不會使人腐化，恐懼才會使人腐化⋯⋯也許是失去權力的恐懼。——約翰·史坦貝克，美國文學家，曾獲諾貝爾文學獎

Power does not corrupt. Fear corrupts ... perhaps the fear of a loss of power.

—John Steinbeck

即使只當一晚國王，也比當一輩子笨蛋好。

——魯珀特·帕普金，出自電影《喜劇之王》

Better to be king for a night, than a schmuck for a lifetime.

—Rupert Pupkin, *The King of Comedy*

他們對權力貪得無厭的程度，只有在他們運用權力時無法治癒的無能可以比擬。

——溫斯頓·邱吉爾，前英國首相

Their insatiable lust for power is only equaled by their incurable impotence in exercising it.

—Winston Churchill

任何一個曾經用放大鏡燒一群螞蟻的人，都能了解權力的吸引力就在於它的完全性與終極性。對那些微小的對象而言，你就是嚴格審判他們悲慘靈魂的永生上帝。雖然當你把對象從螞蟻升級為人類，事情會比較麻煩一點，但一般原則是相同的。只要把你的放大鏡升級成戰斧飛彈跟核子擴散，應該就沒問題了。

我想要的只是張溫暖的床、一句好話，以及無限的權力。
——艾希莉‧布理恩特，美國漫畫家

All I want is a warm bed and a kind word and unlimited power.
—Ashleigh Brilliant, American cartoonist

我會成為一個專制君主，那是我的職業；而上帝會寬恕我，那是祂的職業。——凱薩琳大帝

I shall be an autocrat, that's my trade; and the good Lord with forgive me, that's his.
—Catherine the Great

那些擁有絕對權力的人不只能預言並讓他們的預言成真，他們也可以說謊並讓他們的謊言成真。——艾力‧賀佛爾，美國哲學家。

Those in possession of absolute power can not only prophesy and make their prophecies come true, but they can also lie and make their lies come true.
—Eric Hoffer, American philosopher

權力是終極春藥。 ── 亨利・季辛吉，美國外交官

Power is the ultimate aphrodisiac.

──Henry Kissinger, American diplomat

權力就是當你有充分的理由殺人，而你卻不這樣做。

── 奧斯卡・辛德勒，德國企業家，小說《辛德勒的手提箱》與電影《辛德勒的名單》的靈感來源

Power is when you have every justification to kill someone, and then you don't.

──Oskar Schindler, German industrialist and inspiration for the novel *Schindler's Ark*, and the film *Schindler's List*

逆境造就男人，繁盛造就怪物。

── 維克多・雨果，法國詩人與作家

Adversity makes men, and prosperity makes monsters.

──Victor Hugo, French poet and author

超級強國通常表現得像是兩個全副武裝的盲人在一間房間裡摸索著，雙方都相信對方會帶來生命危險，並以為對方視力良好。

── 亨利・季辛吉，美國外交官

The superpowers often behave like two heavily armed blind men feeling their way around a room, each believing himself in mortal peril

from the other, whom he assumes to have perfect vision.
—Henry Kissinger, American diplomat

　　雖然你的確可以透過把東西炸毀與鐵腕統治來表現權力，但也有更微妙的方式影響他人。透過一個奇妙的字，普通人可以跟總統或國王一樣擁有權力。那個字就是「成功」。
　　像演員、執行長以及低階政治人物之類的成功人士，他們擁有足夠的資金與影響力將他們的意志強加在大眾身上，卻沒有任何人發現他們正在這樣做。所幸他們大多數都忙著耽溺於自以為是的想法，沒時間去用他們的權力做壞事。

成功最糟糕的部分就是，想要找到一個為你開心的人。
—— 貝蒂・蜜勒，美國名歌手，諧星
The worst part of success is to try to find someone who is happy for you.
—Bette Midler

成功往往是在對的方向上踏錯一步而得到的結果。
—— 艾爾・伯恩斯坦，美國體育主播
Success is often the result of taking a misstep in the right direction.
—Al Bernstein, American sportscaster

上帝給了我們兩個部位，一個用來坐，另一個用來思考。成功取決於我們最常用哪一個。——安·蘭德斯，美國專欄作家

The Lord gave us two ends—one to sit on and the other to think with. Success depends on which one we use the most.

—Ann Landers

對我來說成功就是擁有十顆哈密瓜，每一個只吃上面那一半。
——芭芭拉·史翠珊，猶太裔美國歌手與演員

Success to me is having ten honeydew melons and eating only the top half of each one.

—Barbra Streisand

如果努力是通往成功之鑰，多數人寧願直接把鎖撬開。
——竇納樂爵士，英國外交官

If hard work is the key to success, most people would rather pick the lock.

—Claude McDonald, British diplomat

一個成功的人就是能夠用別人丟他的磚頭，造出一個堅固地基的人。——大衛·布林克利，美國新聞主播

A successful man is one who can lay a firm foundation with the bricks others have thrown at him.

—David Brinkley, American newscaster

成功只是很單純的運氣問題，去問任何一個失敗者就知道。

——厄爾·威爾森，美國專欄作家

Success is simply a matter of luck. Ask any failure.

—Earl Wilson, American columnist

別把名氣跟成功搞混了。瑪丹娜是其中一個；海倫凱勒是另一個。——爾瑪·龐貝克，美國幽默作家

Don't confuse fame with success. Madonna is one; Helen Keller is the other.

—Erma Bombeck, American humorist

這輩子你只需要無知與信心，然後就會成功。

——馬克·吐溫，美國作家

All you need in this life is ignorance and confidence, and then success is sure.

—Mark Twain

我的成功方程式就是早起、晚退、不斷開挖油田。

——J·保羅·蓋蒂，美國實業家，創立石油公司

My formula for success is rise early, work late, and strike oil.

—J. Paul Getty, American businessman

根據多數歷史記載，權力是種專門保留給男人的奢侈品。如果你仔細閱讀史料，很快就會發現這可能不是個好主意。

如果是由女人來統治這個世界，耶穌受難、十字軍東征、第二次世界大戰以及九一一恐怖攻擊這類歷史重大事件，我們無法得知是否會有更好的結果。但很難想像它們的結果會更糟。

要顯得有力跟要當個女人是一樣的。如果你必須告訴別人「你是」，那就表示「你不是」。
——瑪格麗特·柴契爾，前英國首相，也是至今為止唯一的女首相

Being powerful is like being a lady. If you have to tell people you are, you aren't.
—Margaret Thatcher

他們在名為普選的美麗承諾裡，忘了女人。這就是他們仍不明白共和政體的最佳證據。
——黛爾芬·德·吉哈丹，法國女作家

Proof that they do not understand the republic is that in their fine promises for universal suffrage, they forgot women.
—Delphine de Girardin, French author

我們女人一直都準備好要成為超級英雄。因為女人想成為英雄，而男人只想幹我們。——芳姬·詹森，荷蘭女演員

We've always been ready for female superheroes. Because women want to be them and men want to do them.
—Famke Janssen, Dutch actress

是否要讓寡婦成為女人通往權力的唯一道路？男人們應該好好考慮清楚。 ——葛羅莉亞‧斯坦能，美國女性主義者
Men should think twice before making widowhood women's only path to power.
—Gloria Steinem, American feminist

事實就是我們不該相信有權力的人。
——詹姆斯‧麥迪遜，美國第4任總統
The truth is that all men having power ought to be mistrusted.
—James Madison

永遠記得運用權力的第一條守則：權力不只是你擁有的東西，還包括敵人認為你有的東西。
——索爾‧阿林斯基，美國社區組織者與作家
Always remember the first rule of power tactics: Power is not only what you have but what the enemy thinks you have.
—Saul Alinsky, American community organizer and writer

當女人憂鬱的時候，她們吃東西或血拼，男人則入侵另一個國家。思考方式完全不同。

——伊蓮‧布斯勒，美國女演員與喜劇演員

When women are depressed, they eat or go shopping. Men invade another country. It's a whole different way of thinking.

—Elayne Boosler, American actress and comedian

第四篇

競爭，到底為了啥？

大家都了解什麼是比賽。你帶著一群孩子隨機對人丟石頭，旁人會側目而視，但是如果你舉辦一場丟石頭大賽，大家就懂了。
——唐‧莫瑞，蘇格蘭足球員

People understand contests. You take a bunch of kids throwing rocks at random and people look askance, but if you go and hold a rock-throwing contest—people understand that.
—Don Murray, Scottish footballer

第十三章
運動

　　對於擁有超乎常人的速度、耐力、力量、協調與專注力的人來說，運動比賽提供了一個永垂不朽的機會；對其他人來說，運動讓人有藉口可以在臉上彩繪、像白癡一樣大叫以及喝裝在塑膠杯裡貴得離譜的啤酒。總之，人人都是贏家。

　　我們很早就迷戀運動。根據體型與技術不同，不論是適合高瘦體型的小孩從事踢球這種快節奏的比賽，或是適合動作慢、過重的小孩進行的溫和競賽，例如神奇寶貝，我們都會被吸引。這種不同的傾向持續到孩子們長大，前者成為運動巨星，而後者變成替他們加油歡呼、喝得醉醺醺的好戰粉絲。

　　撇除他們所扮演的角色完全不同，選手與粉絲倒是有個共同信念：在已知的宇宙中，運動是最重要的一件事。由於在任何特定時間裡，隨時都有賽事正在進行，這也是運動非常獨特的一點：不同類型的運動，可以同時擁有同等重要性。

　　雖然沒有人能確定為什麼人類會想參與這種野蠻競爭，不過許多歷史上的大嘴巴們對這事已經毒舌了一番。

看美式足球就像是看Ａ片。裡頭有很多動作，而且我無法移開視線，但當它結束時，我會納悶：為什麼我要花一下午幹這事？

——路克・薩里斯伯里，美國作家

Watching football is like watching pornography. There's plenty of action, and I can't take my eyes off it, but when it's over, I wonder why the hell I spent an afternoon doing it.

—Luke Salisbury, American author

能力是一門藝術，可以把別人擊出的全壘打全搶來當自己的功勞。 ——凱西・史騰格，美國職棒大聯盟外野手

Ability is the art of getting credit for all the home runs somebody else hits.

—Casey Stengel, MLB outfielder

講到運動，我不是很有興趣。一般而言，除了以陪審團身分參與審判之外，我覺得運動是那些跟我完全沒共通點的人所做的危險又疲勞的活動。

——法蘭・列白維茲，美國作家

When it comes to sports, I am not particularly interested. Generally speaking, I look upon them as dangerous and tiring activities performed by people with whom I share nothing except the right to trial by jury.

—Fran Lebowitz, American author

十月不只是個美麗的月份，還標示著由曲棍球、棒球、籃球與美式足球交織成珍貴卻稍縱即逝的時光。

——傑森·勒夫，美國喜劇演員

October is not only a beautiful month but marks the precious yet fleeting overlap of hockey, baseball, basketball, and football.

—Jason Love, American comedian

我問過一個裁判，他是否能因為我想了些關於他不好的事情判給我技術犯規？他說：「當然不能。」我說：「好吧，我覺得你很臭。」然後他就賞了我一個技術犯規。結論是，你不能相信他們。——吉姆·瓦爾瓦諾，1983年北卡羅萊納大學男子籃球隊教練

I asked a ref if he could give me a technical foul for thinking bad things about him. He said, "Of course not." I said, "Well, I think you stink." And he gave me a technical. You can't trust 'em.

—Jim Valvano, coach of the 1983 North Carolina University men's basketball team

百分之九十的比賽是處於半發瘋狀態。

——吉姆·沃爾福特，美國職棒大聯盟外野手

Ninety percent of the game is half mental.

—Jim Wohford, American major league outfielder

球是人類最災難性的發明，包括汽車在內。
——羅伯特・莫利，英國演員

The ball is man's most disastrous invention, not excluding the wheel.
—Robert Morley, British actor

唯一可致勝的一步就是不要玩。
——WOPR（戰爭作戰計畫反應）**⓱**，出自《戰爭遊戲》

The only winning move is not to play.
—WOPR (War Operation Plan Response), WarGames

人不會因為變老就停止玩樂，只會因為停止玩樂而變老。
——奧利佛・溫德爾・霍姆斯，美國作家

Men do not quit playing because they grow old; they grow old because they quit playing.
—Oliver Wendell Holmes, American writer

　　在美國，參賽者在競賽中受到致命性傷害機率愈多的運動，愈受歡迎。這說明了為什麼板球這唯一一種會為了喝茶而休息的運動，至今還沒受到美國觀眾的青睞。這不是說我們樂於看到有

⓱ 戰爭遊戲為1983年出品的一部科幻電影。WOPR在電影裡為軍方所持有的一部超級電腦，用來預測核子戰爭可能的結果。

人受傷，而是我們不樂於看到「沒」人受傷，這之間有很微妙但很重要的區別。當然，在美國文化裡，那些比較少肢體接觸的運動還是有空間的，但只有跟流血有點關係的運動，才有討論價值。

美式足球比賽跟革命之間有些不同。其中之一，足球比賽通常持續比較久，而且選手都穿著制服；另外，足球比賽中的傷亡也比較多。比賽的目標是把球弄過另一隊的得分線，這樣可以得到六分。撕裂傷、挫傷與擦傷則沒有任何分數，但也不會扣分。「踢」這個動作在足球中很重要。事實上，有些更有熱情的球員甚至會去踢球，偶爾啦。

── 亞佛烈德・希區考克，英國電影導演，以驚悚推理作品聞名世界

There are several differences between a football game and a revolution. For one thing, a football game usually lasts longer and the participants wear uniforms. Also, there are usually more casualties in a football game. The object of the game is to move a ball past the other team's goal line. This counts as six points. No points are given for lacerations, contusions, or abrasions, but then no points are deducted either. Kicking is very important in football. In fact, some of the more enthusiastic players even kick the ball, occasionally.

—Alfred Hitchcock

有些人認為足球是攸關生死的事，但我不喜歡那樣的態度。我可以跟他們保證，足球比那還要嚴肅得多。
——比爾‧辛奇利，英國足球教練

Some people think football is a matter of life and death. I don't like that attitude. I can assure them it is much more serious than that.
—Bill Shankly, British soccer coach

鯊魚跟那些在一月份寒冷的芝加哥比賽中把上衣脫掉的美式足球球迷一樣強壯，不過鯊魚更聰明。
——戴夫‧貝瑞，美國作家與專欄作家

Sharks are as tough as those football fans who take their shirts off during games in Chicago in January, only more intelligent.
—Dave Barry, American author and columnist

拳擊不只是打人，例如，還有不要被打。
——喬治‧福爾曼，美國拳擊手

There's more to boxing than hitting. There's not getting hit, for instance.
—George Foreman, American boxer

他們說，棒球就只是個比賽。的確如此。大峽谷也不過就是個在亞利桑那州的洞。不是所有的洞或比賽，生來就是平等的。
——喬治‧威爾，美國記者

Baseball, it is said, is only a game. True. And the Grand Canyon is only a hole in Arizona. Not all holes, or games, are created equal.

—George Will, American journalist

美式足球結合了美國生活中最糟糕的兩種特質：暴力，和穿插其間的會議。——喬治·威爾，美國記者

Football combines the two worst features of America life: It is violence punctuated by committee meetings.

—George Will, American journalist

橄欖球是紳士玩的野獸運動。足球是野獸玩的紳士運動。美式足球是野獸玩的野獸運動。——亨利·布拉哈，美式足球員

Rugby is a beastly game played by gentlemen. Soccer is a gentleman's game played by beasts. Football is a beastly game played by beasts.

—Henry Blaha, American football player

美式足球終究是種了不起的運動，能釋放你的侵略性、又不用因此坐牢。——海伍德·海爾·布魯恩，美國記者

Football is, after all, a wonderful way to get rid of your aggressions without going to jail for it.

—Heywood Hale Broun, American journalist

足球對粗魯的女孩來說是很好的運動，但不適合纖弱的男孩。
—— 奧斯卡・王爾德，愛爾蘭作家
Football is all very well a good game for rough girls, but not for delicate boys.
—Oscar Wilde

就像人生一樣，國家美式足球聯盟充滿了白癡。
—— 藍迪・克洛斯，前國家美式足球聯盟攻擊前鋒
The NFL, like life, is full of idiots.
—Randy Cross, former NFL offensive lineman

當所有真正的運動員都忙著把彼此打成肉醬，少數幾個基因不良的俗辣卻覺得創造一些屬於他們自己的運動也很有趣，而且比較適合他們這種不擅長運動的人，於是我們有了飛鏢、釣魚、高爾夫與射箭之類的運動。這不是說這類競賽不需要技術，大多數運動都需要；但當你做的最費勁的動作就是把粉弄到一根木杆上的時候，你很難說自己是個運動員。

釣魚很無聊，除非你釣到一隻真正的魚，然後釣魚就變得很噁心了。—— 戴夫・貝瑞，美國作家與專欄作家
Fishing is boring, unless you catch an actual fish, and then it is disgusting.
—Dave Barry, American author and columnist

有兩千萬成熟的美國男人打高爾夫，而他們的老婆卻認為他們是在外面找樂子。——吉姆‧畢夏普，美國記者

Golf is played by 20 million mature American men whose wives think they are out having fun.

—Jim Bishop, American journalist

高爾夫原本是優閒散個步，只是被毀了。——馬克‧吐溫，美國作家

Golf is a good walk spoiled.

—Mark Twain

網球令人沮喪的地方就是無論我變得多厲害，也永遠比不上那面牆。——米奇‧赫貝格，美國喜劇演員

The depressing thing about tennis is that no matter how good I get, I'll never be as good as a wall.

—Mitch Hedberg, American comedian

釣魚，或是像個白癡一樣站在岸邊，兩者只是一線之隔⑱。——史蒂芬‧萊特，美國喜劇演員

There's a fine line between fishing and just standing on the shore like an idiot.

—Steven Wright, American comedian

---

⑱ 這邊的 line 使用了「界線」與「線（釣魚線）」的雙關。

玩馬球就像在地震時努力打高爾夫球。

──席維斯·史特龍，美國演員

Playing polo is like trying to play golf during an earthquake.

—Sylvester Stallone, American actor

滑雪結合了戶外樂趣，並且能用你的臉像打保齡球一樣把樹撞倒。──戴夫·貝瑞，美國作家與專欄作家

Skiing combines outdoor fun with knocking down trees with your face.

—Dave Barry, American author and columnist

高爾夫球是設法把一顆非常小的球打進一個更小的洞裡的運動，就這目的來說，這武器設計得非常差。

──溫斯頓·邱吉爾，前英國首相

Golf is a game whose aim is to hit a very small ball into an even smaller hole, with weapons singularly ill-designed for the purpose.

—Winston Churchill

或許所有的運動都很蠢，不過人類也是這樣。

──羅伯特·林德，愛爾蘭記者

It may be that all games are silly. But then, so are humans.

—Robert Lynd, Irish journalist

除非他們開始讓我們互丟，否則我想鐵餅這運動都無法吸引任何關注。

──阿爾弗雷德‧厄特，美國著名田徑選手，連續四屆奧運鐵餅金牌得主

I don't think the discus will ever attract any interest until they let us start throwing them at one another.

—Al Oerter, Olympic discus champion

只有輸家真心覺得勝利不重要。對其他所有人來說，勝利比呼吸重要得多，這是他們早上醒來的原因，也是他們踏上田徑場的唯一理由。勝利是如此重要，他們甚至願意說謊、作弊甚至偷竊，只為了獲勝。如果他們無法獲勝，那這運動就變得很蠢，而且他們也不想玩了。

任何人在獲勝的那一刻，看起來都像是無敵的。

──喬治‧歐威爾，英國作家與記者

Whoever is winning at the moment will always seem to be invincible.

—George Orwell, British author and journalist

任何人都可能獲勝，除非碰巧有第二個參賽者。

──蕭伯納，愛爾蘭劇作家與作家

Anybody can win, unless there happens to be a second entry.

—George Bernard Shaw, Irish playwright and author

我是雙冠王，我在這裡贏了，在那兒也贏了。那現在幹嘛呢？
——查理·辛，美國演員

I'm bi-winning. I win here, and I win there. Now what?
—Charlie Sheen

如果你把每場比賽都搞得攸關生死，你麻煩大了。你會死很多
次。——迪恩·史密斯，前北卡羅萊納那學男子籃球隊教練

If you make every game a life-anddeath thing, you're going to have
problems. You'll be dead a lot.
—Dean Smith, former coach of the North Carolina University men's
basketball team

對我而言，錢從來不是什麼很大的動機，除了把它當作一種持續
得分的方法。真正的刺激還是在比賽本身。
——唐納·川普，美國商業大亨

Money was never a big motivation for me, except as a way to keep
score. The real excitement is playing the game.
—Donald Trump

如果我是三壘手，然後我媽正往三壘跑，而那一分又會讓我們輸
掉，我會絆倒她。噢，我會扶起她並把她拍乾淨，然後說：「抱
歉，老媽，沒有人可以贏我。」

── 里歐・杜洛克，前美國職棒大聯盟內野手

If I were playing third base and my mother were rounding third with the run that was going to beat us, I'd trip her. Oh, I'd pick her up and brush her off and say, "Sorry, Mom, but nobody beats me."
—Leo Durocher, former Major League infielder

　　人們經常會跟你說人生中有許多事比輸了還糟，不過這些人顯然就是輸家。你很容易就能把這些人與他們成功的對手區分開來，因為輸這件事，讓人受盡折磨，只留下消沉、苦澀與空虛。下次你想安慰這些魯蛇時，或許你可以提議幫他們終結苦難，這應該可以讓他們振作起來。

當你拿到聯賽最後一名時，他們會叫你白癡。但在醫學院以最後一名畢業時，他們會叫你醫生。
　　── 艾伯・雷蒙斯，前奧克拉荷馬市立大學男子籃球隊教練

Finish last in your league and they call you Idiot. Finish last in medical school and they call you Doctor.
—Abe Lemons, former Oklahoma City University men's basketball coach

想到有半打渾身是汗的隊友因為慶祝贏球跳到你身上，應該讓你一顆球都不想進。── 亞瑟・馬歇爾，美式足球員

I would have thought that the knowledge that you are going to be leapt upon by half-a-dozen congratulatory but sweaty teammates would be inducement not to score a goal.

—Arthur Marshall, American football player

如果平手像是親你的姊妹，那輸掉比賽就像是親你沒戴假牙的祖母。——喬治·布瑞特，棒球名人堂三壘手

If a tie is like kissing your sister, losing is like kissing your grandmother with her teeth out.

—George Brett, Hall of Fame third baseman

贏家指責然後原諒；輸家膽小到不敢指責，又因氣量太小而不懂原諒。——席德尼·J·哈里斯，美國記者

A winner rebukes and forgives; a loser is too timid to rebuke and too petty to forgive.

—Sydney J. Harris, American journalist

給我一個好的失敗者，然後我會給你一個白癡。

——里歐·杜洛克，前美國職棒大聯盟內野手

Show me a good loser and I'll show you an idiot.

—Leo Durocher, former Major League infielder

我沒有失敗，我只是找出一萬種不成功的方法。
—— 湯瑪斯·愛迪生

I have not failed. I've just found 10,000 ways that won't work.
—Thomas Edison

我們沒有輸掉比賽，我們只是沒時間了而已。
—— 文斯·隆巴迪，美式足球教練

We didn't lose the game; we just ran out of time.
—Vince Lombardi, American football coach

　　在日常對話中，有些話是大家認定不該說的，這清單相當冗長。但這規則有個例外，就是運動。比賽時，選手與粉絲可以毫無顧忌地對別人說任何他們想說的話，沒有什麼話是太髒、太侮辱人或是太卑鄙，只要它有助於進行賽事，都行。的確，這種目中無人的說話態度可能會導致酒醉鬥毆，但對許多人而言，那正是當初他們去看運動比賽的唯一理由。

他對人跟動物都很好……但你真該聽聽他怎麼跟高爾夫球講話的！—— 淘氣阿丹，出自《淘氣阿丹》

He's nice to people 'n' animals ... but you oughta hear him talkin' to a golf ball!
—Dennis the Menace, *Dennis the Menace*

說髒話的是我的舌頭，不是我的靈魂。

——歐里庇得斯，古希臘悲劇作家。

'Twas but my tongue, 'twas not my soul that swore.

—Euripides

男人講髒話，拯救了自己免於精神崩潰。

——亨利·S·哈斯金斯，美國作家

Many a man's profanity has saved him from a nervous breakdown.

—Henry S. Haskins, American writer

如果髒話可以影響球的飛行，高爾夫球比賽會比現在打得更好。

——荷瑞斯·G·哈欽森，美國高爾夫球選手與作家

If profanity had an influence on the flight of the ball, the game of golf would be played far better than it is.

—Horace G. Hutchinson, American golfer and author

我個人認為我們發展語言是因為我們的內在深處需要抱怨。

——珍·瓦格納，美國作家

I personally think we developed language because of our deep inner need to complain.

—Jane Wagner, American writer

在特定狀況下、緊急狀況下、絕望狀況下，髒話提供了甚至連祈禱都無法提供的慰藉。——馬克·吐溫，美國作家

Under certain circumstances, urgent circumstances, desperate circumstances, profanity provides a relief denied even to prayer.
—Mark Twain

咒罵是在逃跑與戰鬥之間妥協而發明出來的。
——法利·彼得·德昂，美國幽默作家

Swearing was invented as a compromise between running away and fighting.
—Finley Peter Dunne, American humorist

　　運動員有許多特質，包括強壯、迅速、協調、富有，但聰明就是一個他們很少人有的特質。講到踢或丟擲，他們都很厲害，但策略就不行，這時就需要教練：能言善道、夠尖酸、曾經風光過，能夠把一群龍蛇混雜不對盤的人塑造成一支能獲勝的隊伍，當然這一切得建立在他沒先被開除的前提上。

教練規矩愈少，選手會破壞的規矩也愈少。
——約翰·麥登，前美式足球員與教練

The fewer rules a coach has, the fewer rules there are for players to break.
—John Madden, former American football player and coach

如果你沒有贏，你會被開除。如果你贏了，不過是把被開除的那天往後延了。 ── 里歐‧杜洛克，前美國職棒大聯盟內野手

If you don't win, you're going to be fired. If you do win, you've only put off the day you're going to be fired.

—Leo Durocher, former Major League infielder

教練不過就是在你被開除前排除各種失誤。
── 盧‧霍茲，前大學美式足球教練

Coaching is nothing more than eliminating mistakes before you get fired.

—Lou Holtz, former college football coach

我們無法在主場獲勝，也無法在客場獲勝。身為總經理，我的問題就是我想不出別的比賽地點。
── 派特‧威廉斯，奧蘭多魔術隊高階副總裁

We can't win at home and we can't win on the road. My problem as general manager is I can't think of another place to play.

—Pat Williams, senior vice president of the Orlando Magic

練球的那一天就像是過一天健康的生活，對你一點幫助也沒有。

——艾伯·雷蒙斯，前奧克拉荷馬市立大學男子籃球隊教練

One day of practice is like one day of clean living. It doesn't do you any good.

—Abe Lemons, former Oklahoma City University men's basketball coach

運動的成功祕訣在於結合天賦、密集訓練與強烈專注力。但對於世上沒那麼有天賦、比較懶惰的運動員來說，總是有作弊這個選項。與說謊類似，只有當參賽者正在做不正確的事情、而他們也無法說服自己時，才會有風險。如果目標是獲勝，而且你的確獲勝了，那麼你做的事怎麼會被認為是作弊呢？

如果你知道怎麼作弊，現在就開始。

——厄爾·韋弗，巴爾的摩金鶯總經理

If you know how to cheat, start now.

—Earl Weaver, Baltimore Orioles general manager

認為自己比其他人更聰明，你肯定會受騙上當。

——弗蘭索瓦·德·拉·洛舍弗科德，法國作家

The sure way to be cheated is to think one's self more cunning than others.

—François de La Rochefoucauld, French author

讓予免推球[19]：兩個無法推球入洞的輸家之間所作的協議。

——吉姆‧畢曉普，美國記者

Gimme: An agreement between two losers who can't putt.

—Jim Bishop, American journalist

年老與背信會戰勝年輕與技術。——諺語

Old age and treachery will overcome youth and skill.

—Proverb

不，我們不會作弊。就算作弊過，我也永遠不會告訴你。

——湯米‧拉索達，美國職棒大聯盟棒球選手與經理

No, we don't cheat. And even if we did, I'd never tell you.

—Tommy Lasorda, American major league baseball player and manager

為了維持你的自尊，有時候說謊與作弊是必要的。

——羅伯特‧伯恩，美國職業撞球選手與作家

In order to preserve your self-respect, it is sometimes necessary to lie and cheat.

—Robert Byrne, American professional pool player and author

---

[19] Gimme 來自 give me 的變化形。在非正式高爾夫球賽中，球到球洞兩呎內距離，因距離很近不太可能失手，可請求對手給予免除下一桿直接算進洞的權利。

第十四章
戰爭

　　雖然有些爭執可以用猜拳來解決，但有些紛爭就是沒法用外交途徑化解。人類很幸運，我們還沒遇到連老式戰爭都無法解決的問題。就算我們遇到了，反正炸掉它就對了。

　　戰爭的歷史可追溯至我們的祖先。他們發現鄰居擁有過量的食物，於是試圖將鄰居從這不必要的負擔中解放；不過鄰居並不願意放手，於是他們就解放了鄰居們不必要的頭顱並繼續用這種方式恣意橫行。從那個時候起，科技便持續進步，但基本原則沒有進化太多。現在的我們看到某樣喜歡的東西，結果發現那是別人的，我們就開始轟炸，直到他們把東西交出來為止，或是炸到什麼都不剩。這亙古不變的道理再簡單不過，相當具有說服力。

　　由於戰爭的威脅時時都懸在眼前，有人可能會認為所有人整天都縮在防空洞裡。但日復一日，人類依舊繼續他們的生活，世界好像也不會在明天就結束。有些人會說這很令人敬佩；有人則會說這是愚蠢的行為。兩者都對。

我們的炸彈比一般高中生還聰明，至少它們找得到科威特。

——亞倫・惠特尼・布朗，美國作家與喜劇演員

Our bombs are smarter than the average high school student. At least they can find Kuwait.

—Alan Whitney Brown, American writer and comedian

噢，那個啊。我做那個只是為了賺點外快，順便滿足我殺戮與勝利的男性需求。——查理・辛，美國演員

Oh, that. I just do that for the extra money, and to satisfy my male need to kill and win.

—Charlie Sheen

如果我們不成功，我們就冒著失敗的風險。

——丹・奎爾，美國第44任副總統

If we don't succeed, we run the risk of failure.

—Dan Quayle

典型的夢幻運動玩家如果在幻想中獲勝，他們會覺得自己很特別。——唐・利維，澳洲藝術家與電影製作人

The archetypal fantasy-sports player feels that winning at fantasy says something about them.

—Don Levy, Australian artist and film-maker

人類一直以為他們比海豚聰明，因為他們達成了這麼多成就……
汽車、紐約、戰爭……等等，而海豚只是在海裡閒晃過著快樂的
日子。但反過來說，海豚也一直深信牠們遠比人類聰明……理由
幾乎一樣。
——道格拉斯·亞當斯，英國作家，《銀河便車指南》廣播劇連續劇與小說作者

Man has always assumed that he was more intelligent than dolphins
because he had achieved so much ... the wheel, New York, wars, and so
on ... while all the dolphins had ever done was muck about in the water
having a good time. But conversely, the dolphins had always believed that
they were far more intelligent than man ... for precisely the same reason.
—Douglas Adams, British writer and author of the *Hitchhiker's Guide
to the Galaxy* radio series and subsequent novels

他們「錯」低估[20]我了。——喬治·W·布希，前美國總統，為與同樣擔任
過美國總統的父親區別，另稱「小布希」
They misunderestimated me.
—George W. Bush

說戰爭是瘋狂的，就像說性是瘋狂的，對沒國籍、沒卵蛋的人來
說再真確不過，但是在只能悶頭搞定狗屁倒灶的人聽來，這提醒

---

[20] 英文裡並沒有misunderestimate這個字，這個字是典型小布希說錯話的例子之
一。Underestimate為低估的意思，mis用在字首通常為否定後面部分的意思，
所以合起來變成雙重否定，反而像是承認自己的愚蠢。

真是精闢的氣人——約翰·厄普代克，美國小說家

To say that war is madness is like saying that sex is madness: true enough, from the standpoint of a stateless eunuch, but merely a provocative epigram for those who must make their arrangements in the world as given.

—John Updike, American novelist

有些人生來平庸，有些人墮落成平庸，而有些人則被迫接受平庸。——約瑟夫·海勒，美國小說家，此句出自《第22條軍規》

Some men are born mediocre, some men achieve mediocrity, and some men have mediocrity thrust upon them.

—Joseph Heller, American novelist, from *Catch-22*

別在你的敵人犯錯時打斷他們。——拿破崙，法國政治家

Never interrupt your enemy when he is making a mistake.

—Napoleon Bonaparte

戰爭的藝術就在於猜測山丘的另一頭有些什麼。

——亞瑟·韋爾斯利，英國軍人與政治家

The whole art of war consists of guessing at what is on the other side of the hill.

—Arthur Wellesley, British soldier and statesman

不論是兩個小孩在遊樂場上搶球，或是兩個大人在爭論腐爛的恐龍化石，任何紛爭終究是人與人之間的衝突，而這些衝突的複雜性不是找出誰對誰錯就能解決的。複雜的情感因素會開始發酵。一方可能想殺死另一方，但若另一方還沒準備好要死呢？這就是為什麼許多人會選擇討論人類互動過程中的限制，而不是試圖涉入其中。

這就是外交事務邪惡的地方：他們是外國，而且不會總是讓我們隨心所欲。──詹姆斯・雷思頓，美國記者

This is the devilish thing about foreign affairs: They are foreign and will not always conform to our whim.

—James Reston, American journalist

現今美國的問題在於太多人知道太多關於不足的問題。
　　──瑪格麗特・米德，美國人類學家

The problem with America today is that too many people know too much about not enough.

—Margaret Mead

永遠別低估人類愚蠢的能力。──羅伯特・A・海萊因，美國科幻作家

Never underestimate the power of human stupidity.

—Robert A. Heinlein, American science fiction author

我寧可擁有自卑感然後愉快地得到意外驚喜，也不要有優越感然後被粗暴地戳破。──瓦娜‧邦塔，美國作家

I would rather have an inferiority complex and be pleasantly surprised, than have a superiority complex and be rudely awakened.

—Vanna Bonta, American writer

愚蠢是超越國界的個人成就。

── 阿爾伯特‧愛因斯坦，物理哲學家

Stupidity is a personal achievement which transcends national boundaries.

—Albert Einstein

戰爭是上帝教美國人地理的方式。

── 安布羅斯‧比爾斯，美國作家與《魔鬼辭典》的作者

War is God's way of teaching Americans geography.

—Ambrose Bierce, American writer and author of *The Devil's Dictionary*

任何問題直接訴諸武力都是很低劣的解決方式，一般而言，只有小小孩跟大國才會採用。

── 大衛‧佛利民，美國作家

The direct use of force is such a poor solution to any problem, it is generally employed only by small children and large nations.

—David Friedman, American author

男人喜愛戰爭，因為戰爭讓他們看起來很嚴肅，同時也是個可以
讓女人停止嘲笑他們的東西。
—— 約翰‧福爾斯，英國小說家

Men love war because it allows them to look serious. Because it is the
one thing that stops women from laughing at them.
—John Fowles, British novelist

如果能夠光榮地避免打人的話，就不要打，但絕對不要輕輕打。
—— 狄奧多‧羅斯福，美國第 26 任總統，人稱老羅斯福

Don't hit at all if it is honorably possible to avoid hitting, but never hit
soft.
—Theodore Roosevelt

戰犯就是一個試圖殺你卻失敗的男人，然後要求你不要殺他。
—— 溫斯頓‧邱吉爾，前英國首相

A prisoner of war is a man who tries to kill you and fails, and then asks
you not to kill him.
—Winston Churchill

　　攻擊地球另一端的人滿平常的，這比跟住隔壁的混蛋打架要
方便多了。首先，他們超級近；再者，他們可能也花了好幾年計
畫要對你做同樣的事，所以最好先下手為強。

能鄙視鄰居是至高無上的滿足，這種滿足還遠遠超過宗教歧視。想到隔壁的人會下地獄，顯然就是個安慰。
——阿萊斯特・克勞利，英國神學家

The supreme satisfaction is to be able to despise one's neighbor, and this fact goes far to account for religious intolerance. It is evidently consoling to reflect that the people next door are headed for hell.
—Aleister Crowley, British theologian

好鄰居就是會在後院籬笆跟你微笑的人，但不會爬過來。
——亞瑟・貝爾，美國記者

A good neighbor is a fellow who smiles at you over the back fence, but doesn't climb over it.
—Arthur Baer, American journalist

整體而言，愛人類比愛鄰居簡單。——艾力・賀佛爾，美國哲學家
It is easier to love humanity as a whole than to love one's neighbor.
—Eric Hoffer, American philosopher

鄰居問我，他是否可以用我的割草機？我跟他說，當然可以，只要他不把它拿出我的院子。——艾力克・莫克姆，英國喜劇演員
My neighbor asked if he could use my lawn mower, and I told him of course he could, so long as he didn't take it out of my garden.
—Eric Morecambe, British comedian

聖經告訴我們要愛我們的鄰居，也說要愛我們的敵人；或許是因為基本上，他們是同一批人。——G·K·切斯特頓，英國作家

The Bible tells us to love our neighbors, and also to love our enemies; probably because they are generally the same people.

—G. K. Chesterton, British writer

每個男人都被自願當間諜的街坊鄰居包圍。

——珍·奧斯汀，英國女性文學家

Every man is surrounded by a neighborhood of voluntary spies.

—Jane Austen

如果你想惹惱你的鄰居，就說出關於他們的實話。

——彼得羅·阿雷蒂諾，義大利作家

If you want to annoy your neighbors, tell the truth about them.

—Pietro Aretino, Italian author

好籬笆產生出好鄰居。——羅伯特·佛洛斯特，美國詩人，四度獲普立茲獎

Good fences make good neighbors.

—Robert Frost

雖然有些世界領導者是強壯、肌肉發達的人，但衰老的混蛋仍占多數，再加上一個人要征服許多國家當然困難重重，因此組

織軍隊成為必要手段。許多好戰者可以證明，擁有一支軍隊足以完全改變局勢，比方，看似瘋狂的要求突然變得很合理；曾經迴避你的國家，現在想當麻吉。如果你曾有過一把槍，一定知道那種感覺。只要把那感覺乘上一千萬倍。

沒什麼可以比偉大但已死的將軍格言更能撫慰軍人的心。

── 芭芭拉 · W · 塔克曼，一戰歷史學家

Nothing so comforts the military mind as the maxim of a great but dead general.

—Barbara W. Tuchman, World War I historian

身處軍隊就像是身處男童軍隊，只是男童軍有大人監督。

── 農夫法蘭，出自電影《呆呆向前衝》

Being in the army is like being in the Boy Scouts, except that the Boy Scouts have adult supervision.

—Farmer Fran, *The Waterboy*

我不知道這些男人可以對敵軍造成什麼影響，但我的天，他們嚇死我了。── 威靈頓公爵

I don't know what effect these men will have upon the enemy, but, by God, they terrify me.

—Duke of Wellington

沒了紀律，軍隊就只是一群穿同樣顏色衣服的男人。

—— 法蘭克・伯恩斯，出自美國電視影集《外科醫師》

Without discipline the army would just be a bunch of guys wearing the same-color clothing.

—Frank Burns, *M*A*S*H*

經過一天辛苦的基礎訓練，你可以吞掉一條響尾蛇。

—— 「貓王」艾維斯・普利斯萊，美國知名歌手

After a hard day of basic training, you could eat a rattlesnake.

—Elvis Presley

如果我的士兵開始思考，他們沒有一個人會繼續留在軍隊。 ——

腓特烈二世，史稱「菲特烈大帝」，普魯士國王

If my soldiers were to begin to think, not one of them would remain in the army.

—Frederick II

由獅子帶領的驢子軍隊比由驢子帶領的獅子軍隊好。

—— 喬治・華盛頓，美國國父

An army of asses led by a lion is better than an army of lions led by an ass.

—George Washington

戰爭是件很嚴肅的事，所以不能委託給軍人。

——喬治·克列孟梭，法國政治家

War is too serious a matter to entrust to military men.

—Georges Clemenceau, French statesman

為什麼他們不讓同性戀進軍隊 **❷** ？我個人認為他們只是害怕會有一千個手持M16步槍的人說：「你叫誰死同性戀 **❷** ？」

——喬恩·史都華，美國政治諷刺作家

Why can't they have gay people in the army? Personally, I think they are just afraid of a thousand guys with M16s going, "Who'd you call a faggot?"

—Jon Stewart, American political satirist

士兵會為了一條彩色緞帶進行漫長艱辛的戰鬥。

——拿破崙，法國政治家

A soldier will fight long and hard for a bit of colored ribbon.

—Napoleon Bonaparte

---

❷ 自1994年至2010年，美軍有「不問、不說」（Don't ask, don't tell.）的同性戀政策，如果同性戀不說，長官無權過問性傾向，也不得試圖揭露其性傾向並逐出軍隊。此政策於2011年廢除，同性戀者可公開服役。

❷ Faggot為俚語中歧視男同性戀的稱呼。

想到饑荒、疾病、死亡、愛國主義等這些戰爭帶來的副作用，就讓人不舒服，但令人吃驚的是，還是有人對這些永遠不會膩。比起為了生存而參戰，有些該死的傢伙活著就是為了參戰。一般人可以很輕易地看出他們根本瘋了，但進一步審視的話，就可以充分理解他們為什麼會有這種錯誤的執著。多數好戰者連距離戰場一千英哩以內的地方都沒踏入過。如果有，他們大概沒法活到足以改變想法的那一天。

不論對國家多有利，建立任何想廢止戰爭的模式，都會拔除政府裡最賺錢的部門。
──湯瑪斯・潘恩，美國記者與開國元勳

To establish any mode to abolish war, however advantageous it might be to Nations, would be to take from such Government the most lucrative of its branches.
—Thomas Paine, American journalist and Founding Father

戰爭的目的不是讓你為了你的國家而死，而是讓其他混蛋為了他的國家而死。
──喬治・S・巴頓，美國陸軍四星上將

The object of war is not to die for your country but to make the other bastard die for his.
—George S. Patton

當我採取行動，我不會把一枚兩百萬美金的飛彈發射到一個十元美金的空帳篷並擊中一隻駱駝的屁股。這必須是決定性的。

── 喬治‧W‧布希，美國第四十三任總統，為與同樣擔任過美國總統的父親區別，另稱「小布希」

When I take action, I'm not going to fire a $2 million missile at a $10 empty tent and hit a camel in the butt. It's going to be decisive.

—George W. Bush

一如既往，我覺得我們會屠殺他們。

── 穆罕默德‧賽義德‧薩哈夫，伊拉克外交官與政治家

My feelings—as usual—we will slaughter them all.

—Mohammed Saeed al-Sahaf, Iraqi diplomat and politician

我親愛的美國同胞，我很高興跟你們宣布，我剛簽署了法律，規定蘇聯永久違法。五分鐘後將會開始轟炸。

── 羅納德‧雷根，美國第40任總統，麥克風測試時所說

My fellow Americans, I am pleased to tell you I just signed legislation which outlaws Russia forever. The bombing will begin in five minutes.

—Ronald Reagan, while performing a microphone test

一旦征服了最後一個敵人，獲勝的將軍終於可以獲取他的獎勵：一片充滿飢荒與瘟疫的焦土。直到此刻，他才終於明白戰爭的本質。那感覺爛透了，而且不是那種「可惡，我把湯灑到褲子上了」的爛法。戰爭爛到沒有任何語言的任何字眼可以形容它，雖然這並沒有阻止那幾個雜碎繼續嘗試。

也許這個世界是另一個星球的地獄。
　　——奧爾德斯·赫胥黎，英國作家
Maybe this world is another planet's hell.
—Aldous Huxley, British author

你無法打贏一場戰爭，就像你無法打贏一場地震一樣。
　　——吉納特·藍欽，女國會議員
You can no more win a war than you can win an earthquake.
—Jeannette Rankin, congresswoman

為了和平去打仗，就像是為了童貞而亂搞。
　　——喬治·卡林，美國喜劇演員
Fighting for peace is like screwing for virginity.
—George Carlin, American comedian

軍事情報^㉓就字面上來說是自相矛盾的。

——格魯喬·馬克斯，美國電影與喜劇演員

Military intelligence is a contradiction in terms.

—Groucho Marx

這顯示了我們在伊拉克的戰爭有多奇怪，而且我們從一開始就知道：出兵伊拉克的時候，德國並不想參與。德國，戰爭界的麥可·喬登，居然不參加！

——喬恩·史都華，美國政治諷刺作家

Here's how bizarre the war is that we're in in Iraq, and we should have known this right from the get-go: When we first went into Iraq, Germany didn't want to go. Germany. The Michael Jordan of war took a pass.

—Jon Stewart, American political satirist

當學校有所有必需的經費，而空軍得義賣蛋糕來籌錢買轟炸機，那將會是美好的一天。

——羅伯特·傅剛，美國作家

It will be a great day when our schools have all the money they need, and our air force has to have a bake sale to buy a bomber.

—Robert Fulghum, American author

㉓ Intelligence 在此指情報。格魯喬說字面上自相矛盾是因為 intelligence 另有智慧之意。

戰爭一開始像個漂亮女孩,每個男人都想跟她調情,結束時則像是個醜陋老女人,拜訪她的人都會覺得難受而哭泣。
——塞繆爾‧哈納吉德,西班牙猶太教法典學者

War begins like a pretty girl with whom every man wants to flirt and ends like an ugly old woman whose visitors suffer and weep.
—Samuel HaNagid, Spanish Talmudic scholar

在戰爭這種令人厭惡的行為裡打轉了幾千年後,幾個有遠見的人想知道如果他們拒戰會發生什麼事。雖然大部分的人都立刻被殺死了,但這潮流開始有了一股牽引力,讓人類逐漸停止毫無意義地攻擊。不過,他們很快就對和平感到厭倦,又退回去互砍。

雖然自然的人類狀態一直是場持續的戰爭,但不時還是會有和平的小區域出現。只是沒有人會去談論它,因為擔心那會激起所有人再度開打。

我對強制性的食人行為深具信心。如果人被迫吃下他們殺死的對象,就不會再有戰爭。
——艾比‧霍夫曼,青年國際黨共同創辦人

I believe in compulsory cannibalism. If people were forced to eat what they killed, there would be no more wars.
—Abbie Hoffman, cofounder of the Youth International Party

沒有任何國家像美國這樣，在和平時期飽受戰爭及其毀滅的折磨。──愛德華‧達赫伯格，美國小說家

No country has suffered so much from the ruins of war while being at peace as the American.

—Edward Dahlberg, American novelist

我為了和平而來。我沒有帶任何火炮，但我用眼裡的淚水懇求你：如果你敢搞我，我就殺光你們全部。

──詹姆斯‧馬蒂斯，美國海軍陸戰隊將軍

I come in peace. I didn't bring artillery. But I'm pleading with you, with tears in my eyes: If you fuck with me, I'll kill you all.

—James Mattis, United States Marine Corps general

我們必須尊重其他同胞的宗教，但只在合理範圍內，像是他老婆很美、孩子很聰明的說法，我們會尊重。

──H‧L‧曼肯，美國記者

We must respect the other fellow's religion, but only in the sense and to the extent that we respect his theory that his wife is beautiful and his children smart.

—H. L. Mencken, American journalist

原諒你的敵人，但永遠別忘記他們的名字。

——約翰‧F‧甘迺迪，美國第35任總統

Forgive your enemies, but never forget their names.

—John F. Kennedy

每個人在戰爭與戰爭之間都是和平主義者。就像在兩頓飯之間是素食主義者一樣。——科爾曼‧麥卡錫，美國記者與講師

Everyone's a pacifist between wars. It's like being a vegetarian between meals.

—Colman McCarthy, American journalist and lecturer

我的願望是由男同性戀來治理這個世界，因為這樣就不會有戰爭，只會更加重視軍裝。

——羅斯安妮‧巴爾，美國女演員、作家、導演

My hope is that gays will be running the world, because then there would be no war. Just a greater emphasis on military apparel.

—Roseanne Barr

第十五章
政治

　　只要存在著一群和平共存的人，你大可放心，距離變成完全徹底的狗屎狀態還有一步之遙。沒人知道什麼時候會發生，但總會有人建議建立可依據的生活規矩是必要的，然後他們當然也得想出一些罰則來處罰那些無視規矩的人。難免會有少數人認為那些規矩很蠢，並提議改寫。誰有這份榮幸來建立罰則或者改寫？經過一番爭論後，兩個候選人出現了，然後我們這些歹命的公民就得投票。早在明白這件事之前，我們的烏托邦社會就已經發明了政治，當然也包括它們自己的毀滅。

　　不論你生活在什麼樣的政治制度裡，可能你對於結果都不會太興奮。但這沒什麼好擔憂的，歷史上幾乎所有人也都這樣覺得。除了天氣和運動之外，政治永遠都是王八蛋們最喜歡的話題。

我痛恨所有拙劣的工作就像我痛恨罪惡，但我特別痛恨政治上的拙劣，因為那會造成成千上萬的人的痛苦與毀滅。

—— 約翰・沃爾夫岡・馮・歌德，德國作家

I hate all bungling as I do sin, but particularly bungling in politics, which leads to the misery and ruin of many thousands and millions of people.

—Johann Wolfgang von Goethe, German writer

犯罪毋需付出代價，政治也是。

—— 阿爾弗雷德・E・紐曼，《瘋狂雜誌》吉祥物

Crime does not pay ... as well as politics.

—Alfred E. Neuman, mascot for *MAD Magazine*

理想的政府形式是民主，以及伴隨而來的暗殺。

—— 伏爾泰，法國哲學家

The ideal form of government is democracy tempered with assassination.

—Voltaire, French philosopher

民意調查無法取代思想。 —— 華倫・巴菲特，美國商人

A public-opinion poll is no substitute for thought.

—Warren Buffett, American businessman

我喜歡去華盛頓，只是為了想靠近我的錢。

—— 鮑伯・霍伯，美國著名演員

I love to go to Washington—if only to be near my money.

—Bob Hope

唯一讓我輸掉這場選舉的方法就是，我被逮到跟一個死掉的女孩或活著的男孩上床。

—— 愛德溫・愛德華，前路易斯安那州州長

The only way I can lose this election is if I'm caught in bed with a dead girl or a live boy.

—Edwin Edwards, former governor of Louisiana

政治的實況就是忽視事實。

—— 亨利・亞當斯，美國記者、美國第6任總統亞當斯的孫子

Practical politics consists in ignoring facts.

—Henry Adams, American journalist and grandson to John Quincy Adams

誠實的外交是天方夜譚。

—— 約瑟夫・史達林，前蘇聯領導人

A sincere diplomat is like dry water or wooden iron.

—Joseph Stalin

政治就是熟練使用鈍器。

　　——萊斯特·鮑爾斯·皮爾遜，加拿大歷史學家與政治家

Politics is the skilled use of blunt objects.

—Lester Bowles Pearson, Canadian historian and politician

一般而言，治理眾人的藝術在於盡可能從一群公民那裡拿錢給另
一群。——伏爾泰，法國哲學家

In general, the art of government consists in taking as much money as
possible from one party of the citizens to give to the other.

—Voltaire, French philosopher

　　多年來，人類發明了幾種政治制度，光這點就預示了制度本
身不可避免的缺點。如果它們其中之一有什麼優點，那就不需要
其他的制度了。我們仍然必須與現行制度合作，即使選擇性沒那
麼多。

　　雖然你在政治行動上的選擇的確受限於政府形式，但公開發
表對制度的看法還是很重要的，因為如果沒意外，當結果不如你
預期時，你會有抱怨的權利。

拒絕參與政治的懲罰之一，就是你會被比你差的人統治。

　　——柏拉圖，古希臘哲學家

One of the penalties for refusing to participate in politics is that you end up being governed by your inferiors.

—Plato

奇怪的女人躺在池塘裡分送劍，絕對不該是政府制度的基礎！

──丹尼斯，出自電影《聖杯傳奇》

Strange women lying in ponds distributing swords is no basis for a system of government!

—Dennis, *Monty Python and the Holy Grail*

民主就是允許投票給你最不討厭的候選人。

──羅伯特·伯恩，美國職業撞球選手與作家

Democracy is being allowed to vote for the candidate you dislike least.

—Robert Byrne, American professional pool player and author

共產主義就像是禁酒令：它是個好主意，但沒有用。

──威爾·羅傑斯，美國喜劇演員與演員

Communism is like prohibition: It's a good idea, but it won't work.

—Will Rogers, American comedian and actor

什麼是委員會？從不適合的人裡挑出一群不甘願的人，來做不必要的事。──理查·哈克尼斯，美國記者

What is a committee? A group of the unwilling, picked from the unfit, to do the unnecessary.

—Richard Harkness, American journalist

政治或許是唯一一種被認為不需要準備的職業。

——羅伯特・路易斯・史蒂文森，蘇格蘭文學家

Politics is perhaps the only profession for which no preparation is thought necessary.

—Robert Louis Stevenson

不論我們和政客知不知道，大自然都有參與我們的政策與決定，她擁有比我們更多的投票權、更長遠的記憶以及更嚴格的正義感。——溫德爾・貝瑞，美國作家

Whether we and our politicians know it or not, Nature is party to all our deals and decisions, and she has more votes, a longer memory, and a sterner sense of justice than we do.

—Wendell Berry, American writer

與其給政客進入城市的鑰匙，換鎖可能會比較好。

——道格・拉森，美國專欄作家。

Instead of giving a politician the keys to the city, it might be better to change the locks.

—Doug Larson, American columnist

　　民主政治的美好在於它帶有一種與生俱來的選擇。不是要在兩個混蛋之間做選擇，反正這只不過是個幻覺。真正的選擇在於你是要說服自己，你的參與是重要的？還是忽視所有與政治沾上任何一點邊的東西？

　　不管你的選擇是哪個，結果通常是一樣的，某些不值得握有權力的人還是會得到權力。所有投給他的人會抱怨他沒有遵守承諾，而沒投給他的人則會說：我早告訴你了吧。

沒有什麼背信忘義、卑賤的事是政黨做不出來的，因為在政治裡沒有榮譽可言。

——本傑明・迪斯雷利，前英國首相。

There is no act of treachery or meanness of which a political party is not capable; for in politics there is no honor.

—Benjamin Disraeli, former British prime minister

從下雨也能得到功勞的政黨，如果對手把乾旱怪到他們頭上，那也不用太驚訝。——德懷特・莫羅，美國參議員

Any party which takes credit for the rain must not be surprised if its opponents blame it for the drought.

—Dwight Morrow, United States senator

讀者，假設你是個白癡，假設你是個國會議員，我居然講了重複的東西。——馬克·吐溫，美國作家

Reader, suppose you were an idiot; and suppose you were a member of Congress; but I repeat myself.

—Mark Twain

我們都想投給最好的人，但他從來都不是候選人。

——法蘭克·麥金尼·哈伯德，以「金·哈伯」為筆名，美國漫畫家

We'd all like to vote for the best man, but he's never a candidate.

—Frank McKinney "Kin" Hubbard, American cartoonist

如果眾神確有打算讓我們投票，祂們應該會給我們候選人。

——霍華德·津恩，美國歷史學家

If the gods had intended for people to vote, they would have given us candidates.

—Howard Zinn, American historian

委員會是一群無法獨自做任何事的人所組成，他們聚集在一起可以做的就是，決定他們無法做任何事。

——佛瑞德·亞倫，美國喜劇演員

A committee is a group of people who individually can do nothing but together can decide that nothing can be done.

—Fred Allen, American comedian

強化一個人智力的唯一辦法就是讓心智成為所有思想通行的大道，別在任何事上打定主意，包括別成為單一黨派的過道。
—— 約翰・濟慈，英國詩人

The only means of strengthening one's intellect is to make up one's mind about nothing / to let the mind be a thoroughfare for all thoughts. Not a select party.
—John Keats

你可以把一個人帶到國會，但你無法讓他思考。
—— 米爾頓・伯利，美國喜劇演員與演員

You can lead a man to Congress, but you can't make him think.
—Milton Berle, American comedian and actor

要在一個政黨裡成功，必須培養坐著不動，以及當蠢人講廢話時還要保持禮貌的能力。
—— 莫頓・布萊克威爾，共和黨社會運動家

To succeed inside a political party, one must cultivate an ability to sit still and remain polite while foolish people speak nonsense.
—Morton Blackwell, Republican activist

批評政客腐化，跟你因為狗拉大便在地毯上而罵牠是很像的。牠知道你在為某件事生氣，但你能讓牠理解為什麼生氣的機會卻很渺茫。儘管一點用也沒有，但大眾還是為了希望能夠改變政治現狀而持續指責及抗議。雖然這可能可以吸引你看一下地方晚間新聞，但事實證明，往他們口袋裡塞大把的鈔票更有效。如果你沒有大把的鈔票可用，那就抱怨一下他們吧，雖然完全沒有效果可言，但至少還有療癒的功能。

魔術師跟政客有很多共通點，他們同樣都是把我們的注意力從他們真正在做的事轉移。——本‧奧克瑞，奈吉利亞詩人
The magician and the politician have much in common: They both have to draw our attention away from what they are really doing.
—Ben Okri, Nigerian poet

他什麼都不懂，卻認為自己什麼都懂。很明顯，他適合從政。
——蕭伯納，愛爾蘭劇作家與作家
He knows nothing and thinks he knows everything. That points clearly to a political career.
—George Bernard Shaw, Irish playwright and author

在墨西哥，冷氣被稱為「政客」，因為製造很多噪音，又沒什麼用。——連恩‧戴頓，英國歷史學家

In Mexico, an air conditioner is called a "politician," because it makes a lot of noise but doesn't work very well.

—Len Deighton, British historian

他從不選擇意見，他只穿那些正在流行的東西。

—— 列夫・托爾斯泰，俄國小說家

He never chooses an opinion; he just wears whatever happens to be in style.

—Leo Tolstoy

你擁有所有受歡迎政治家的特質：可怕的聲音、不好的血統以及粗俗的態度。

—— 阿里斯托芬，古希臘喜劇作家

You have all the characteristics of a popular politician: a horrible voice, bad breeding, and a vulgar manner.

—Aristophanes

如果有什麼事是公僕討厭做的，那就是為公眾做事。

—— 法蘭克・麥金尼・哈伯德，以「金・哈伯」為筆名，美國漫畫家

If there's anything a public servant hates to do, it's something for the public.

—Frank McKinney "Kin" Hubbard, American cartoonist

你在華盛頓想要有朋友？養隻狗吧。

——哈瑞・S・杜魯門，美國第 34 任副總統

You want a friend in Washington? Get a dog.

—Harry S. Truman

與政客打交道時，記得，千萬別把愚蠢誤以為是陰謀。雖然有些政客的確用褲袋撈了不少不義之財，但他們當初連怎麼穿上褲子都還搞不清楚。所以在你開始抱怨華盛頓那幫金玉其外、敗絮其中的人之前，別白費唇舌才是比較明智的。或者至少要用你的國會議員可以理解的字句，最好是用動畫火柴人跟明亮的顏色來表達。

政治只是醜人的演藝事業。

——傑・雷諾，美國電視節目主持人

Politics is just show business for ugly people.

—Jay Leno

有些傢伙，因為保守而獲得信任，其實他們只是愚蠢。

——法蘭克・麥金尼・哈伯德，以「金・哈伯」為筆名，美國漫畫家

Some fellows get credit for being conservative when they are only stupid.

—Frank McKinney "Kin" Hubbard, American cartoonist

政客到哪兒都一樣。即使那邊根本沒有河流，他們也會承諾要蓋橋。 —— 尼基塔・赫魯雪夫，前蘇聯共產黨第一書記，史達林的繼任者

Politicians are the same all over. They promise to build bridges even when there are no rivers.

—Nikita Khrushchev, former First Secretary of the Communist Party of the Soviet Union and successor to Joseph Stalin

房間裡有十五位民主黨員，而你會得到二十種意見。

—— 派屈克・萊希，佛蒙特州參議員

You get fifteen Democrats in a room, and you get twenty opinions.

—Patrick Leahy, Vermont senator

老實說，任何一個對複雜議題有強烈意見的人，我都抱持懷疑的態度。 —— 史考特・亞當斯，美國漫畫家與漫畫《呆伯特》的創作者

Frankly, I'm suspicious of anyone who has a strong opinion on a complicated issue.

—Scott Adams, American cartoonist and creater of The *Dilbert* comics

政客就像尿布。他們需要經常更換，而且更換理由也一樣。

—— 來源不詳

Politicians are like diapers. They both need changing regularly and for the same reason.

—Unknown

你知道的，大腦，在共和黨裡是可疑份子。
——沃爾特・利普曼，美國作家與政治評論家

Brains, you know, are suspect in the Republican Party.

—Walter Lippmann, American writer and political commentator

每州有兩個參議員的原因，是因為這樣其中一個就可以當指定駕駛。——傑・雷諾，美國脫口秀節目主持人

The reason there are two senators for each state is so that one can be the designated driver.

—Jay Leno

應該要有一天，一天就好了，開放全民可以參加「參議員狩獵季」。——威爾・羅傑斯，美國喜劇演員與演員

There ought to be one day—just one—when there is open season on senators.

—Will Rogers, American comedian and actor

　　到頭來，政治應該是件嚴肅的事。我們選出來、送進政府機關的人，真的可以毀滅或者拯救這個世界，就看他們怎麼決定。所以，為什麼他們要像個白天肥皂劇裡的角色一樣，不斷演出滑稽的行為？從在浴室隔間上演的火辣辣風流韻事到祕密竊聽及洗錢，這樣的政治人物沒辦法給我們太多信心。如果他們把花在掩

蓋自己不檢點行為的時間的一半拿來治理國家，我們也許真的可以有些進步。

最高法院已經裁定在華盛頓特區不能佈置耶穌誕生的場景，並非因為任何宗教因素，而是因為他們找不到三位智者與一位處女。
—— 傑‧雷諾，美國脫口秀節目主持人

The Supreme Court has ruled that they cannot have a nativity scene in Washington, D.C. This wasn't for any religious reasons. They couldn't find three wise men and a virgin.
—Jay Leno

噢，我不怪國會。如果有六兆美金任我使用，我也會很不負責的。—— 喬治‧利屈堤，美國漫畫家

Oh, I don't blame Congress. If I had $600 billion at my disposal, I'd be irresponsible, too.
—George Lichty, American cartoonist

任何一個政黨如果名字裡有「民主」兩個字的，肯定不民主。
—— 派屈克‧莫瑞，美國政治家

Any political party that includes the word *democratic* in its name, isn't.
—Patrick Murray, American politician

如果湯瑪斯・傑佛遜❷認為課稅卻沒有代議制度是不好的，他應該看看現在的代議狀況。

—— 拉什・林博，美國保守主義電台名人

If Thomas Jefferson thought taxation without representation was bad, he should see how it is with representation.

—Rush Limbaugh, American conservative radio personality

當幽默作家沒什麼訣竅，尤其當你有整個政府替你工作的時候。

—— 威爾・羅傑斯，美國喜劇演員與演員

There's no trick to being a humorist when you have the whole government working for you.

—Will Rogers, American comedian and actor

政治笑話的問題就在於他們是被選出來的。

—— 蕭伯納，愛爾蘭劇作家與作家

The problem with political jokes is that they get elected.

—George Bernard Shaw, Irish playwright and author

❷ 美國第 3 任總統，也是獨立宣言的起草人，開國元勳中最具影響力的一位。

在所有可得的政治職位當中，沒有一個像美國總統這樣令人夢寐以求。在自由世界裡，它是最有權力的位置，所以不意外它會吸引一些美國能提供的超級蠢貨、大爛人及混蛋。

每四年我們就會看到一個裝滿候選人的聚寶盆，然後被削減到兩個，然後一個，唯一存活下來的混帳。這是個很優雅的制度，最後結果無可避免地會是國家百分之五十一的人得到他們想要的，剩下的百分之四十九則再抱怨個四年。可能不是很完美，但目前這就是我們所有的全部了。

全國擁有最棒工作的人就是副總統了。他要做的事情只有每天早上起床，然後說：「總統好嗎？」
——威爾·羅傑斯，美國喜劇演員與演員

The man with the best job in the country is the vice president. All he has to do is get up every morning and say, "How is the president?"
—Will Rogers, American comedian and actor

在美國，任何人都可以當總統。這是你當美國人的其中一個風險。 ——阿德萊·史蒂文森，前伊利諾州州長

In America, anybody can be president. That's one of the risks you take.
—Adlai Stevenson, former governor of Illinois

美國人有不同的講話方式。他們講電梯，我們講升降梯❷⁵……他們講總統，我們講心理變態的笨飯桶。

——阿列克謝・塞爾，英國喜劇演員

Americans have different ways of saying things. They say elevator, we say lift ... they say president, we say stupid psychopathic git.

—Alexai Sayle, British comedian

我還是個小男孩的時候，他們跟我說任何一個人都可以當總統；現在，我開始相信了。

——克萊倫斯・蘇厄德・丹諾，美國律師，為教授演化論的高中生物老師約翰・T・斯科普斯辯護，也是後來著名的「斯科普斯猴子審判」

When I was a boy, I was told that anybody could become president; I'm beginning to believe it.

—Clarence Seward Darrow, American lawyer famous for his defense of John T. Scopes in the "Scopes Monkey Trial"

如果是總統來做，這種手段就不違法。

——理查・尼克森，美國第 37 任總統

When the president does it, that means it's not illegal.

—Richard Nixon

---

❷⁵ Lift 為英式英語中的電梯。

同胞們，總統需要休息，他就像美國百工牌的灰塵惡魔吸塵器一樣。如果不幫他充電，他就沒辦法吸[26]了。
── 史蒂芬・荷伯，美國政治諷刺作家

Folks, the president needs a break. He's like a Black & Decker cordless Dirt Devil vacuum. If you don't recharge his batteries, he can't suck.
—Stephen Colbert, American political satirist

　　美國小孩從小就被告知美國是地球上最偉大的國家，許多人震驚地發現事實可能不是如此。因為全世界還有其他一百九十五個政治實體並不這麼想。

　　整體來說，美國在其他地區的表現不太好。那些目前沒在跟我們打仗的國家，傾向認為我們是沒安全感的遊樂場惡霸，不顧一切想偷走所有人的玩具。雖然我們自然而然地會想抹煞這些說法，但比較明智的行動或許是聽聽看他們想說什麼。那樣子，當我們無可避免地入侵他們國家時，會更具有毀滅性。

我不喜歡談論政治，因為我的財產裡不包含一支擁有二十萬士兵的軍隊。── 法蘭茲・李斯特，匈牙利作曲家

I am not fond of speaking about politics because I don't have in my possession an army of 200,000 soldiers.
—Franz Liszt, Hungarian composer

---

[26] 此處的 suck 亦為雙關語，前面講吸塵器，因此字面上是吸的意思，實則為 suck 的很爛的意思，暗喻總統就沒辦法繼續爛了。

自由不過是種混亂，只是燈打得比較好。

——亞倫‧迪恩‧福斯特，美國科幻作家與原版《星際大戰》小說作者

Freedom is just chaos, with better lighting.

—Alan Dean Foster, American science-fiction writer and author of the original *Star Wars* novel

我發現了欺騙外交官的技巧。我跟他們說實話，而他們完全不相信我。——卡米洛‧迪‧加富爾，義大利首相

I have discovered the art of deceiving diplomats. I tell them the truth and they never believe me.

—Camillo Di Cavour, Italian prime minister

一個靠搶劫彼得來付保羅錢的政府，永遠都能仰賴保羅的支持。

——蕭伯納，愛爾蘭劇作家與作家

A government that robs Peter to pay Paul can always depend on the support of Paul.

—George Bernard Shaw, Irish playwright and author

在民主體制下，一個政黨總是把它主要的心力放在試圖證明另一個政黨不適合執政。通常雙方都會成功，也都是對的。

——H‧L‧曼肯，美國記者

Under democracy one party always devotes its chief energies to trying

to prove that the other party is unfit to rule—and both commonly succeed, and are right.
—H. L. Mencken, American journalist

社會主義從未在美國紮根是因為窮人不認為自己是被剝削的無產階級，而是暫時蒙羞的百萬富翁。
—— 約翰‧史坦貝克，美國作家

Socialism never took root in America because the poor see themselves not as an exploited proletariat but as temporarily embarrassed millionaires.
—John Steinbeck

我認為那是個不錯的想法。 —— 聖雄甘地，帶領印度脫離英國殖民的民族領袖。此為被問到他對西方文明看法時的回答。

I think it would be a good idea.
—Mahatma Gandhi, when asked what he thought of Western civilization

每一段知識份子與共產黨之間的婚姻，都以通姦作結。
—— 尼可拉斯‧戈梅茲‧達維拉，哥倫比亞作家

Every marriage of an intellectual with the Communist Party ends in adultery.
—Nicolás Gómez Dávila, Colombian writer

外交官總是能記得女人的生日，卻不會記得她的年紀。

── 羅伯特・佛洛斯特，美國詩人，四度獲普立茲獎。

A diplomat is a man who always remembers a woman's birthday but never remembers her age.

—Robert Frost

第五篇

女人、男人

有時候我懷疑男人跟女人是否真的適合彼此。或許他們應該比鄰而居，偶爾拜訪一下彼此就好。
——凱薩琳‧赫本，美國電影女演員，有「美國影壇第一夫人」之稱。

Sometimes I wonder if men and women really suit each other. Perhaps they should live next door and just visit now and then.
—Katharine Hepburn

第十六章
約會

　　沒人說過約會很容易。事實上，約會其實蠻恐怖的。每次你踏出家門尋找真愛時，你都要面對窘迫、愚蠢以及人類最害怕的事：拒絕。

　　即使你心儀的對象同意跟你約會，也不代表你就此一帆風順。即使是成功展開交往，都會伴隨著許多尷尬沉默的窘境，還有背上不受控制冒出的汗水。不論情況有多荒謬或多複雜，當你明白在你之前還有其他人有相同經歷，並用了極不入流、沒風度的尖酸嘲諷來毒舌約會這檔事，而且簡直是只有史上最混蛋的王八蛋才講得出來的話，你會舒坦許多。

　　這些混蛋對約會到底有什麼意見？你可以在這章找到全部的對話，但我們先從這裡開始。

在你們之中有多少人開始約會，是因為懶得去自殺？
　　——茱蒂・泰努塔，美國喜劇演員

How many of you have ever started dating because you were too lazy to commit suicide?

—Judy Tenuta, American comedian

我愛你，就像胖孩子愛蛋糕一樣。 ——五角，美國饒舌藝術家

I love you like a fat kid loves cake.

—50 Cent, American rap artist

被信任是比被愛更大的讚美。 ——喬治·麥克唐納，蘇格蘭奇幻作家

To be trusted is a greater compliment than being loved.

—George MacDonald, Scottish fantasy author

基本上我們是來自一條成功調情的長遠血脈的後裔，而且這已經深植在我們的大腦裡。如果不展開與另一個性別的聯繫，我們就無法繁殖，然後種族就會滅絕。

——凱特·福克斯，英國社會人類學家

Basically we are descended from a long line of successful flirts and it is hard-wired into our brains. If we didn't initiate contact with the opposite sex, then we wouldn't reproduce, and the species would die out.

—Kate Fox, British social anthropologist

在愛情裡總有些瘋狂，但在瘋狂中也總是有些理性。

——弗里德里希·尼采，德國哲學家

There is always some madness in love. But there is also always some reason in madness.

—Friedrich Nietzsche

看著你的女兒被約會對象接走，那感覺就像是把一把價值一百萬
美金的史特拉底瓦里❷名琴交給一隻猩猩。

——吉姆‧畢夏普，美國記者

Watching your daughter being collected by her date feels like handing
over a $1 million Stradivarius to a gorilla.

—Jim Bishop, American journalist

在愛情萌芽階段，你必須小心走路；飛奔過原野投進愛人的懷抱
這種事，只能發生在你確定你跌倒時，他們不會笑出來。

——喬納森‧卡羅爾，美國作家

You have to walk carefully in the beginning of love; the running across
fields into your lover's arms can only come later when you're sure they
won't laugh if you trip.

—Jonathan Carroll, American author

我很自私、沒耐心，又有點沒安全感。我會犯錯、會失控，有時
候很難搞。但如果你無法接受我最糟的一面，那顯然你也不值得
我最美好的模樣。 ——瑪麗蓮‧夢露

I'm selfish, impatient, and a little insecure. I make mistakes, I am out
of control and at times hard to handle. But if you can't handle me at

---

❷ 史特拉底瓦里為17-18世紀義大利著名的弦樂器製造師，現存由他製造的琴都
相當名貴。

my worst, then you sure as hell don't deserve me at my best.

—Marilyn Monroe

親吻是一種讓兩個人因太靠近彼此而無法看到對方任何缺點的手段。—— 芮妮・雅斯內克。

Kissing is a means of getting two people so close together that they can't see anything wrong with each other.

—Rene Yasenek

我嫁給我親吻的第一個男人。當我告訴小孩這件事時，他們快吐了。—— 芭芭拉・布希，老布希總統的太太

I married the first man I ever kissed. When I tell this to my children, they just about throw up.

—Barbara Bush

沒有人可以打贏性別戰爭，因為太常與敵人調情了。

—— 亨利・季辛吉，美國外交官

No one will win the battle of the sexes; there is too much flirting with the enemy.

—Henry Kissinger, American diplomat

如果你把電視劇跟電影當成指南，約會看起來就會很簡單：你只需要認識一個不擅長社交的人，精通某些他或她覺得很有魅力的難解嗜好，然後從此過著幸福快樂的日子。當然，這些完全不是約會的真實樣貌。如果他們誠實地拍一部關於約會的電影，那部電影長度會只有十分鐘。一對情侶相識，然後跳到他們在不同張沙發上看電視。其中一個放了個屁，另一個笑說：「怎麼搞的！電影不是這樣演的。」接著上片尾名單。所以或許你可以替自己省掉談戀愛的麻煩，只要讀讀羅曼史就好。

任何一段關係追根究柢都是場權力鬥爭，掌握權力的就是比較不愛另一半的那個人。

—— 查客・克勞斯特曼，美國作家

Every relationship is fundamentally a power struggle, and the individual in power is whoever likes the other person less.

—Chuck Klosterman, American writer

別讓一個漂亮的女人用甜言蜜語哄騙、引誘及欺騙你，她的目標是你的穀倉。

—— 赫西俄德，古希臘詩人

Do not let a flattering woman coax and wheedle you and deceive you; she is after your barn.

—Hesiod, Greek poet

愛情就是在任何時間隱藏你的真實樣貌，包括睡覺在內。愛情就是化著妝上床睡覺，到樓下的漢堡王大便，還有把酒藏在香水瓶裡。那就是愛情。—— 潔娜・瑪若妮，出自美國情境喜劇《超級製作人》

Love is hiding who you really are at all times. Even when you're sleeping. Love is wearing makeup to bed, and going downstairs to the Burger King to poop. And hiding alcohol in perfume bottles. That's love.

—Jenna Maroney, *30 Rock*

每個男人的夢想都是可以沉溺於一個女人的懷抱，卻又能夠同時不落入她的掌控之中。—— 傑利・路易斯，美國喜劇演員、歌手

Every man's dream is to be able to sink into the arms of a woman without also falling into her hands.

—Jerry Lewis

愛情總是充滿樂趣及玩樂，直到某人瞎了眼或者懷孕。
—— 吉姆・柯爾，美國大學美式足球教練

Love is all fun and games until someone loses an eye or gets pregnant.

—Jim Cole, American college football coach

愛情就像是駕駛雪車穿越凍原時不幸翻車，還被困在車底。到了夜裡，冰原黃鼠狼出現了。
—— 馬特・格朗寧，美國漫畫家與《辛普森家庭》的創作者

Love is like racing across the frozen tundra on a snowmobile which flips over, trapping you underneath. At night, the ice weasels come.
—Matt Groening, American cartoonist and creator of *The Simpsons*

愛情是一種很嚴重的精神疾病。
—— 柏拉圖，古希臘哲學家
Love is a serious mental disease.
—Plato

　　要描述墜入愛河的過程有些困難，但這樣想或許會有點幫助：想像一下，盯著一個水泥游泳池，裡面的水都替換成活的狼獾，而所有的救生員都長得像是《玉米田的孩子》裡的小孩。不顧既有的風險，你還是潛進去了。
　　地球上沒有任何單身者會建議另一個人談戀愛，但不知為何情況正好完全相反，愛情還是持續發生。在你奔向夕陽追尋愛情之前，你也許會想聽聽在你之前失敗的人是怎麼說的。

愛情是兩個頭腦，沒有一點思想。
—— 菲力普·貝瑞，美國劇作家
Love is two minds without a single thought.
—Philip Barry, American playwright

友誼與愛情的不同之處在於你可以傷對方多深。

—— 艾希莉·布理恩特，美國漫畫家

The difference between friendship and love is how much you can hurt each other.

—Ashleigh Brilliant, American cartoonist

永遠別在上床睡覺時生氣。別睡覺，快吵架。

—— 菲莉絲·狄樂，美國喜劇演員與女演員

Never go to bed mad—stay up and fight.

—Phyllis Diller, American comedian and actress

愛情就像沙漏，填滿心的同時，腦袋也空了。

—— 儒勒·雷納爾，法國作家

Love is like an hourglass, with the heart filling up as the brain empties.

—Jules Renard, French author

愛情就像葡萄酒，啜飲很棒，喝光整瓶則會頭痛。

—— 胡立歐·伊格萊西雅斯，西班牙歌手

Love is like wine: To sip is fine, but to empty the bottle is a headache.

—Julio Iglesias, Spanish singer

當你垂釣愛情時，用你的心當餌，而不是你的腦袋。

—— 馬克‧吐溫，美國作家

When you fish for love, bait with your heart, not your brain.

—Mark Twain

　　不管別人讓你信了些什麼，為了人類的繁衍，男人還是個必要的變數。我們應該要感謝這個事實，不然女人大概不會讓我們長久待在她們身邊。

　　男人擅長許多事，但當個細心體貼的好夥伴絕非其中的一項。除非有來自第三者的競爭，不然在短期之內，我們大概不會有任何改變。多數女人只是翻個白眼繼續前進，不過還是有某些女人願意讓我們盡一下本分的。

真命天子就要出現了，但他人在非洲，而且是用走的。

—— 歐普拉‧溫芙蕾，美國電視節目脫口秀主持人

Mr. Right is coming. But he's in Africa and he's walking.

—Oprah Winfrey

男性是可以馴養的動物，只要堅定溫柔地對待他們，就可以訓練他們做大部分的事情。—— 吉莉‧庫柏，英國作家

The male is a domestic animal which, if treated with firmness and kindness, can be trained to do most things.

—Jilly Cooper, British author

當個女人是個極為困難的任務，因為這任務大部分是由應付男人所組成的。
—— 約瑟夫・康拉德，生於波蘭的英國小說家

Being a woman is a terribly difficult task since it consists principally in dealing with men.
—Joseph Conrad

女人想要平庸的男人，而男人則努力盡其所能地變平庸。
—— 瑪格麗特・米德，美國人類學家

Women want mediocre men. And men are working hard to become as mediocre as possible.
—Margaret Mead

你可以想像沒有男人的世界嗎？沒有任何犯罪，還有許多快樂的胖女人。
—— 瑪麗森・史密斯，美國作家

Can you imagine a world without men? No crime and lots of happy, fat women.
—Marion Smith, American author

男人的更年期比女人的更年期有趣多了。女人的更年期會變胖還有潮熱；男人的更年期是跟年輕美眉約會與騎重機。
——麗塔‧羅德納，美國女演員與喜劇演員

Male menopause is a lot more fun than female menopause. With female menopause you gain weight and get hot flashes. Male menopause—you get to date young girls and drive motorcycles.
—Rita Rudner, American actress and comedian

雖然我們會崇拜某個男人，但我們也同意當他們聚一起時，實在很蠢。——班克斯太太，出自《歡樂滿人間》

Though we adore men individually, we agree that as a group they're rather stupid.
—Mrs. Banks, *Mary Poppins*

　　雖然男人在物種間的互動上極為糟糕，女人也不是沒有她們的缺點。當她們不忙於把男人的心磨成肉泥時，她們會喜怒無常、優柔寡斷、欲求不滿、膚淺而且充滿控制慾。這些，還是她們好的一面。

　　一次又一次，男人換過一個又一個女人，始終深信下一個會不一樣。最後我們終將找到一個女孩，她會忽視我們阮囊羞澀的銀行戶頭與變寬的腰圍，全心全意愛著我們的真實樣貌。不幸地，十之八九這些無益的追尋都會以失意的辱罵告終，下面這些蠢蛋們就是證據。

大多數男人的問題在於他們是王八蛋，大多數女人的問題則在於她們忍受那些王八蛋。——雪兒，美國女演員、歌手

The problem with most men is they're a**holes. The problem with most women is they put up with those a**holes.

—Cher

當一個年輕人抱怨一名年輕小姐沒心沒肺時，可以確定她已擄獲他的心。——喬治・丹尼森・普倫提斯，美國記者

When a young man complains that a young lady has no heart, it's pretty certain that she has his.

—George Dennison Prentice, American journalist

她是那種會吃光你所有的腰果，然後只留下花生跟榛果給你的女生。——雷蒙・錢德勒，美國小說家

She was the kind of girl who'd eat all your cashews and leave you with nothing but peanuts and filberts.

—Raymond Chandler, American novelist

女孩就像蛞蝓，她們有某些目的，但很難想像那目的是什麼。——卡爾文，出自漫畫《卡爾文與霍布斯》

Girls are like slugs. They serve some purpose, but it's hard to imagine what.

—Calvin, *Calvin and Hobbes*

女人生命中只需要三樣東西：食物、水與讚美。

——克里斯・洛克，美國喜劇演員

There are only three things women need in life: food, water, and compliments.

—Chris Rock, American comedian

每個女孩都可以很有魅力，妳只需要站著別動跟看起來呆呆的。

——海蒂・拉瑪，澳洲女演員

Any girl can be glamorous. All you have to do is stand still and look stupid.

—Hedy Lamarr, Austrian actress

從生物學上來說，如果什麼東西咬了你，比較可能是母的。

——德斯蒙德・莫利斯，英國動物學家

Biologically speaking, if something bites you, it is more likely to be female.

—Desmond Morris, British zoologist

要跟一個男人快樂地在一起，妳必須很了解他，然後少愛他；要跟一個女人快樂地在一起，你必須很愛她，然後別想了解她。

——海倫・羅蘭德，美國記者

To be happy with a man, you must understand him a lot and love him a little. To be happy with a woman, you must love her a lot and not try

to understand her at all.
—Helen Rowland, American journalist

女人的心比男人的乾淨許多，因為她常常變心。
—— 奧利佛‧赫福特，美國作家與插畫家
A woman's mind is cleaner than a man's. She changes it more often.
—Oliver Herford, American writer and illustrator

女人會在任何事上面說謊，只為了保持練習。
—— 菲力普‧馬羅，出自《漫長的告別》
A woman will lie about anything, just to stay in practice.
—Philip Marlowe, *The Long Goodbye*

女人和貓隨心所欲做自己，而男人和狗就應該放輕鬆，對他們習
以為常。 —— 羅伯特‧A‧海萊因，美國科幻作家
Women and cats will do as they please, and men and dogs should relax
and get used to the idea.
—Robert A. Heinlein, American science fiction author

女人的直覺是幾百萬年來不去思考的結果。
—— 魯伯特‧休斯，美國歷史學家

Women's intuition is the result of millions of years of not thinking.
—Rupert Hughes, American historian

　　如果你已經疲於像是在酒吧相遇或是在雜貨店尷尬交流這種傳統約會管道，線上約會這個選項就像是在絕望與寂寞荒野上的一道希望之光。但當你從潛在對象的汪洋中篩選時，記住，你眼前看到的不一定就是你會得到的。鏡頭可能會讓人看起來比實際胖了十磅，但用適當的角度與朦朧的燈光，也可以讓人看起來輕兩百磅。所以，在你進入線上約會世界之前，請先有心理準備，萬一你的約會對象跟你看到的照片不太一樣，而且眼前的他像是一頭曬傷的海象時，你要說些什麼？

女士，妳今天看起來格外醜陋，是因為我們已經有伴了嗎？
——阿爾弗雷德・雅里，法國作家
You're looking exceptionally ugly tonight, Madam; is it because we have company?
—Alfred Jarry, French writer

要延長你的命，就少吃點。
——班傑明・富蘭克林，美國政治家
To lengthen thy life, lessen thy meals.
—Benjamin Franklin

我不知道她是否賢慧，但她很醜，不過有個女人在身邊就夠瞧的了。 ——海因里希·海涅，德國詩人

I do not know if she was virtuous, but she was ugly, and with a woman that is half the battle.

—Heinrich Heine, German poet

有些人不論到哪總是帶來歡笑，其他人則是離開後才會有歡笑。 ——奧斯卡·王爾德，愛爾蘭作家

Some cause happiness wherever they go; others whenever they go.

—Oscar Wilde

我發現只有一種方法可以顯瘦，跟胖子混在一起。 ——羅德尼·丹傑菲爾德，美國喜劇演員

I found there was only one way to look thin: Hang out with fat people.

—Rodney Dangerfield, American comedian

一個肥肚腩永遠無法孕育出好的想法。 ——聖耶柔米，古代西方教會聖經學者

A fat stomach never breeds fine thoughts.

—Saint Jerome

我去過這麼多次盲目約會，應該得到一隻導盲犬[28]。
—— 溫蒂·利布曼，美國喜劇演員
I've been on so many blind dates, I should get a free dog.
—Wendy Liebman, American comedian

噢，她是慾望的解藥。
—— 威廉·康格里弗，英國劇作家及詩人
O, she is the antidote to desire.
—William Congreve, English playwright and poet

美麗是膚淺的，但醜陋會深到骨子裡。 —— 桃樂絲·帕克，美國詩人
Beauty is only skin-deep, but ugly goes clean to the bone.
—Dorothy Parker, American poet

　　我們都曾是小孩，我們從小就被灌輸每個人都會有命中注定的另一半這樣的觀念。不論你碰巧長得多醜、多畸形，只要你內心是美麗的，就能找到真愛……

　　小孩就是這麼好騙。

　　目前的事實就是有很多人完全沒有會可約。在社會的邊緣形

---

[28] 因為是盲目（blind）約會，所以這邊的狗指導盲犬。盲目約會是一種約會型式，通常由親友介紹認識，初約會時雙方互不認識，但沒有相親這麼嚴肅認真。

成一股永遠孤單的蠢蛋次文化。既然他們沒有人可以約會，在徹底的孤寂之中，他們就讓自己耽溺在《魔獸世界》或編織迷你貓毛衣。不過在你開始同情他們之前，想想他們永遠也不會經歷的心痛以及他們銀行戶頭裡那些多出來的錢，再問問你自己：「到底誰才像是輸家？」

獨自一人！不論你喜不喜歡，獨處都會是你經常要面對的。
——蘇斯博士，美國著名童書作家、漫畫家

All alone! Whether you like it or not, alone is something you'll be quite a lot.
—Dr. Seuss

不要批評自慰。那是跟某個我愛的人的性愛。
——伍迪・艾倫，美國電影導演

Don't knock masturbation. It's sex with someone I love.
—Woody Allen

知識份子就是發現某件事比性愛還有趣的人。
——愛德嘉・華萊士，英國小說家

An intellectual is someone who has found something more interesting than sex.
—Edgar Wallace, British novelist

對我而言，愛自己很簡單，但對女士們來說就完全是另一回事了。——強尼‧維加斯，英國喜劇演員

It is easy for me to love myself, but for ladies to do it is another question altogether.

—Johnny Vegas, British comedian

我們有理由相信，男人一開始直立行走是為了要騰出雙手來自慰。——莉莉‧湯姆琳，美國女演員、作家

We have reason to believe that man first walked upright to free his hands for masturbation.

—Lily Tomlin

關於節育，我靠的是我的個性。
——米爾特‧艾貝爾，美國喜劇演員

For birth control, I rely on my personality.

—Milt Abel, American comedian

如果你不會太久，我會一輩子在這等你。
——奧斯卡‧王爾德，愛爾蘭作家

If you are not too long, I will wait here for you all my life.

—Oscar Wilde

最持久的愛情是那些再也不會回頭的愛。

—— 威廉‧薩默塞特‧毛姆，英國劇作家

The love that lasts the longest is the love that is never returned.

—W. Somerset Maugham, British playwright

第十七章
上床

　　雖然在沙灘上來個漫長的散步以及在浪漫的夜晚吟詩是很好，但對大部分精蟲衝腦的傢伙來說，他們只想進入最後一個階段而已。如果順著他們的意，多數的約會會直接從自我介紹跳到房間。這並不是說這些混球不想先了解妳，只是這樣做對於他們想要的結果其實沒有任何影響。當大部分的王八蛋把他們真正的意圖小心翼翼地隱藏起來時，有些好心人會揭露他們對於自己性事運氣不佳的真正感受。

「唯一一個為了上床等上一個月的理由，就是她的年紀是十七歲又十一個月。

——巴尼・史廷森，出自《老爸老媽的浪曼史》

The only reason to wait a month for sex is if she's seventeen years, eleven months old.

—Barney Stinson, *How I Met Your Mother*

在學校實施性教育是個不錯的想法，但我不認為小孩應該要有家庭作業。──比爾‧寇司比，美國諧星

Sex education may be a good idea in the schools, but I don't believe the kids should be given homework.

─Bill Cosby

女人比男人更具有通靈能力，她們是第一個知道你是不是想上床的人。──保羅‧羅德里奎，墨西哥喜劇演員與演員

Girls are much more psychic than guys. They're the first to know if you're going to get laid.

─Paul Rodriguez, Mexican comedian and actor

花錢買的性與免費的性最大差別在於，花錢買的性通常比較便宜。──布倫丹‧貝漢，愛爾蘭作家

The big difference between sex for money and sex for free is that sex for money usually costs a lot less.

─Brendan Behan, Irish author

兒子，女人就像啤酒。她們很好聞也很好看，你會踩過自己的老媽只為了得到一個女人！但你不會只停在一個女人身上。你還會想喝另一個女人！──荷馬‧J‧辛普森，出自《辛普森家庭》

Son, a woman is like a beer. They smell good, they look good, you'd step over your own mother just to get one! But you can't stop at one. You wanna drink another woman!

—Homer J. Simpson, *The Simpsons*

我把我貧乏的性生活歸咎於我媽。她唯一告訴過我的只有：「男人在上面，女人在下面。」這三年來，我跟我老公都睡上下鋪。

── 瓊·瑞佛斯，美國演員、電視節目主持人

I blame my mother for my poor sex life. All she told me was "The man goes on top and the woman underneath." For three years my husband and I slept in bunk beds.

—Joan Rivers

男人在十八歲達到他們的性顛峰，女人在三十五歲達到性顛峰。是不是會讓人覺得上帝在狠狠跟我們開玩笑？

── 麗塔·羅德納，美國女演員與喜劇演員。

Men reach their sexual peak at eighteen. Women reach theirs at thirty-five. Do you get the feeling that God is playing a practical joke?

—Rita Rudner, American actress and comedian

給我貞潔與節制，但不是現在！ ──聖奧古斯丁，羅馬帝國末期神學家

Give me chastity and continence, but not yet!

—Saint Augustine

表達感受是要看時間跟地點的，例如你的狗過世或是有人超你的車時。而你最不該展露激動情緒的地方就是臥室。因為沒什麼比無法控制的啜泣更讓人掃興的了，哪怕那是喜極而泣。

　　有些時候性就只是性。兩個人（有時更多人）同時覺得飢渴難耐並決定要解決這個問題。上帝保佑那些勇於承認這件事的人。

一天一高潮，醫生遠離我。
——梅・蕙絲，美國演員
An orgasm a day keeps the doctor away.
—Mae West

這是個適合非常緊身短褲的場合。
——布雷吉特・瓊斯，出自《BJ單身日記》
This is an occasion for genuinely tiny knickers.
—Bridget Jones, *Bridget Jones's Diary*

我付錢給她們不是為了上床，而是為了請她們離開。
——查理・辛，美國演員
I don't pay them for sex. I pay them to leave.
—Charlie Sheen

當你聽到女孩們說：「啊，老天，我昨晚真的喝得太醉了，我不該跟那傢伙上床的。」你知道嗎？我們可能是那個錯誤！
—— 塞斯，出自電影《男孩我最壞》

You know when you hear girls say, "Ah man, I was so shitfaced last night; I shouldn't have fucked that guy"? We could be that mistake!
—Seth, *Superbad*

一個男人可以跟任何一個女人快樂地在一起，只要他不愛她。
—— 奧斯卡·王爾德，愛爾蘭作家

A man can be happy with any woman as long as he does not love her.
—Oscar Wilde

我認為性是用錢可以買到的最美好、最自然、最有益健康的東西。—— 史提夫·馬丁，美國電影演員、喜劇演員

I believe that sex is one of the most beautiful, natural, wholesome things that money can buy.
—Steve Martin

一個硬挺的男人，值得去尋找。
—— 梅·蕙絲，美國演員

A hard man is good to find.
—Mae West

一般人的性生活跟看棒球賽非常像：一直坐在那兒等待著某件事發生，不時穿插短暫的刺激。當一切都結束時，你卻希望你待在家裡用電視看比賽就好。但有少數特定的人，他們的性生活則像是太陽馬戲團。在看過秀的好幾個星期後，你還是無法百分之百確定自己到底看了些什麼。

他們叫「狂野女孩」㉙而不叫「狂野女人」是有理由的。當女孩狂野時，她們會露出胸部；當女人狂野時，她們殺死男人並把小孩淹死在浴缸裡。
——路易斯‧C‧K，美國喜劇演員
There's a reason it's called "girls gone wild" and not "women gone wild." When girls go wild, they show their tits. When women go wild, they kill men and drown their kids in a tub.
—Louis C. K., American comedian

如果真的抽掉我的肋骨，我會在《兩小無猜》播出時，忙著吸我自己的老二而不是追求薇妮‧庫柏。另外，我也不會在舞台上吸別人的老二，我會吸我自己的。再說，當你可以吸自己的老二時，誰還會有空去殺小狗狗？明早我要打個電話給我的外科醫生。——瑪麗蓮‧曼森，美國搖滾音樂家

㉙ Girls gone wild 是一間出產色情影片的公司。

If I really got my ribs removed, I would have been busy sucking my own dick on *The Wonder Years* instead of chasing Winnie Cooper. Besides, I wouldn't have sucked other people's dicks on stage, either. I would have been sucking my own. Plus, who really has time to be killing puppies when you can be sucking your own dick? I think I'm gonna call the surgeon in the morning.

—Marilyn Manson, American rock musician

當局警告你性行為的危險時，有一個必須要學會的教訓，就是不要跟當局有性關係。

── 馬特・格朗寧，美國漫畫家與《辛普森家庭》的創作者

When the authorities warn you of the dangers of having sex, there is an important lesson to be learned. Do not have sex with the authorities.

—Matt Groening, American cartoonist and creator of *The Simpsons*

許多我的同行認為我是個古怪的雙性戀，就像我身上可能有一支氨填充的觸手一樣。那無所謂。

── 小勞勃道尼，美國演員

A lot of my peer group think I'm an eccentric bisexual, like I may even have an ammonia-filled tentacle somewhere on my body. That's okay.

—Robert Downey Jr., American actor

我的想法是，任何人的性生活如果被播放出來，都很難不驚世駭俗。——威廉·薩默塞特·毛姆，英國劇作家

My own belief is that there is hardly anyone whose sexual life, if it were broadcast, would not fill the world at large with surprise and horror.
—W. Somerset Maugham, British playwright

記住，如果你在完事後抽菸，那就是你做太快了。
——伍迪·艾倫，美國電影導演

Remember, if you smoke after sex, you're doing it too fast.
—Woody Allen

你要知道，當我恨你時，是因為我愛你愛到那熱情讓我的靈魂錯亂。——茉莉·德·萊斯皮納斯，18世紀法國名媛

You know that when I hate you, it is because I love you to a point of passion that unhinges my soul.
—Julie de Lespinasse, eighteenth-century French socialite

　　有一個鮮為人知吸引潛在伴侶的祕訣。你可以是世上最胖、最醜的怪物，但只要你把自己表現得像是上天賜給人類的禮物，還是有人會跟你上床。人們經常因為你難看的痘疤跟左肩上畸形的凸起而覺得掃興，再沒什麼比自信更能讓人燃起慾望的了。

所有人都能因為一頭濃密的頭髮感到充滿自信。但面對一個自信的光頭男人，那就是你未經琢磨的鑽石。

——拉里・大衛，美國喜劇演員

Anyone can be confident with a full head of hair. But a confident bald man—there's your diamond in the rough.

—Larry David, American comedian

一個男人可以是矮肥短外加禿頭，但如果他擁有熱情，女人就會喜歡他。——梅・蕙絲，美國演員

A man can be short and dumpy and getting bald, but if he has fire, women will like him.

—Mae West

跳舞是水平慾望的垂直表現。

——蕭伯納，愛爾蘭劇作家

Dancing: the vertical expression of a horizontal desire.

—George Bernard Shaw, Irish playwright and author

男人的年紀取決於他身邊女人的年紀。

——格魯喬・馬克斯，美國電影與喜劇演員

A man's only as old as the woman he feels.

—Groucho Marx

別人對你的看法不一定要成為你的現實。

—— 萊斯・布朗，美國勵志演說家

Other people's opinion of you does not have to become your reality.

—Les Brown, American motivational speaker

很少有什麼事會比在城裡一夜狂歡、醒來時發現有陌生人半裸著身體跟你躺在同一張床上感覺還要好。即使你已經不記得發生什麼事了，但照理說一切順利。不過這種揚揚得意的感覺，可能會在他或她翻身時讓你發現對方可能是、也可能不是人類的時候急踩煞車。雖然你的確可以挑個好一點的，但記住你自己也沒多好也是很重要的。到頭來，性就是性，即使在某些州可能會被認為是人獸交。

當狒狒想要回他的屁股時，你該做出什麼樣的表情？

—— 來源不詳

What are you gonna do for a face when the baboon wants his ass back?

—Unknown

他的大頭跟臉，醜到幾乎讓人覺得神魂顛倒。

—— 艾茵・蘭德，俄國小說家

He had a big head and a face so ugly it became almost fascinating.

—Ayn Rand, Russian novelist

美麗可能只在表層，而醜陋會明顯地從骨子展露出來。

　　——瑞德・福克斯，美國喜劇演員

Beauty may be skin deep, but ugly goes clear to the bone.

—Redd Foxx, American comedian

一開始我以為他在遛狗，後來我才發現那是他的女伴。

　　——庫朵斯・考文司基，出自電影《奇味吵翻天》

At first I thought he was walking a dog. Then I realized it was his date.

—Cuddles Kovinsky, *Polyester*

他擁有贏家般的笑容，但其他部分都是輸家。

　　——喬治・坎貝爾・史考特，美國演員

He had a winning smile, but everything else was a loser.

—George C. Scott, American actor

我從不忘記人的長相，但你的話，我會破例忘記一下。

　　——格魯喬・馬克斯，美國電影與喜劇演員

I never forget a face, but in your case I'll make an exception.

—Groucho Marx

我可以與妳共舞到牛群回家……重新考慮後，我寧可與牛共舞，然後妳回家。──格魯喬·馬克斯，美國電影與喜劇演員

I could dance with you until the cows come home ... on second thoughts, I'll dance with the cows and you go home.

―Groucho Marx

她酷似米洛的維納斯：很老、沒有牙齒，黃皮膚上還有白斑。──海因里希·海涅，德國詩人

She resembles the Venus de Milo: she is very old, has no teeth, and has white spots on her yellow skin.

―Heinrich Heine, German poet

上週我宣稱這個女人是我見過最醜的女人。在那之後她的姊姊就持續來拜訪我……現在我希望能撤回那項聲明。──馬克·吐溫，美國作家

Last week I stated this woman was the ugliest woman I had ever seen. I have since been visited by her sister ... and now wish to withdraw that statement.

―Mark Twain

　　有些幸運的傢伙只需要眨眨眼睛或撥個頭髮就可以吸引潛在追求者，不過我們大多數的人都必須經歷閒聊這段災難。只要你

可以講出一個完整句子及避免換氣過度，你也許就能體驗成功的感覺，但你的魅力與機智難免還是有發揮不了作用的時候。幸好，即使他或她對你沒那麼有興趣，只要你肯出擊，就會有回報。

妳很美麗，卻很空洞。
——安東尼·德·聖-艾修伯里，法國作家
You are beautiful, but you are empty.
—Antoine de Saint-Exupéry, French writer

沒有人比他這個欠缺基本禮貌的人還令人難以忍受。
——布萊恩特·H·麥吉爾，美國作家
No one is more insufferable than he who lacks basic courtesy.
—Bryant H. McGill, American author

以你的外表而言，你現在這樣算很好看了。
——蘇斯博士，美國著名童書作家、漫畫家
You're in pretty good shape for the shape you are in.
—Dr. Seuss

即使學過整頁的多音節詞彙，可能都無法像直接說某個女人是賤貨或某個男人是混蛋一樣有效地表達出那個概念。
——艾瑞克・伯恩，加拿大精神病學家

A whole page of learned polysyllables may not convey as much as the statement that a certain woman is a bitch, or that a certain man is a jerk.
—Eric Berne, Canadian psychiatrist

她是如此地純潔，摩西連她的雙腿膝蓋都打不開。
——瓊・瑞佛斯，美國演員、電視節目主持人

She's so pure; Moses couldn't even part her knees.
—Joan Rivers

或許你不會記得你在某個晚上表現得像個雜碎，但我們會。
——羅伯・羅倫克，職業酒保

If you act like an a**hole one night, (you) might not remember it. But we will.
—Rob Lorenc, professional bartender

我不太懂演戲，我只是個極有天分的騙子。
——小勞勃道尼，美國演員

I know very little about acting. I'm just an incredibly gifted faker.
—Robert Downey Jr., American actor

口頭避孕猜一個字：我要一個女生跟我上床，她說「不」。
——伍迪・艾倫，美國電影導演

A fast word about oral contraception. I asked a girl to go to bed with me and she said no.
—Woody Allen

你看起來就像是政府製造用來阻擋老二的巨大機器人。
——哥倫布，出自電影《屍樂園》

You're like a giant cock-blocking robot made by the government.
—Columbus, *Zombieland*

你知道女人想上床時的樣子嗎？我也不知道。
——德魯・加利，美國喜劇演員、演員與遊戲節目主持人

You know that look women get when they want sex? Me neither.
—Drew Carey, American comedian, actor, and game show host

　　男人會跟所有會動的東西做愛不是什麼祕密，但多數女人不懂的是，其實男人的標準比那還要低上許多。會動很好，但那不是必備條件。追求性愛時，男人降低標準的程度可說是沒有下限，尤其如果已經有一段時間沒做愛的話。雖然把男人歸類為豬再容易不過，但對於這種高尚的動物來說不太公平。稱男人為男人就已經夠侮辱人了。

我不是在親她，我只是在她嘴裡說悄悄話。

——奇可・馬克斯，美國演員，格魯喬・馬克斯的兄弟

I wasn't kissing her. I was whispering in her mouth.

—Chico Marx, American actor and brother of Groucho Marx

男人在女人身上第一個注意到的是她的眼睛。然後，當她的眼睛沒看到的時候，他們就會注意她的胸部。

——柯南・奧布萊恩，美國喜劇演員與夜間電視住持人

The first thing men notice about a woman is her eyes. Then, when her eyes aren't looking, they notice her breasts.

—Conan O'Brien, American comedian and late-night television host

我去酒吧時，不會找一個知道緬因州首府是哪的女人。

——戴維・布倫納，美國喜劇演員

When I go to a bar, I don't go looking for a girl who knows the capital of Maine.

—David Brenner, American comedian

一千個男人裡面只選得出一個領導者，因為其餘九百九十九個都跟隨女人。——格魯喬・馬克斯，美國電影與喜劇演員

Only one man in a thousand is a leader of men, the other 999 follow women.

—Groucho Marx

沒有哪個男人把手放在女孩的洋裝上，只是為了找一張借書證。

—— 瓊·瑞佛斯，美國演員、電視節目主持人

No man has ever put his hand up a girl's dress looking for a library card.

—Joan Rivers

你看，問題就在於上帝給了男人大腦跟老二，但血液的量卻只夠一次跑去一個地方。 —— 羅賓·威廉斯，美國演員

See, the problem is that God gives men a brain and a penis, and only enough blood to run one at a time.

—Robin Williams

我熱切地渴望回到子宮裡。任何人的子宮。

—— 伍迪·艾倫，美國電影導演

I have an intense desire to return to the womb. Anybody's.

—Woody Allen

　　當女孩長大時，母親通常會警告她們，男人只對一件事有興趣。她們沒被告知究竟是哪件事，只有說她們不該讓男人得逞。幾年之後她們終於搞清楚究竟是什麼事。雖然部分的女孩安分守己地聽從母親的建議，少數幾個卻屈服於誘惑，想一探究竟有什麼好大驚小怪。男人的確是只對性有興趣，但她們的母親卻忘了提一件重要的事，女人同樣有權利只對一件事有興趣。

為了避免被說是個賣弄風騷的人，她總是很容易屈服。

—— 查理，塔列蘭伯爵，法國外交官

In order to avoid being called a flirt, she always yielded easily.

—Charles, Count Talleyrand, French diplomat

如果所有參加哈佛－耶魯比賽的女孩們都首尾相連地躺在一塊，
我也不會太驚訝。—— 桃樂絲·帕克，美國詩人

If all the girls who attended the Harvard-Yale game were laid end to
end, I wouldn't be surprised.

—Dorothy Parker, American poet

妳就是兩腿開開來到這世上的，她們會用一個Y型棺材把妳送進
墳墓裡。—— 佛雷德利·拉斐爾，美國作家

You were born with your legs apart. They'll send you to the grave in a
Y-shaped coffin.

—Frederic Raphael, American writer

耶穌說：「當彼此相愛。」他沒說要愛全世界。

—— 德蕾莎修女

Jesus said, "Love one another."

He didn't say love the whole world.

—Mother Teresa

昨晚她擦了太多胭脂而穿太少衣服，女人絕望的時候就是那樣。

—— 奧斯卡·王爾德，愛爾蘭作家

She wore too much rouge last night and not quite enough clothes. That is always a sign of despair in a woman.

—Oscar Wilde

飢渴是不分性別的。

—— 藍迪·K·米爾荷蘭，美國漫畫家，最有名作品為網路漫畫《來點積極正面的》

Desperate is not a sexual preference.

—Randy K. Milholland, American cartoonist most famous for the webcomic, *Something Positive*

她就像違警罪法庭上的聖經，經常被輕吻，而親她的跟親聖經的差不多是同一類的人。 —— 羅伯遜·戴維斯，加拿大作家

She has been kissed as often as a police-court Bible, and by much the same class of people.

—Robertson Davies, Canadian author

那個女人會說八國語言，卻不會說任何一種語言的不。

—— 桃樂絲·帕克，美國詩人

That woman speaks eight languages and can't say no in any of them.

—Dorothy Parker, American poet

她坐過的大腿比用過的衛生棉還多。

　——華特・溫徹爾，美國專欄作家

She's been on more laps than a napkin.

—Walter Winchell, American columnist

我從沒想過會有這麼一天，看到女孩們現在被曬傷的地方。

　——威爾・羅傑斯，美國喜劇演員與演員

I never expected to see the day when girls would get sunburned in the places they now do.

—Will Rogers, American comedian and actor

　　直到最近，男人與女人可以盡情地與他們找到的伴侶發生不安全的性行為。當然，最糟的狀況就是結束後的接下來的幾週，尿尿都有灼熱感。如今，做愛比在你淘氣的部位塗滿蜂蜜再裸奔跑過熊的國度還要危險。至少你還有可能可以逃過熊爪的摧殘。

　　考慮到這一點，這個週末插上古老的電視遊樂器，享受一個人的美好時光或許是個明智的選擇。你的生殖器官會感謝你。

我在我的每部電影裡都有個戀愛對象：一把槍。

　——阿諾・史瓦辛格，美國演員，曾任加州州長

I have a love interest in every one of my films: a gun.

—Arnold Schwarzenegger

由愛故生憂，由愛故生怖；若離於愛者，無憂亦無怖。
—— 佛陀

He who loves fifty people has fifty woes; he who loves no one has no woes.
—Buddha

幹嘛結婚只折磨一個男人，我維持單身，就足以讓成千上萬的男人陷入悲慘的境地。—— 嘉莉‧斯諾，美國喜劇演員

Why get married and make one man miserable when I can stay single and make thousands miserable?
—Carrie Snow, American comedian

語言……創造出「寂寞」這個字表達單身的痛苦；而語言也創造出「獨處」這個字來表達單身的榮耀。—— 保羅‧田立克，德國哲學家

Language ... has created the word "loneliness" to express the pain of being alone. And it has created the word "solitude" to express the glory of being alone.
—Paul Tillich, German philosopher

女人就只是女人，但一支好雪茄卻是火辣的享受。
—— 魯德亞德‧吉卜林，生於孟買的英國作家

A woman is just a woman, but a good cigar is a smoke.
—Rudyard Kipling

我愛米老鼠勝過任何一個我認識的女人。

── 華特・迪士尼，美國著名電影製片人

I love Mickey Mouse more than any woman I have ever known.

─Walt Disney

如果你愛一樣東西，就放它自由。不過當它帶著皰疹回來時，不需要太驚訝。── 恰克・帕拉尼克，美國小說家

If you love something, set it free. Just don't be surprised if it comes back with herpes.

─Chuck Palahniuk, American novelist

第十八章
被甩

一直到最近，男人與女人在狀況差的時候，仍沒太多選擇。女人等待並希望可以活得比她們的伴侶久，同樣的，男人也希望另一半快點死，除此之外，雙方都別無它法。兩種性別都有的最普遍選項就是：忍耐並假裝一切都很好。當你寧可用嘴咬下自己的手，也不想跟這個人多相處一秒的時候，這些都不是什麼好選項。

直到甩人與離婚的想法獲得認可，我們才終於能夠隨心所欲。雖然沒人喜歡被甩，但被甩絕對比被枕頭悶死來得好。

對現在的年輕男女來說，被踢到一旁可說是人生必經儀式。它有助於塑造某種性格，讓你作好準備，掌控未來，勇於面對無法逃避的失意。而且如果你夠幸運，有一天，你甚至有權當甩人的那個。

雖然人真的不應該把快樂建築在別人的痛苦之上，但如果那些人活該的話，這句話就不適用。即使他們目前什麼也沒做錯，他們很可能終究有一天會犯錯。

所以不論你是在方程式的哪一邊，甩人的或被甩的，都可從這些苦澀、失戀的爛咖嘴吐出的缺德話得到慰藉。

我一直都覺得記憶渲染事實的方式很神奇。

—— 黛安‧索耶，美國新聞主播

I'm always fascinated by the way memory diffuses fact.

—Diane Sawyer, American news anchor

我從沒結過婚，但我都會宣稱我離婚了，好讓他們不會覺得我哪裡有問題。—— 伊蓮‧布斯勒，美國女演員與喜劇演員

I've never been married, but I tell people I'm divorced so they won't think something is wrong with me.

—Elayne Boosler, American actress and comedian

給我一個沒有愧疚感的女人，然後我會給你一個男人。

—— 埃麗卡‧容，美國作家

Show me a woman who doesn't feel guilty and I'll show you a man.

—Erica Jong, American author

為什麼你一定要跟她分手？當個男人，別再打給她就好了。

—— 喬伊，出自《六人行》

Why do you have to break up with her? Be a man. Just stop calling.

—Joey, *Friends*

憎恨是盲目的，愛情也是。——奧斯卡‧王爾德，愛爾蘭作家

Hatred is blind, as well as love.

—Oscar Wilde

有個很好的分手方式，但不包括便利貼。——凱莉，出自《慾望城市》

There is a good way to break up with someone and it doesn't include a Post-it.

—Carrie, *Sex and the City*

跟我的前妻一起出去很輕鬆，因為她已經知道我是個白癡。
——華倫‧湯瑪斯，美國喜劇演員

It's relaxing to go out with my exwife because she already knows I'm an idiot.

—Warren Thomas, American comedian

　　想到追求的過程會有多可怕，就能理解為什麼大部分的人寧可留在一段失敗的關係裡也不願冒著被甩的風險。當然，你們已不再相愛，也已經好幾個月沒一起睡覺，但如果你又要開始約會，你就慘了。

　　不論你多努力想維持現狀，有些時候你還是會經歷分手時冷漠無情的反手回擊。我可以告訴你，狀況並沒有聽起來的那麼糟，不過以下這些傢伙可不會同意。

再見，我要離開了，因為我覺得很無聊。 ——喬治‧山德斯，俄國演員
Goodbye. I am leaving because I am bored.
—George Sanders, Russian actor

不論妳是在第一次約會就跟他上床還是等到第十次，男人都可以
輕易地甩了妳。 ——莎曼珊，出自《慾望城市》
A guy can just as easily dump you if you fuck him on the first date as
he can if you wait until the tenth.
—Samantha, *Sex and the City*

你知道被拒絕最糟糕的事情是什麼嗎？就是不能控制。如果你可
以控制被甩的地點跟方式，看起來就不會那麼糟了。
——羅伯‧弗萊明，出自電影《失戀排行榜》
You know what is the worst thing about being rejected? The lack of
control. If I could only control the where and how of being dumped, it
wouldn't seem as bad.
—Rob Fleming, *High Fidelity*

妳的心就是我的皮納塔[30]。 ——恰克‧帕拉尼克，美國小說家
Your heart is my piñata.
—Chuck Palahniuk, American novelist

---

[30] 皮納塔是一種紙糊的容器，裡面裝滿玩具或糖果讓人用棍棒打擊，打破時玩具
或糖果就會掉出來。

女人或許可以假裝高潮，男人卻可以假裝整段關係。

——莎朗‧史東，美國女演員

Women might be able to fake orgasms, but men can fake whole relationships.

—Sharon Stone, American actress

　　有一個很常見的誤解是，提分手的人可能就是有問題的那一方。但這顯然是錯的。「是我的問題，不是你」這台詞就跟由小雞雞男人構成的社會所強調的「尺寸並不重要」一樣荒謬。如果你被甩了，保證其他人會認為你要不是做錯事，就是沒辦法把事情做對。

我永遠都會愛你在我心目中的假象。

——艾希莉‧布理恩特，美國漫畫家

I will always love the false image I had of you.

—Ashleigh Brilliant, American cartoonist

維繫一段關係並不容易。它就像是份全職工作，而我們也應該要把它視為全職工作來對待。如果你的男朋友或女朋友要離開你，他們應該要提早兩週通知，還應該要有遣散費，而且在他們離開之前，應該要替你找個臨時僱員。——鮑伯‧艾廷格，美國專欄作家

Relationships are hard. It's like a full-time job, and we should treat it like one. If your boyfriend or girlfriend wants to leave you, they should give you two weeks' notice. There should be severance pay, and before they leave you, they should have to find you a temp.

—Bob Ettinger, American columnist

很多好看的人很笨。有那麼多白癡看起來這麼好看，這件事超可怕的。——狄恩‧凱恩，美國演員

A lot of beautiful people are stupid. There are a tremendous number of idiots who look so good. It's frightening.

—Dean Cain, American actor

愛情是一種男人看事情完全與事實相反的狀態。

——弗里德里希‧尼采，德國哲學家

Love is a state in which a man sees things most decidedly as they are not.

—Friedrich Nietzsche

女人一旦把她的心交給你，你就再也無法擺脫她身體的其他部位了。——約翰‧凡布魯爵士，英國建築家

Once a woman has given you her heart, you can never get rid of the rest of her body.

—Sir John Vanbrugh, British architect

我怎麼會跟這奇怪的男人上床……顯然只有真愛可以合理解釋我為何如此缺乏品味。

── 瑪格麗特‧愛特伍，加拿大作家

How could I be sleeping with this peculiar man. ... Surely only true love could justify my lack of taste.

—Margaret Atwood, Canadian author

如果你們收藏的唱片種類大相逕庭，又或者，如果在派對上也不會彼此聊起你們最愛的電影，這樣還要假裝一段關係會有未來，其實一點好處也沒有。

── 羅伯‧弗萊明，出自電影《失戀排行榜》

It's no good pretending that any relationship has a future if your record collections disagree violently or if your favorite films wouldn't even speak to each other if they met at a party.

—Rob Fleming, *High Fidelity*

每當我看著妳，我都會有強烈的渴望想要獨自一人。

── 奧斯卡‧黎凡特，美國音樂家與演員

Every time I look at you, I get a fierce desire to be lonesome.

—Oscar Levant, American musician and actor

在經歷一次嚴重受傷的分手後，你很自然地會去反省這段關係，試圖找出哪裡出了錯。如果你想不起來任何不忠的例子或是明顯的錯誤，那麼你每週五花時間玩拼字遊戲及看《CSI犯罪現場》重播可能沒什麼幫助。

就像所有的事情一樣，如果你不努力保持新鮮有趣，關係就會開始變得無聊。不管是打扮好出去跳個舞，或是在電影院後面親熱，變化就是生活的情趣。不然你就會像這些可悲的傢伙一樣孤老終生。

偶爾外遇對婚姻是有益的。外遇可以增添情趣，讓婚姻不會變乏味……我應該要知道的。
——貝蒂・戴維斯，美國電影、電視、戲劇女演員

An affair now and then is good for a marriage. It adds spice, stops it from getting boring. ... I ought to know.
—Bette Davis

我的妻子瑪麗，跟我結婚四十七年了，我們不曾吵架吵到鬧離婚。想謀殺對方？有，但離婚，從來沒有。
——傑克・班尼，美國喜劇演員

My wife, Mary, and I have been married for forty-seven years and not once have we had an argument serious enough to consider divorce; murder, yes, but divorce, never.
—Jack Benny, American comedian

他的婚姻很幸福，但他老婆的不是。—— 維克多・伯治，丹麥喜劇演員

He was happily married—but his wife wasn't.

—Victor Borge, Danish comedian

男人應該要像面紙，柔軟、強韌，而且可用完即丟。
—— 雪兒，美國女演員、歌手

Men should be like Kleenex: soft, strong, and disposable.

—Cher

某種純真似乎是消逝了。嗯……新奇的要素已經不見一陣子了。
—— 查理・辛，美國演員

There's an innocence that has kind of gone away. Umm ... the novelty factor hasn't been there for a while.

—Charlie Sheen

我喜歡在一段不好的關係結束之後去購物。我不知道為什麼。我買一件新衣服，那確實可以讓我感覺好很多，它就是可以。有時候如果我看到一件真的很漂亮的衣服，我就會故意與某個人分手。—— 麗塔・羅德納，美國女演員與喜劇演員

I love to shop after a bad relationship. I don't know. I buy a new outfit and it makes me feel better. It just does. Sometimes if I see a really great outfit, I'll break up with someone on purpose.

—Rita Rudner, American actress and comedian

雖然沒有人願意相信他們的另一半有能力背叛，事實就是多數人確保有了B計畫以後，才會結束一段既存的關係。但奇怪的是，比起為了B計畫而離開我們的另一半，通常我們對踢爛B計畫的牙齒更有興趣。

除非你誤以為你的另一半已死，不然偷吃是沒有任何藉口的。除非，那個人真的超辣，或者你真的很醉，或者你只是那晚很無聊。進一步考慮之後，如果下面這些混蛋可以當成某種指標的話，那麼偷吃就完全可被接受。

告訴他，我真搞的太忙了，或者反過來說也行❸。
——桃樂絲‧帕克，美國詩人
Tell him I've been too fucking busy—or vice versa.
—Dorothy Parker, American poet

妳的忠誠觀就是同一時間床上只會有一個男人。
——佛雷德利‧拉斐爾，美國作家
Your idea of fidelity is not having more than one man in bed at the same time.
—Frederic Raphael, American writer

❸ 這句話要反過來說就是 Tell him I'm too busy fucking，忙著與別人上床。

為什麼我跟她在一起？因為她讓我想起妳。事實上，她比妳更能讓我想起妳！——格魯喬・馬克斯，美國電影與喜劇演員

Why was I with her? She reminds me of you. In fact, she reminds me more of you than you do!

—Groucho Marx

開放的婚姻是宇宙要告訴你：你該離婚了。

——安・蘭德斯，美國專欄作家

An open marriage is nature's way of telling you that you need a divorce.

—Ann Landers

我愛同一個女人已經四十九年了。如果我老婆發現這件事，她會殺了我的！——漢尼・楊曼，英國喜劇演員

I've been in love with the same woman for forty-nine years. If my wife ever finds out, she'll kill me!

—Henny Youngman, British comedian

一個男人可以四處上床而沒有任何問題，但如果一個女人犯了十九或二十個錯，她就成了蕩婦。

——瓊・瑞佛斯，美國演員、電視節目主持人

A man can sleep around no questions asked, but if a woman makes nineteen or twenty mistakes, she's a tramp. 　　　　—Joan Rivers

別讓一個男人猜太久，他絕對會去別處尋找答案。

——梅・蕙絲，美國演員

Don't keep a man guessing too long—he's sure to find the answer somewhere else.

—Mae West

有婦之夫出軌時，他真的是個好情人。

——瑪麗蓮・夢露

Husbands are chiefly good lovers when they are betraying their wives.

—Marilyn Monroe

我們的婚姻裡有三個人，所以實在是有點擠。

——黛安娜王妃。

There were three of us in this marriage, so it was a bit crowded.

—Princess Diana

有個狀況我會直接分手解決，就是如果她逮到我跟另一個女人在一起。我不會忍受這件事。

——史提夫・馬丁，美國電影演員、喜劇演員

There is one thing I would break up over, and that is if she caught me with another woman. I won't stand for that.

—Steve Martin

我終於開始跟某人發生關係，然後我就被解雇了。
——湯米‧柯克，美國演員

Eventually I became involved with somebody, and I was fired.
—Tommy Kirk, American actor

如果妳嫁給一個曾背叛妻子的男人，那麼妳就是嫁給一個會背叛妳的男人。——安‧蘭德斯，美國專欄作家

If you marry a man who cheats on his wife, you'll be married to a man who cheats on his wife.
—Ann Landers

　　雖然被男朋友或女朋友甩掉可能很像世界末日，至少你還能保有你的房子。但如果你犯下了先結婚的重大錯誤，可能就沒那麼幸運了。

　　記不記得，過去每一段感情分手後，都會有一箱裝滿你重要的東西放了下來，就像得到安慰獎一樣？嗯，離婚就像那樣，不過你得把箱子換成信封，而你的東西代換成一疊清單，詳細列出你現在欠世上最恨你的人多少錢。

任何一樁失敗婚姻最明顯的解釋就是兩個人已到了水火不容的地步；意即，一個是男人，另一個則是女人。
——安娜‧昆德倫，美國專欄作家

The clearest explanation for the failure of any marriage is that the two

people are incompatible; that is, one is male and the other female.
—Anna Quindlen, American columnist

我從未恨一個男人恨到把鑽石還給他。
——莎莎‧嘉寶，匈牙利裔美國演員
I never hated a man enough to give his diamonds back.
—Zsa Zsa Gabor

贍養費就像是買燕麥給一匹死馬。 ——亞瑟‧貝爾，美國記者
Alimony is like buying oats for a dead horse.
—Arthur Baer, American journalist

贍養費是快樂付給惡魔的贖金。 ——H‧L‧曼肯，美國記者
Alimony—the ransom that the happy pay to the devil.
—H. L. Mencken, American journalist

我不認為我會再結婚。我只會找一個我不喜歡的女人並給她一棟
房子。 ——路易斯‧格里薩德，美國喜劇演員
I don't think I'll get married again. I'll just find a woman I don't like
and give her a house.
—Lewis Grizzard, American comedian

每當我跟一個男人約會，我就會想，這個會是我希望我的孩子跟他共度週末的男人嗎？

——麗塔‧羅德納，美國女演員與喜劇演員

Whenever I date a guy, I think, Is this the man I want my children to spend their weekends with?

—Rita Rudner, American actress and comedian

啊，是的，離婚……在拉丁文裡，這個字的意思是透過男人的錢包扯下他的生殖器。

——羅賓‧威廉斯，美國演員

Ah, yes, divorce ... from the Latin word meaning to rip out a man's genitals through his wallet.

—Robin Williams

好一段時間，我們在商量是要渡個假還是離婚。後來我們都同意，去百慕達旅行，大不了兩個星期內就結束了，但離婚是可以一輩子擁有的。

——伍迪‧艾倫，美國電影導演

For a while we pondered whether to take a vacation or get a divorce. We decided that a trip to Bermuda is over in two weeks, but a divorce is something you always have.

—Woody Allen

我是個了不起的家管。每次我離開一個男人，我都能保有他的房子❸。——莎莎‧嘉寶，匈牙利裔美國演員

I am a marvelous housekeeper. Every time I leave a man I keep his house.
—Zsa Zsa Gabor

在好萊塢，如果一段婚姻可以維持比牛奶的效期限還久，就是成功的婚姻了。——麗塔‧羅德納，美國女演員與喜劇演員

In Hollywood a marriage is a success if it outlasts milk.
—Rita Rudner, American actress and comedian

　　你以為你已經遇到了此生的摯愛，但當你忙著替未出世的孩子命名時，她正忙著思考要裝死逃過這一切。不過別因此而沮喪，事情總有可能會更糟。例如，她大可繼續跟你約會。
　　大體而言，只要想想所有你可以重拾的美好事物，被甩可能會是一段關係中最棒的一件事。你可以在外面逗留到很晚，或是在洗澡的時候喝啤酒，你甚至可以依照大自然的本意讓馬桶蓋保持掀起來的樣子！到頭來，還是單身比較好。

當一個男人跟你老婆偷情時，沒有比讓他把她留在身邊更好的復仇了。——薩卡‧圭特瑞，演員與導演

---

❸ 這裡玩弄了 housekeeper（家管）與 keep house 的雙關。

When a man steals your wife, there is no better revenge than to let him keep her.

—Sacha Guitry, actor and director

一段良好的關係就像煙火：喧囂、易爆，而且握太久可能會讓你重傷。── 傑夫・雅克，網路漫畫《可疑內容》的製作人

A good relationship is like fireworks: loud, explosive, and liable to maim you if you hold on too long.

—Jeph Jacques, producer of the webcomic *Questionable Content*

我跟某個人分手了，她說：「你再也找不到像我一樣的人了。」而我卻想著：「希望不要！」有誰會在結束一段爛關係時說：「順便問一下，妳有雙胞胎姊妹嗎？」── 拉里・米勒，美國演員

I broke up with someone, and she said, "You'll never find anyone like me again." And I'm thinking, "I hope not!" Does anybody end a bad relationship and say, "By the way, do you have a twin?"

—Larry Miller, American actor

後來妳才明白，就算跟一個男人在一起覺得很幸福，也不一定可以證明妳愛他。── 瑪格麗特・莒哈絲，法國作家

It's afterward you realize that the feeling of happiness you had with a

man didn't necessarily prove that you loved him.
—Marguerite Duras, French writer

想要浪漫的愛情一直延續下去，最終一定搞砸。
—— 奧斯卡‧王爾德，愛爾蘭作家
They spoil every romance by trying to make it last forever.
—Oscar Wilde

　　每個人處理分手的方式不太一樣。有些人坐在家裡對著茶杯哭，再喝下自己的眼淚；有些人選擇更有效率的方式應對，比如用藥物或酒精來麻痺他們的痛苦。的確，這可能沒辦法解決任何問題，但至少他們會遇見一堆比他們更可悲的人。

　　無論你選擇的應對機制是什麼，重要的是，要回到約會的世界裡並提醒自己：不是每個人都是說謊、偷吃的爛貨，只是絕大多數的人都是而已。

悲傷時扯自己的頭髮是愚蠢的，彷彿痛苦會因為禿頭減少似的。
—— 西塞羅，古羅馬哲學家
It is foolish to tear one's hair in grief, as though sorrow would be made less by baldness.
—Cicero, Roman philosopher

終於發現單身可以如此不寂寞，這是多麼迷人的驚喜。

──艾倫‧鮑絲汀，美國女演員

What a lovely surprise to finally discover how unlonely being alone can be.
—Ellen Burstyn, American actress

我愛男人，即使他們都是說謊、偷吃的爛人。

──葛妮絲‧派特洛，美國女演員

I love men, even though they're lying, cheating scumbags.
—Gwyneth Paltrow, American actress

好女人的供應量遠超過配得上她們的男人數量。

──羅伯特‧格雷夫斯，英國詩人與小說家

The supply of good women far exceeds that of the men who deserve them.
—Robert Graves, British poet and novelist

或許我會找一個比妳好的女孩；擁有同樣聰明的眼神，但親切多了；有一樣柔軟的雙唇，但更真誠；而且我敢說，她一定比妳更好。 ──魯伯特‧布魯克，英國詩人，出自「契爾騰家族」

And I shall find some girl perhaps, and a better one than you, With eyes as wise, but kindlier, and lips as soft, but true, and I daresay she will do.
—Rupert Brooke, British poet, "The Chilterns"

第十九章
婚姻

你跟一個人交往久到你忘了喜歡對方的什麼，這時你有兩個選項：放棄或結婚。人們可能會認為前者是再明顯不過的選擇，但其實有許多變數需要考量。

首先最重要的就是年紀。二十多歲時，汰舊換新或許可以是你的選項，但如果你指關節上的毛已經長得比你頭上的毛還多，前景就沒那麼看好。第二，雖然你可能已不再喜歡你的伴侶，但你有「不喜歡」他或她嗎？有不少成功的婚姻是建立在相敬如「冰」之上，這事實也許會讓你吃驚。最後，你有其他更好的利用時間計畫嗎？

的確，這一連串假設的情境描繪了一個相當無情殘忍的婚姻前景，但如果我把婚姻描繪成一輩子的愛斯基摩親吻[33]及在床上吃早餐，那就是在幫倒忙了。就像所有已婚的人會告訴你，婚姻生活有它的好處，但實在不多。

你可以相信我說的，有許多比我有見識的討厭鬼可以證實婚姻生活的磨練與苦難。

---

[33] 愛斯基摩親吻是一種用自己的鼻尖去碰觸對方鼻尖的親吻方式。

婚姻是一場法律或宗教的儀式，儀式中兩個不同性別的人鄭重同意騷擾並監視對方九十九年，或直到他們加入死亡的行列。

——艾爾伯特·哈伯德，美國作家

Marriage: A legal or religious ceremony by which two persons of the opposite sex solemnly agree to harass and spy on each other for ninety-nine years, or until death do them join.

—Elbert Hubbard, American writer

妳就是我們的小孩這麼醜的原因。

——格魯喬·馬克斯，美國電影與喜劇演員

You're the reason our kids are so ugly.

—Groucho Marx

單身漢比已婚男人更了解女人；若非如此，他們也會結婚。

——H·L·曼肯，美國記者

Bachelors know more about women than married men; if they didn't, they'd be married, too.

—H. L. Mencken, American journalist

婚姻美滿的祕訣仍是個祕密。 ——漢尼·楊曼，英國喜劇演員

The secret of a happy marriage remains a secret.

—Henny Youngman, British comedian

我們會有成千上萬個機會遇見漂亮的姑娘，但她們全被結婚這個想法沖昏頭，還把矜持拋到腦後。

—— 傑瑞米・格雷，出自電影《婚禮終結者》

We are gonna have tons and tons of opportunities to meet gorgeous ladies that get so aroused by the thought of marriage that they'll throw their inhibitions to the wind.

—Jeremy Grey, *Wedding Crashers*

穿過耳洞的男人對婚姻的準備更充分，他們已經經歷過痛苦及買珠寶。 —— 麗塔・羅德納，美國女演員與喜劇演員

Men who have pierced ears are better prepared for marriage. They've experienced pain and bought jewelry.

—Rita Rudner, American actress and comedian

一個戀愛中的男人直到結婚時才會完整，然後，他就完了。

—— 莎莎・嘉寶，匈牙利裔美國演員

A man in love is incomplete until he has married. Then he's finished.

—Zsa Zsa Gabor

如果一個已婚男人喝的威士忌比他單身時所喝的品質還糟，他就是不快樂。 —— H・L・曼肯，美國記者

No married man is genuinely happy if he has to drink worse whisky than he used to drink when he was single.

—H. L. Mencken, American journalist

　　既然每年都有成千上萬的人結婚，按理說，這項傳統一定有
什麼實質好處。一項針對此事的調查結果顯示：你付的稅會比較
少。

　　婚姻生活中還有幾件小小的邊際效益，像是你可以在另一個
人面前放屁而不用道歉，或是隨時可以開上共乘車道。但很多時
候，婚姻就像自己一個人玩「餵食小河馬」的玩具一樣無趣。這
可能解釋了為什麼那麼多人強烈反對婚姻。

據說「我是」是英語裡最短的句子。那有沒有可能「我願意」是
最長的句子？

　　——喬治·卡林，美國喜劇演員

I am is reportedly the shortest sentence in the English language. Could
it be that I do is the longest sentence?

—George Carlin, American comedian

我是由法官證婚，我應該要求有陪審團。

　　——格魯喬·馬克斯，美國電影與喜劇演員

I was married by a judge. I should have asked for a jury.

—Groucho Marx

是我的妻子讓我有了信仰。因為娶了她之後，我才相信有地獄存在。——哈爾·洛屈，美國導演

My wife converted me to religion. I never believed in hell until I married her.

—Hal Roach, American director

我太太講話有點障礙，偶爾她會停下來呼吸。
——吉米·杜蘭特，美國演員與音樂家

My wife has a slight impediment in her speech—every now and then she stops to breathe.

—Jimmy Durante, American actor and musician

當一個男人替他老婆開車門時，要不這是輛新車，要不這是個新老婆。——菲利普親王，英國女王伊莉莎白二世夫婿

When a man opens the car door for his wife, it's either a new car or a new wife.

—Prince Philip

一個男人的妻子對丈夫的權力比州政府還多。
——拉爾夫·沃爾多·愛默生，美國文學家。

A man's wife has more power over him than the state has.

—Ralph Waldo Emerson

關於結婚，的確有些事困擾著我……像是擁有一個丈夫。

——羅斯安妮‧巴爾，美國女演員、作家、導演。

Some stuff does bother me about being married ... like having a husband.

—Roseanne Barr

悲劇並不是愛無法持續，而是那種持續不斷的愛。

——雪莉‧海札德，澳洲作家。

The tragedy is not that love doesn't last. The tragedy is the love that lasts.

—Shirley Hazzard, Australian author

我太尊重女人了，所以無法娶她。

——席維斯‧史特龍，美國演員。

I respect a woman too much to marry her.

—Sylvester Stallone, American actor

對我而言，女人就像大象，好看，但我不會想擁有。

——W‧C‧菲爾茲，美國喜劇演員

Women are like elephants to me: nice to look at, but I wouldn't want to own one.

—W. C. Fields, American comedian

如果你曾經咬一口三明治然後想說：「老天，這是我吃過最難吃的三明治了，我一定要跟每個我認識的人分享這可怕的經驗！」那你對於婚姻生活就已經有點概念了。

　　若以我們認知的婚姻為基礎，合理的結論應該是婚姻已不存在，但婚姻制度卻前所未有的強健，甚至同志平權社運人士不惜跟他們的異性戀朋友們一樣悲慘，只為了爭取婚姻而奮鬥不懈。儘管沒人可以確定為什麼我們會湧向婚姻制度，但幾個有遠見的人們確實是盡了他們最大的努力試著引領我們遠離婚姻。

孤獨的恐懼遠超過束縛的恐懼，所以我們選擇結婚。
──西里爾·康諾利，英國作家

The dread of loneliness is greater than the dread of bondage, so we get married.
─Cyril Connolly, British author

任何讀了婚約之後還會想要踏進婚姻的聰明女人，都活該要去承擔所有後果。
──伊莎朵拉·鄧肯，美國舞蹈家

Any intelligent woman who reads the marriage contract, and then goes into it, deserves all the consequences.
─Isadora Duncan, American dancer

愛情只是暫時的瘋狂，可被婚姻治癒。

—— 安布羅斯‧比爾斯，美國作家與《魔鬼辭典》的作者

Love is temporary insanity curable by marriage.

—Ambrose Bierce, American writer and author of *The Devil's Dictionary*

戀愛中的人跑去結婚，真是蠢到極點。

—— 蕭伯納，愛爾蘭劇作家與作家

It is most unwise for people in love to marry.

—George Bernard Shaw, Irish playwright and author

婚禮上演奏的音樂，總讓我想起那些即將奔赴沙場的士兵。

—— 海因里希‧海涅，德國詩人

Music played at weddings always reminds me of the music played for soldiers before they go into battle.

—Heinrich Heine, German poet

我寧可當一個單身乞丐，也不願當結婚的女皇。

—— 英國女王伊麗莎白一世，終生未婚

I would rather be a beggar and single than a queen and married.

—Elizabeth I

婚姻沒有任何保障。如果你尋求的是這個，去跟汽車電池一起生活吧。── 爾瑪·龐貝克，美國幽默作家

Marriage has no guarantees. If that's what you're looking for, go live with a car battery.

—Erma Bombeck, American humorist

為了性而結婚，就像是為了免費花生而去買一架波音747。
── 傑夫·法克斯渥西，美國喜劇演員

Getting married for sex is like buying a 747 for the free peanuts.

—Jeff Foxworthy, American comedian

結婚過後，丈夫與妻子就成了硬幣的兩面，他們無法面對彼此，卻仍然在一起。── 海門特·喬西，印度傳播學教授

After marriage, husband and wife become two sides of a coin; they just can't face each other, but still they stay together.

—Hemant Joshi, Indian communications professor

　　雖然的確有近半的婚姻以失敗告終，但那也表示有過半的已婚人口可能是幸福的。從中扣掉約百分之七十五的人，他們只是拖在那期待婚姻會有改善，還是有不少人與另一半的相處並不那麼悲慘。雖然這不是有史以來最令人振奮的統計數據（也不是最正確的），但知道還有幾十對夫婦真正適合彼此，仍令人欣慰。

一個女人值得擁有的最佳丈夫就是考古學家。她越老，他就對她越有興趣。

—— 阿嘉莎・克莉絲蒂，英國推理小說家

An archaeologist is the best husband a woman can have. The older she gets, the more interested he is in her.

—Agatha Christie

我從未對我的妻子不忠，因為我真的很喜歡我的房子。

—— 鮑伯・孟克豪斯，英國喜劇演員與演員

I'd never be unfaithful to my wife for the reason that I love my house very much.

—Bob Monkhouse, British comedian and actor

有些人問我維持婚姻長久的祕訣。我們一週會花點時間去兩次餐廳，來一點燭光、晚餐、輕柔的音樂及跳舞。她星期二去；我星期五去。

—— 漢尼・楊曼，英國喜劇演員

Some people ask the secret of our long marriage. We take time to go to a restaurant two times a week. A little candlelight, dinner, soft music, and dancing. She goes Tuesdays; I go Fridays.

—Henny Youngman, British comedian

要讓人妻保持愉悅只需要兩件事：一是讓她認為她可以隨心所欲，另一件就是讓她隨心所欲。 —— 林登・B・詹森，美國第36任總統

Only two things are necessary to keep one's wife happy. One is to let her think she is having her own way, and the other is to let her have it.
—Lyndon B. Johnson

我是在婚姻裡首次領略非暴力抗爭的概念。 —— 聖雄甘地，帶領印度脫離英國殖民的民族領袖

I first learned the concepts of nonviolence in my marriage.
—Mahatma Gandhi

你認為的浪漫，就是在遠離我的臉的地方打開汽水罐。 —— 羅斯安妮・巴爾，美國女演員、作家、導演

Your idea of romance is popping the can away from my face.
—Roseanne Barr

　　由於童年時接觸太多童話故事，我們很多人在成長過程中因而認定我們最終會與王子或公主結婚，並從此過著幸福快樂的日子。隨著時間過去，我們決定可以屈就於明星或是運動員；最後我們會把期望值降到任何一個擁有大學學歷及擁有一口健康漂亮恆齒的人。如果我們的父母讀給我們聽的是分類廣告而不是童話故事，我們對無法避免的命運，也許可以有更充足的心理準備。

很有趣的是，一個男人在世上沒什麼事好操心的時候，他就會去結婚。——羅伯特‧佛洛斯特，美國詩人，四度獲普立茲獎

It's a funny thing that when a man hasn't anything on earth to worry about, he goes off and gets married.

—Robert Frost

無論如何都要結婚。如果你娶了一個好老婆，你會很快樂；如果你娶了一個壞老婆，你會成為哲學家。——蘇格拉底，古希臘哲學家

By all means marry; if you get a good wife, you'll be happy; if you get a bad one, you'll become a philosopher.

—Socrates

身為金髮女孩是一件很棒的事。當人們對妳沒什麼期望時，妳很容易就可以讓他們驚訝。

——潘蜜拉‧安德森，美國女演員與模特兒

It is great to be a blonde. With low expectations it's very easy to surprise people.

—Pamela Anderson, American actress and model

所有人都知道男人總是結得了婚，不論他是一○二歲、一文不值還是喪失所有身體功能。總會有些女人願意在這些男人身上賭一把。——艾咪‧范德比爾特，美國作家與禮儀權威

Everyone knows that a man can always marry even if he reaches 102, is penniless, and has all his faculties gone. There is always some woman willing to take a chance on him.

—Amy Vanderbilt, American author and authority on etiquette

我有我的標準。雖然可能很低，但我還是有我的標準。
—— 貝蒂·蜜勒，美國名歌手，諧星

I have my standards. They may be low, but I have them.

—Bette Midler

交往與婚姻的差異，就像是種子目錄圖片與真正長出來的差別。
—— 詹姆斯·沃頓，美國國會議員

The difference between courtship and marriage is the difference between the pictures in a seed catalog and what comes up.

—James Wharton, U.S. congressman

就像是跟一隻奶油球火雞相擁。
—— 傑夫·法克斯渥西，美國喜劇演員

It's like cuddling with a Butterball turkey.

—Jeff Foxworthy, American comedian

在每個成功男人的背後，都有一個驚訝的女人。

——瑪麗詠‧皮爾森，加拿大第 14 任總理之妻

Behind every great man, there is a surprised woman.

—Maryon Pearson, wife of the 14th Canadian prime minister

愛情並不是找到一個完美的人，而是把一個不完美的人視為完美。——山姆‧金恩，美國作家與教授

Love isn't finding a perfect person. It's seeing an imperfect person perfectly.

—Sam Keen, American author and professor

　　健康婚姻的祕訣不是信任或理解，也不是妥協跟誠實。而是操弄。

　　從你說「我願意」的那一刻起，直到你們其中一個死掉或是你們厭倦彼此為止，你都得跟這個人在一起。唯一能將這樣的狀況變得比較能忍受的方法，就是把他或她塑造成你心目中理想配偶的模樣。雖然你也可以坐下來把你們的問題討論清楚，但透過微妙的背叛還是比較好的方式。如果你做得夠漂亮，你的配偶甚至不會意識到你做了什麼事。

讓大部分丈夫去做某件事的最好方式就是告訴他們，他們可能年紀太大了，不適合做那件事。 ──安妮‧班克勞馥，美國女演員

The best way to get most husbands to do something is to suggest that perhaps they're too old to do it.

──Anne Bancroft, American actress

誠實是一段關係的關鍵。如果你可以裝誠實，你就贏了。

──理查‧傑尼，美國喜劇演員與演員

Honesty is the key to a relationship. If you can fake that, you're in.

──Richard Jeni, American comedian and actor

當你看到一對夫婦沿著街走來，走在前面三步併兩步的就是氣呼呼的那一個。

──海倫‧羅蘭德，美國記者

When you see a married couple coming down the street, the one who is two or three steps ahead is the one that's mad.

──Helen Rowland, American journalist

丈夫就是情人褪去激情之後剩餘的部分。

──海倫‧羅蘭德，美國記者

A husband is what is left of the lover after the nerve is extracted.

──Helen Rowland, American journalist

只有在男人還是嬰兒時，女人才能真正成功地改變一個男人。
—— 娜妲麗・華，美國電影、電視演員，《西城故事》是代表作

The only time a woman really succeeds in changing a man is when he is a baby.
—Natalie Wood

我喜愛結婚。找到那個你想煩他一輩子的人，真的很棒。
—— 麗塔・羅德納，美國女演員與喜劇演員

I love being married. It's so great to find that one special person you want to annoy for the rest of your life.
—Rita Rudner, American actress and comedian

  儘管婚姻的一開始是興奮地結合辦家家酒與研究你們可以在多少地方舒服地做愛這兩件事，但那段蜜月期一般在七十二小時之內就會完結。然後呢？

  雖然有些夫妻試圖用一些聰明的方式來增加變化，例如生小孩或是有趣的扮裝，但最好的方式還是坦然接受那無法避免的不足。知道每個星期二是肉卷之夜以及每個星期四你都會玩黑白棋，確實很讓人安心。

  我媽曾經告訴我，如果一對已婚夫婦在新婚的第一年裡，每一次做愛就把一美分放進罐子裡，一年後每做一次愛就從罐裡拿出一

美分，他們永遠也拿不完罐裡的硬幣。

—— 亞米斯德・莫平，美國作家

My mother once told me that if a married couple puts a penny in a pot for every time they make love in the first year, and takes a penny out every time after that, they'll never get all the pennies out of the pot.

—Armistead Maupin, American author

你知道當你晚上回到家，面對的是一個只給你少許愛意、少許熱情、少許溫柔的女人時代表什麼嗎？代表你走錯房子了。

—— 漢尼・楊曼，英國喜劇演員

Do you know what it means to come home at night to a woman who'll give you a little love, a little affection, a little tenderness? It means you're in the wrong house.

—Henny Youngman, British comedian

女人講話是因為她們想講話，而男人只在受到外力驅使時才講話，例如，找不到任何乾淨襪子的時候。

—— 琴・柯爾，美國作家與劇作家

Women speak because they wish to speak, whereas a man speaks only when driven to speech by something outside himself—like, for instance, he can't find any clean socks.

—Jean Kerr, American author and playwright

我老婆跟我試過要一起吃早餐，但我們後來必須停止這樣，不然我們的婚姻會完蛋。 ——溫斯頓・邱吉爾，前英國首相

My wife and I tried to breakfast together, but we had to stop or our marriage would have been wrecked.

—Winston Churchill

結婚很像是泡進一缸熱水裡。你習慣之後，水就沒那麼熱了。
——米妮・波爾，美國女演員

Getting married is a lot like getting into a tub of hot water. After you get used to it, it ain't so hot.

—Minnie Pearl, American actress

我嫁的人比我低一等，所有的女人都一樣。
——南茜・阿斯特，英國政治家

I married beneath me; all women do.

—Nancy Astor, British politician

女人所承受的非自願性愛總量中，婚姻裡占的比例可能比賣淫還多。 ——伯特蘭・羅素，英國哲學家

The total amount of undesired sex endured by women is probably greater in marriage than in prostitution.

—Bertrand Russell, British philosopher

後記

讀完這本貫穿歷史的名人王八蛋們提及人生要事的概略，你大概已經能得出一些結論：

- 混蛋總是喜歡聽自己講話；
- 地球會耗盡許多東西：樹木、石油、可呼吸的空氣，但混蛋永遠不會少。

第一個是已知的事實。你只要跑一趟當地的酒吧，甚至連乳臭未乾的小王八蛋都很樂意拿各種事開講，從總統幹得有多爛講到治不好的疹子有多可怕，講到你耳朵爛掉。

儘管第二個觀察結果乍聽之下，可能會讓人覺得有點沮喪，但其實它是個你能接受的事實。起初你可能還會想，也許有一天王八蛋們會因為選擇性育種或強烈的催眠暗示而被淘汰，但面對並接受消滅他們是無望的這個事實時候到了。而且，現在你應該也已經意識到，其實這不一定是壞事。

想想看，歷史上的爛人已經幫了你一個大忙。首先，他們讓你看起來像是個全能的大好人；而且，如果你早上買咖啡時排在一個混蛋後面，很有可能咖啡師會特別小心煮好你點的咖啡；最後，我們不得不老實承認，那些王八蛋就是有種把你只敢放在心裡想、卻不敢說出來的話講出來。光是這點，我們就欠他們一個感謝。

所以在我們結束探索王八蛋的各個面向之前，我想再給你最後幾則來自於歷史上偉大人物們的經典省思。畢竟，有誰可以比他們講得更好？

只有兩件事可能是沒有極限的：宇宙及人類的愚蠢。不過前者我還不太敢確定。—— 阿爾伯特‧愛因斯坦，物理哲學家

Only two things are infinite, the universe and human stupidity, and I'm not sure about the former.

—Albert Einstein

你怎麼稱呼愛、恨、仁慈、復仇、人性、寬大、原諒？它們是來自於同一個動機的不同結果，那個動機就是：自我肯定的必要性。—— 馬克‧吐溫，美國作家

What do you call love, hate, charity, revenge, humanity, magnanimity, forgiveness? Different results of the one master impulse: the necessity of securing one's self-approval.

—Mark Twain

他能用最多的話語來闡述任何人說過、最微不足道的觀點。
—— 亞伯拉罕‧林肯，美國第 16 任總統

He can compress the most words into the smallest idea of any man I know.

—Abraham Lincoln

你只能年輕一次，但你永遠都可以不成熟。

——戴夫・貝瑞，美國作家與專欄作家

You can only be young once. But you can always be immature.

—Dave Barry, American author and columnist

我們必須嘲笑別人才能避免為他哭泣。

——拿破崙，法國政治家

We must laugh at man to avoid crying for him.

—Napoleon Bonaparte

沒有人是完美的。好吧，曾經有一個完美的傢伙，但我們殺了他……。——克里斯多福・摩爾，美國作家

Nobody's perfect. Well, there was this one guy, but we killed him. ...

—Christopher Moore, American author

沒話說，也克制自己閉嘴，避免證實這個客觀事實的人，我獻上無上祝福。——喬治・艾略特，英國小說家

Blessed is the man who, having nothing to say, abstains from giving us wordy evidence of the fact.

—George Elliot, British novelist

我割到自己的手指是悲劇，而你跌入下水道溺斃可就是喜劇了。

——梅爾·布魯克斯，美國喜劇演員、導演

Tragedy is when I cut my finger. Comedy is when you fall into an open sewer and die.

—Mel Brooks, American comedian, director, and actor

如果有什麼東西比循規蹈矩的人更會讓不墨守成規的人痛恨的，就是另一個不墨守成規的人竟不遵守離經叛道的主流標準。

——比爾·渥恩，美國專欄作家

If there is anything the nonconformist hates worse than a conformist, it's another nonconformist who doesn't conform to the prevailing standard of nonconformity.

—Bill Vaughan, American columnist

一個五歲的孩子都能懂，派人去找個五歲的孩子來。

——格魯喬·馬克斯，美國電影與喜劇演員

A child of five would understand this. Send someone to fetch a child of five.

—Groucho Marx

你保重，希望我開車的時候能撞見你❸。
──羅德尼‧丹傑菲爾德，美國喜劇演員

You take care and I hope I'll run into you—when I'm driving.
—Rodney Dangerfield, American comedian

當然，文字是人類所使用過最強大的毒品。
──魯德亞德‧吉卜林，生於孟買的英國作家

Words are, of course, the most powerful drug used by mankind.
—Rudyard Kipling

你無法想像，全然放空有多麼愉悅：我的腦袋裡沒有任何想法，
你甚至可以滾一顆球穿過它！──列夫‧托爾斯泰，俄國小說家

You can't imagine what a pleasure this complete laziness is to me: not a
thought in my brain—you might send a ball rolling through it!
—Leo Tolstoy

有些日子甚至連我的幸運火箭內褲都幫不上忙。
──卡爾文，出自漫畫《卡爾文與霍布斯》

Some days even my lucky rocketship underpants won't help.
—Calvin, *Calvin and Hobbes*

---

❸ Run into 有多種意思，一種是「偶然遇見」，一種是「撞到」，這句乍看之下是
　說想偶遇，實則是想開車撞對方。

首先，先確保擁有一份獨立收入，然後再來實踐美德。
—— 希臘諺語

First secure an independent income, then practice virtue.

—Greek proverb

衡量一個男人是否誠實的最佳方式，不是他的所得稅退稅，而是他完全沒有調整浴室裡的體重計。
—— 亞瑟·C·克拉克，英國科幻作家

The best measure of a man's honesty isn't his income tax return. It's the zero adjust on his bathroom scale.

—Arthur C. Clarke, British science-fiction author

如果他們可以從發霉的麵包做出盤尼西林，他們一定也可以從你身上做出些什麼。 —— 穆罕默德·阿里，美國拳擊手

If they can make penicillin out of moldy bread, they can sure make something out of you.

—Muhammad Ali

愚蠢可以充分解釋的事，絕對不要歸因於惡意。
—— 尼克·迪亞墨斯，美國作家

Never attribute to malice what can be adequately explained by stupidity.

—Nick Diamos, American author

如果我的批評者看到我沿著泰晤士河散步，他們會說那是因為我不會游泳。

——瑪格麗特·柴契爾，前英國首相，也是至今為止唯一的女首相

If my critics saw me walking over the Thames, they would say it was because I couldn't swim.

—Margaret Thatcher

如果你想要毀掉世上任何想法的話，找個委員會來研議它就好了。——查爾斯·F·凱特林，美國發明家

If you want to kill any idea in the world, get a committee working on it.

—Charles F. Kettering, American inventor

一張照片勝過一千個否認。

——羅納德·雷根，美國第40任總統

One picture is worth 1,000 denials.

—Ronald Reagan

你以為我會把介紹你用的那段話收回來嗎？

——格魯喬·馬克斯，美國電影與喜劇演員

Do you suppose I could buy back my introduction to you?

—Groucho Marx

每當我開始覺得我變老了，而且漸漸走近墳墓時，就會發生別的
事。——「貓王」艾維斯‧普利斯萊，美國知名歌手

Every time I think that I'm getting old, and gradually going to the
grave, something else happens.

—Elvis Presley

如果這是茶，請給我一些咖啡……但如果這是咖啡，請給我一些
茶。——亞伯拉罕‧林肯，美國第16任總統

If this is tea, please bring me some coffee ... but if this is coffee, please
bring me some tea.

—Abraham Lincoln

就算把羽毛塞進你的屁股，也不會讓你變成一隻雞。
——布萊德‧彼特

Shoving feathers in your ass does not make you a chicken.

—Brad Pitt

我不信任任何人，甚至是我自己。
——約瑟夫‧史達林，蘇聯前領導人

I trust no one. Not even myself.

—Joseph Stalin

我發展出了一種新哲學⋯⋯我一次只害怕一天。

——查爾斯・舒茲，美國漫畫家與漫畫《花生》的創作者

I've developed a new philosophy ... I only dread one day at a time.

—Charles Schulz

我不認為被稱為不可知論者是一種侮辱，我反而覺得那是種恭維。我不會假裝我懂那麼多無知的人們相信的事。這就是不可知論的意思。

——克萊倫斯・蘇厄德・丹諾，美國律師，為教授演化論的高中生物老師約翰・T・斯科普斯辯護，也是後來著名的「斯科普斯猴子審判」

I do not consider it an insult but rather a compliment to be called an agnostic. I do not pretend to know where many ignorant men are sure—that is all that agnosticism means.

—Clarence Seward Darrow, American lawyer famous for his defense of John T. Scopes in the "Scopes Monkey Trial"

如果你不能友善以對，至少可以相應不理。

——大衛・鮑爾斯，美國第35任總統約翰・甘迺迪的特別助理

If you can't be kind, at least be vague.

—David Powers, special assistant to John F. Kennedyassistant to John F. Kennedy

人類是最聰明的動物，也是最蠢的。
—— 第歐根尼，古希臘哲學家

Man is the most intelligent of the animals—and the most silly.
—Diogenes, Greek explorer

人們試圖設計某樣極度簡單、傻瓜也會用的東西時，常犯的錯誤就是低估了純傻瓜的聰明才智。
—— 道格拉斯・亞當斯，英國作家，廣播劇《銀河便車指南》的作者

A common mistake that people make when trying to design something completely foolproof is to underestimate the ingenuity of complete fools.
—Douglas Adams, British writer and author of *The Hitchhiker's Guide to the Galaxy*

人道主義者一直是偽君子。 —— 喬治・歐威爾，英國作家與記者
A humanitarian is always a hypocrite.
—George Orwell, English author and journalist

愚蠢、自私與健康是快樂的三要素，但如果少了愚蠢，一切就無法成立。 —— 古斯塔夫・福樓拜，法國作家
To be stupid, selfish, and have good health are three requirements for happiness, though if stupidity is lacking, all is lost.
—Gustave Flaubert, French writer

我想我就是喜歡看事物的陰暗面。杯子總是一半是空的,而且還破了,我的嘴唇剛被它割破,然後又在一顆牙齒上弄出個洞。
—— 詹尼安・吉勞法羅,美國喜劇演員與女演員

I guess I just prefer to see the dark side of things. The glass is always half empty. And cracked. And I just cut my lip on it. And chipped a tooth.
—Janeane Garofalo, American comedian and actress

想要好天氣請上天堂,要有人作伴的請下地獄。
—— 馬克・吐溫,美國作家

Go to Heaven for the climate, Hell for the company.
—Mark Twain

我沒有任何偏見,我一視同仁地討厭每個人。
—— W・C・菲爾茲,美國喜劇演員

I am free of all prejudices. I hate everyone equally.
—W. C. Fields

她在引述別人的話時很有天分,這可以有效替代機智。
—— 威廉・薩默塞特・毛姆,英國劇作家

She had a pretty gift for quotation, which is a serviceable substitute for wit.
—W. Somerset Maugham, British playwright

如果事實證明上帝存在，我不會認為祂是邪惡的。關於祂，你能說的最惡劣評價就是祂基本上是個低成就者。

—— 伍迪·艾倫，美國電影導演

If it turns out that there is a God, I don't think that he's evil. But the worst that you can say about him is that basically he's an underachiever.

—Woody Allen

由於氫的數量龐大，一些科學家宣稱氫是構成宇宙的基本元素，但我反駁這說法。我認為愚蠢的量遠超過氫，愚蠢才是構成宇宙的基本元素。

—— 法蘭克·札帕，美國搖滾音樂家

Some scientists claim that hydrogen, because it is so plentiful, is the basic building block of the universe. I dispute that. I say there is more stupidity than hydrogen, and that is the basic building block of the universe.

—Frank Zappa, American rock musician

只有平庸的人能永遠保持他們的最佳狀態。

—— 尚·季洛杜，法國作家

Only the mediocre are always at their best.

—Jean Giraudoux, French writer

壞事發生在你身上只有一個原因，因為你是個笨蛋。

—— 瑞德‧弗爾曼，出自美國電視影集《70年代秀》

The only reason bad things happen to you is because you're a dumbass.
—Red Forman, *That 70's Show*

死亡可以解決所有問題。沒有人，就沒有問題。

—— 約瑟夫‧史達林，蘇聯前領導人

Death is the solution to all problems. No man—no problem.
—Joseph Stalin

一句機智的諺語無法證明任何事。

—— 伏爾泰，法國哲學家

A witty saying proves nothing.
—Voltaire, French philosopher

如果這裡有任何人我還沒侮辱到的，我會請求他的原諒。

—— 約翰尼斯‧布拉姆斯，德國作曲家

If there is anyone here whom I have not insulted, I beg his pardon.
—Johannes Brahms, German composer

現在你已經學會王八蛋的說話藝術了，出去用他們的話讓別人有自知之明吧，或是用王八蛋的話低聲抱怨也行。一切取決於你！

　　不過，現我要用英國演員喬治‧桑德斯的名言來跟你告別：「再見。我要離開了，因為我覺得很無聊。」

這些話，爲什麼這麼有哏?!
—— 名人毒舌語錄1200句

作　　者—— 艾瑞克·格茲莫考斯基　　發 行 人—— 蘇拾平
　　　　　（Eric Grzymkowski）　　　總 編 輯—— 蘇拾平
譯　　者—— 王定春　　　　　　　　　編 輯 部—— 王曉瑩
特約編輯—— 陳心怡　　　　　　　　　行 銷 部—— 陳詩婷、曾志傑、蔡佳妘、廖倚萱
　　　　　　　　　　　　　　　　　　業 務 部—— 王綬晨、邱紹溢、劉文雅

出 版 社—— 本事出版
　　　　　　台北市松山區復興北路333號11樓之4
　　　　　　電話：(02) 2718-2001　傳眞：(02)2718-1258
　　　　　　E-mail：andbooks@andbooks.com.tw
發　　行—— 大雁文化事業股份有限公司
　　　　　　地址：台北市松山區復興北路333號11樓之4
　　　　　　電話：(02)2718-2001
　　　　　　傳眞：(02)2718-1258
美術設計—— COPY
內頁排版—— 陳瑜安工作室
印　　刷—— 上晴彩色印刷製版有限公司
2015年10月初版
2023年5月10日二版2刷
定價　420元

THE QUOTABLE A**HOLE: More Than 1,200 Bitter Barbs, Cutting Comments, and
Caustic Comebacks for Aspiring and Armchair A**holes Alike by Eric Grzymkowski
Copyright © 2011 by F+W Publications, Inc.
Complex Chinese translation copyright © 2015 by Motifpress Publishing, a division of
AND Publishing Ltd.
Published by arrangement with Adams Media, an imprint of Simon & Schuster, Inc.
through Bardon-Chinese Media Agency
ALL RIGHTS RESERVED.

版權所有，翻印必究
ISBN 978-957-9121-71-2
ISBN 978-957-9121-99-6（EPUB）

缺頁或破損請寄回更換
歡迎光臨大雁出版基地官網 www.andbooks.com.tw 訂閱電子報並塡寫回函卡

國家圖書館出版品預行編目資料
這些話，爲什麼這麼有哏?! —— 名人毒舌語錄1200句
艾瑞克·格茲莫考斯基（Eric Grzymkowski）/ 著　王定春 / 譯
---.二版.－臺北市；本事出版　：大雁文化發行，　2021年12月
　面　；　公分.－
譯自：THE QUOTABLE A**HOLE: More Than 1,200 Bitter Barbs, Cutting Comments,
　　　　and Caustic Comebacks for Aspiring and Armchair A**holes Alike
ISBN 978-957-9121-71-2（平裝）
1. 言論集
079.52　　　　　　　　　　　　　　　　　　　　109009048

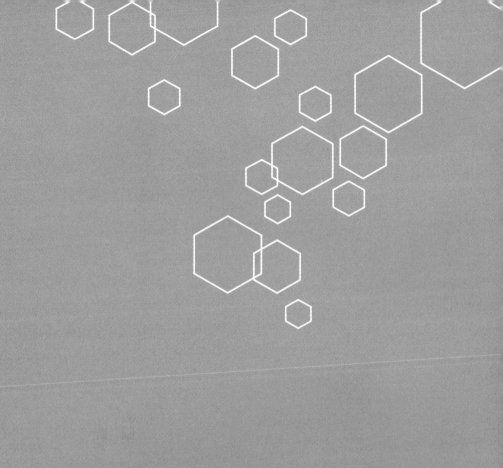

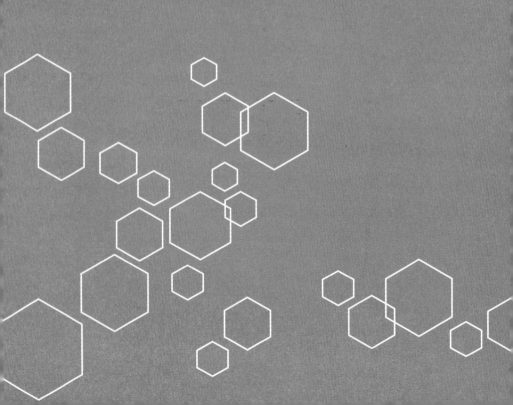

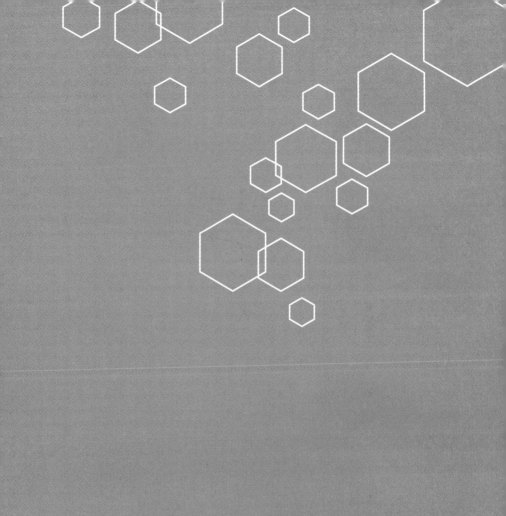

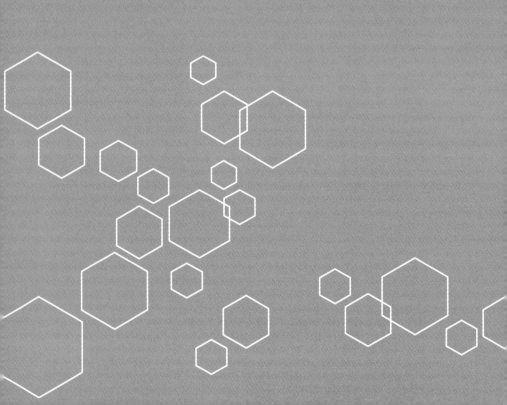